Macmillan

Macmillan Professional Masters

Titles in the series

Data Processing

Second edition

John Bingham

Senior Management Consultant

MACMILLAN

First edition published in 1983 as *Mastering Data Processing* by
MACMILLAN EDUCATION LTD
Houndmills, Basingstoke, Hampshire RG21 2XS
and London
Companies and representatives
throughout the world

ISBN 0–333–48980–2 hardcover
ISBN 0–333–44646–1 paperback
ISBN 0–333–44647–X paperback export

A catalogue record for this book is available
from the British Library

Printed in Hong Kong

Second edition (fully revised and updated) published 1989
10   9   8   7   6   5   4
00 99 98 97 96 95 94 93 92 91

Contents

Part V   THE APPLICATIONS OF DATA PROCESSING

Preface to the First Edition

The so-called 'information explosion' and 'computer revolution' have combined to raise data processing to a new level of importance in every organisation. New technology, not only in computers but also in data communications and office equipment, has simultaneously made the subject much more technical and complex than ever before. No longer is it possible, however, to leave these subjects entirely to specialists because part of the impact of the latest developments has been to make modern means of data processing available to users throughout the organisation. Mini-computers, microcomputers and terminals connected to remote mainframes have all contributed to this process which seems certain not only to continue but also to accelerate.

The consequence of these developments is that almost everyone working in commerce, industry or government is likely to become involved in using the new technology. It is only by understanding the basic concepts that underlie data processing that it will be possible to take full advantage of the opportunities available. Certainly, no accountant, administrator, banker, engineer, manager or scientist can consider him or herself to be fully prepared for the challenges of the coming years without a thorough grounding of data processing theory, techniques, equipment and practice.

It is to provide such a grounding that this book has been written. Aimed at both the advanced student and the general reader who wishes to broaden his or her knowledge of this important subject, the book covers all the main topics in this fascinating area.

The book is divided into five distinct parts, each dealing with a separate facet of the subject. Part I, An Introduction to Data Processing, examines the interaction between data processing and computers. Part II, The Tools of Data Processing, looks at the equipment, dealing with both the so-called 'Hardware' and 'Software'. Part III, Developing Systems, considers how an organisation can go about the task of analysing its activities to see whether they can economically and practically be performed by computers and details the steps and techniques necessary to achieve that aim. Part IV, Making Data Processing Work, examines the practical problems of data processing in an organisation, and Part V, The Applications of Data Processing, discusses the main uses of computers for data processing and identifies some of the most important systems-design features.

Although the five Parts follow a natural sequence, each may be read separately, in any sequence, if more appropriate to the existing knowledge or course of study being pursued by the reader.

Like all technological subjects, data processing has its own vocabulary which may at first encounter confuse the reader. The most important terms are explained at the appropriate place in the text, but as an aid to the reader a Glossary has been included and reference should be made to this when an unfamiliar term is encountered elsewhere in the text.

JOHN BINGHAM

Preface to the Professional Masters Edition

In the five short years since the first edition was published, the pace of development in data processing has continued unabated, and the impact upon people employed in a wide variety of occupations has increased. Indeed, it has even affected the author, since the handwritten document which provided the first draft of the first edition has been superseded by direct use of a word processing package on a personal computer. Among the most significant developments have been the convergence of computing and communications, the growth in the use of relational databases, and perhaps above all the explosion in the use of micro or personal computers.

In preparing this edition, I have tried to include those developments which have most changed the face of commercial data processing and at the same time to eliminate or de-emphasise those aspects of the subject which are no longer as relevant as they were. I have nevertheless retained the same basic structure, which is designed to integrate the technical and practical aspects of the subject into a coherent whole.

JOHN BINGHAM

Acknowledgements

I should like to thank all those who have assisted me in writing this book. In particular my thanks are due to John Cockroft and Gerald Janes, who assisted in aspects of my research; Geoff Carrington and Bob Jarvis, who reviewed and commented upon material within the areas of their special competence; and, above, all, Ron Breeden, who reviewed the entire draft and made numerous valuable suggestions about both content and presentation.

My greatest debt is, however, once again to my wife Mollie, who not only typed the entire manuscript, but also carried out much of the research and data collection necessary.

In preparing the second edition my principal collaborators have been Gerald Janes and my colleague Allan Dolgow. To them both I would like to express my thanks.

J. B.

data processing (n.): the converting of raw data to machine readable form and its subsequent processing (as storing, updating, combining, re-arranging or printing out) by a computer; data processor (n.).

Webster's New Collegiate Dictionary

Part 1

An Introduction to Data Processing

1 Data Processing and the Role of Computers

1.1 What is Data Processing?

Almost any organisation has a certain amount of administrative work that must be carried out: staff must be paid, raw materials or finished goods have to be ordered and customers have to be invoiced for items they have purchased. In addition, records have to be maintained of the personnel employed, the tax deducted from their pay, suppliers, orders placed with suppliers but not yet fulfilled, customers, customers' orders that have not yet been satisfied and a hundred and one other items in order that the organisation may work efficiently and meet its legal obligations.

It was during the 1950s that the term 'data processing' came into widespread use to describe all these administrative processing and record-keeping functions which had, of course, existed since the beginning of commerce as we know it today. Although the activities included in the term 'data processing' were diverse, they nevertheless shared some common features. Among these were:

* the need to maintain accurate record or files
* the need to sort, merge and tabulate the records in the files
* the need to carry out basic calculations
* the large volume of records handled
* the routine and repetitious nature of much of the manipulation performed on the records.

Given these common features it was natural that machines should be developed to help in the processing with the objectives of improving accuracy, reducing tedious manual work, speeding up the work and, above all, reducing the costs involved. The use of machines in what is now called data processing has, in fact, a long history. As early as the 1890s a punched card machine devised by Dr Herman Hollerith was in use to count responses to questions posed in the American Census.

The machines used for data processing until the 1950s were mechanical or electro-mechanical. It became apparent, however, that the electronic computers that had been developed during the 1940s for mathematical computation and owing their basic concepts to Babbage and his 'Differencing Engine' of over a hundred years before could be adapted for commercial data processing. In 1951 the world's first commercial data processing computer was developed by the British food company Lyons to perform some of the commercial tasks described above. This machine, called the *L*yons *E*lectronic *O*ffice, or LEO for short, was the forerunner of the computers which perform so much of the administrative work of business organisations today. A period of rapid development followed and a significant point was reached in 1959 when IBM introduced the 1401 computer. This machine, designed especially for commercial work, established new levels of cost effectiveness and became to data processing what the Model T Ford had been to road transport – popularising and extending the use of computers many times over.

With the widespread use of computers for data processing work, the terms 'electronic data processing' (EDP) and 'automatic data processing' (ADP) came into use to distinguish data processing carried out using the new tools from that using the (then) conventional tools. Today it is doubtful if this distinction still exists and in most people's minds the term data processing includes the use of computers where appropriate.

The flexibility of computers has also caused the scope of the term data processing to be broadened and today it often includes such activities as scheduling the work to be performed in manufacturing plants, calculating statistics, monitoring the performance of industrial plant or machinery and analysing a wide range of technical facts and figures. The features common to all these activities are, however, the same as those described above.

The question, 'What is data processing?' is probably best answered by stating that it is a term used to describe a wide range of activities which have certain characteristics in common, namely the collection, processing, output and (usually) storage of quantities of data with most of these activities being performed on a routine or semi-regular basis. In modern usage the term data processing usually, though not always, implies the use of computers for at least some of these activities.

The study of data processing is, therefore, the study of the organisation and techniques for the collection, processing, storage and output of data. The data processing practitioner needs skills in addition to those of a computer technician since it is only when the capabilities of the machine are properly integrated into a complete business system that the full benefits of the technology are obtained.

1.2 **The Need for Information**

So far we have considered data processing in the context of the administration of an organisation, but this is not its only use. A second major area of activity is ensuring that the management of the organisation receives the necessary information in order that decisions may be taken on a rational basis rather than on the basis of intuition. Should prices be raised? Should more of product *A* be produced? Should a cheaper raw material be substituted for one already in use? These are all typical decisions constantly facing managers. The right decision in these and hundreds more cases can only be made if the manager concerned has up-to-date and reasonably accurate information.

For decision-making purposes absolute accuracy may be less important than timeliness. Obviously it must be accurate enough to enable the right decision to be made, but information which is delayed is likely to be less valuable than information which is available almost instantly. Moreover, information tends to become less valuable after it has been produced – a point which has considerable importance in the design of systems and one to which we will return when considering the types of system that can be developed.

So far the terms 'data' and 'information' have been used but no explanation of the distinction between them has been given. There is, however, a marked distinction. To use an analogy, data may be likened to a raw material and information to a finished product – the two being separated by a *'process'*. This relationship is shown for system 1 in Figure 1.1. In our analogy the process may be either manufacturing (for example, the machining of a casting into a finished part) or assembly (for example, the joining of a body to the engine/gearbox unit to produce a car). In either example it will be easily appreciated that the 'finished product' of one process can readily become the 'raw material' for another (an engine, for example, is a collection of manufactured sub-assemblies which in turn becomes an input or 'raw material' for the complete car). Similarly, with data, the information which is output from one process can often become the data or 'raw material' for another process. This situation is a key characteristic of data processing and information systems. Returning to the model in Figure 1.1 it can be seen that the output from system 1 is both used as it stands by the user and forms input (showed by the dotted line) to system 2. Thus an output from a payroll system which quantifies the direct labour cost of a particular cost centre could become input to a costing system.

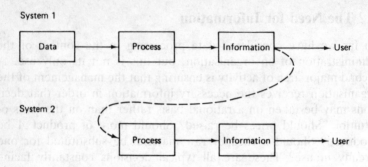

Fig 1.1 *the data-information model*

The processing which occurs to transform data into information will include manipulation (sorting, merging, tabulating) as well as calculation, and will frequently entail the use of stored data as well as newly collected data.

A more complete model of the data/information cycle is shown in Figure 1.2, while Figure 1.3 gives a highly simplified example of how a costing system may use input from a payroll system.

Much of the information that an organisation requires for decision-making purposes does, of course, arise from the administrative systems discussed in the previous section. It would be a mistake, however, to believe that this is always the case. Some '*decision-making*' or '*information*' systems are completely independent of any administrative system. The economics of such systems (a subject to which we will return in Chapter 2) are always difficult to ascertain, but suffice it to say, at this stage, that they exist and can be justified in many cases.

Before we leave this point it is essential to stress again that the 'process' box of our simple data-to-information model as shown in Figure 1.1 does not *necessarily* mean the use of a computer. Clerical labour or other machines can be used instead or in conjunction with a computer. Indeed, in principle, for administrative and decision-making purposes, there is nothing that computers can do which *cannot* be done by clerical effort. The difference is that computers enable things to be done which were uneconomical until recently. Computers are, moreover, faster and more accurate for repetitive work than either clerical personnel or less sophisticated machines and for this reason can perform analyses of information which had not previously been practical.

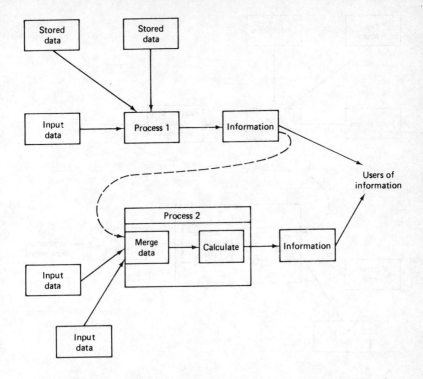

Fig 1.2   *the data-information model expanded to show the use of stored data and a subdivision of the processing performed*

1.3 **Characteristics of Computers**

In the foregoing summary of the nature of data processing and the need for information it has been stated that in many cases computers are used in these activities. Since their introduction into commercial life computers have come to be the focal point of many government and company operations. Moreover, as computers become more sophisticated, become available in a wider variety of sizes and configurations and above all become less expensive, the trend to make use of them is not only continuing but increasing. Soon, with the initial cost of microcomputers becoming so low, it will be rare for even the smallest organisation not to make use of computers. What then are the particular attributes making computers valuable and explaining the dramatic increase in their use?

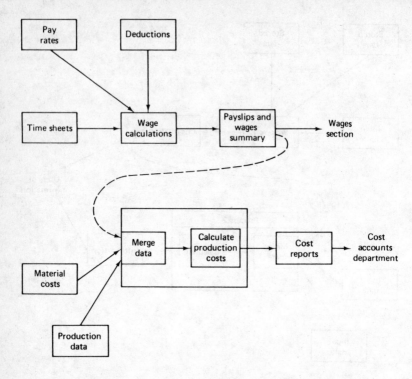

Fig 1.3 *the data-information model applied to a simplified payroll and costing example*

In this section the basic characteristics of computers will be reviewed to show that they offer a good match to many of an organisation's data processing and information needs.

In general terms computers can be said to have four main features:

* speed
* accuracy and consistency
* ability to store and access large volumes of data
* imposition of a formal approach to working methods.

(a) Speed
Many people associate computers with speed and this association is well founded. Computers operate at speeds which are typically quoted in milli, micro or nano seconds (one thousandth, one millionth or one thousand millionth of a second). This means that

computers are able to operate at great speed to process or manipulate data. In practice the speed of the computer itself is often limited by the speed of the peripheral devices which perform such functions as reading data into the computer at much slower speeds.

(b) Accuracy and consistency

Human beings are, by nature, prone to make errors. Computers are, by contrast, extremely accurate. In addition to the intrinsic accuracy of their electronic components, computers are designed in such a way that many of the inaccuracies which could arise due to the malfunctioning of the equipment are detected and their consequences avoided in a way which is completely transparent to the user. The importance of accuracy in dealing with large quantities of data need hardly be stressed.

A closely related concept is that of consistency. Not only are computers more accurate than human beings, but they are also more consistent. That is to say that given the same data and the same instructions they will produce the same answer every time that particular process is repeated. This is in contrast to the all-too-common human tendency to produce a different answer every time a column of figures is added!

(c) Ability to store and access large volumes of data

A further characteristic of computers is their ability to store and access large volumes of data. Strictly speaking data (and preprocessed information) are not normally stored 'in the computer' except when it is actually being used. It is retained on various *media* (magnetic tape and disks are the most common) which may be held *on-line* (that is to say already mounted on the computer available for almost instant use) or *demounted* and stored in a data library. The key point is that these media give the opportunity of storing very large quantities of data. The capacity of a magnetic disk may be up to 5000 million characters (figures, letters or special signs) of data and a computer may have eight or more of these disks on-line and many more in a special store or 'library'. Similarly, a standard reel of magnetic tape may contain several million characters of data. It is not unusual for a computer installation having a dozen tape drives on-line to have a library of several hundred tapes.

Clearly the organisation of large quantities of data in such a way that the required characters can be found quickly, and without the need to search through lots of unwanted data, is a major subject in its own right and will be discussed in detail in Chapter 12. For the moment we should merely note that not only can large volumes of data be stored, but they can also be arranged so that ready access to each piece of data and, more importantly, various combinations of data can be obtained.

(d) Imposition of a formal approach to working methods

At first sight it may seem somewhat strange to include this feature as a key characteristic of computers. Because a computer can only work with a strict set of rules (a *program*) it *necessarily* forces the identification and imposition of rigid rules for dealing with the data it is given to process. This feature therefore imposes a level of formalisation on the processing of data to which it may not previously have been subjected. Indeed some leading writers on management have gone so far as to say that this formalisation is the most important effect that computers have had on business and government. Whilst it is not necessary to go that far, it is certainly true that formalisation of data processing procedures is an important effect caused by the use of computers.

It is doubtful if man has yet devised any machines which have no negative features to set against their positive characteristics. Certainly, computers have a number of inherent limitations. Although there is a good match between the requirements of data processing and the features of computers discussed so far, a knowledge of these limitations is essential if the systems designed utilising computers are to be more effective.

Two of these limitations arise from the need for computers to be *programmed*, that is, given precise, detailed instructions in a language that the computer can 'understand'. The first limitation is that *programming* takes a considerable amount of time and usually has to be performed by specialist personnel. We shall see in later chapters that the process of putting a system on to a computer actually involves much more than writing the programs. This serves to extend the time frame yet further and leads directly to the frequently heard complaint from computer users about the length of time it takes to develop or modify a system. For example, with a manual data processing system, procedures can often be changed as quickly as it is possible to tell the staff concerned. With a computer program, however, it is necessary not only to explain the change, but also to make the amendment, *compile* the program (input it into the computer and translate it into the computer's internal code) and test it as well as making a record of the change.

The second limitation is also connected with the need for a computer to be programmed. Precisely because the computer needs exact, detailed instructions there is a tendency for it to become inflexible in its use. With data all being processed according to the same rigid rules, it is difficult to make changes or exceptions in the way a human being can. This is the basic reason why computers can so often appear stupid to the man in the street. Despite the stories that sometimes appear in the popular press about the capabilities of computers, they cannot think. They analyse data in strict accordance with sets of rules defined in a *program*. Thus the gas or electricity bill for £0.00p is due to the rigidity with which the computer is applying the rules it has been given to produce a stupid result. This type of example can be overcome by sensible system design (such as testing for £0.00 and passing exceptional data to a human operator for special attention), but the basic point of rigidity remains.

A third limitation is that computers require data to be presented to them in a form they can understand! Obvious though this point may be, it is also extremely inconvenient because that form is not one that humans can readily comprehend! Much progress has been made in capturing data as a byproduct of some other operation and a great deal of ingenuity has been exercised in developing ways in which documents that humans can understand can be directly used as a computer input. The majority of data used in computers however, still have to be translated into a suitable code on a computer readable media – a process which is not only time-consuming but also expensive.

1.4 **Practical Problems**

In addition to the three limitations discussed in the preceding section which stem directly from the nature of the computer as a machine, there are three practical implications which face any organisation making use of computers. Each of these is important enough to merit a chapter of its own. For completeness, however, they are introduced here. The three points are:

* the need for specialised personnel
* the organisational changes implied by centralised data processing
* the level of costs incurred.

(a) The need for specialised personnel
We have already mentioned that computer programs are usually written by specialised personnel – usually called *programmers*. This, however, is only part of the story. For all but the smallest installations, a specialist staff will be employed to operate the computer,

for data preparation and to design the systems used. Paradoxically, using computers is a labour-intensive activity! The full range of skills needed to operate a computer service is given in Chapter 13.

(b) The organisational changes implied by centralised data processing
The introduction of a computer into an organisation inevitably causes changes in the structure of that organisation. The most obvious change is usually the creation of a specialised data processing department. There are however, other more subtle changes as other departments accommodate to the changes involved in dealing with a centralised computing service. These changes may include adjustments to the working pattern to reflect the daily, weekly or monthly processing cycle of the computer system and the introduction of appropriate communications methods for getting the data to the computer and receiving the output from it. Changes of this nature will occur even if a number of computers are distributed throughout an organisation instead of a single installation. In Chapter 3 the impact of data processing on the organisation will be considered.

(c) The level of costs incurred
Computers may be getting cheaper but all those of practical use for data processing purposes are still expensive items of equipment in absolute terms. Moreover, many of them (especially the larger machines) require a special computer room having a controlled air-conditioned environment and raised floors so that the connecting cables can be kept out of the way. As we have seen, specialist staff are also necessary and their costs (which are by no means insignificant) must be added to the total cost of introducing and running a computer. These costs, of course, must be compared with the benefits and it is this comparison we shall discuss in Chapter 2.

So far computers have been referred to as if the term represented a single limited range of equipment. In fact, the range of machines included in the term is enormous. At the time of writing, computers available on the British market range in cost from about £100 to sums measured in millions. Their capacities and capabilities also vary in similar proportions. In Chapter 5 some of the many types of machines available and their specific features will be considered, but it is worth remembering that this range of equipment exists and with it the possibility of matching the data processing needs of a wide variety of organisations.

2 The Economics of Data Processing

One of the meanings of the word 'economics' is 'consideration of cost and return' and it is in this sense that data processing will be considered in this chapter.

In the first section the various costs that an organisation incurs in using computers for data processing will be identified and discussed; this will be followed by a review of the returns or benefits that may accrue from that use. Finally, the way in which the balance between the various elements in the economic equation may be evaluated will be considered.

2.1 The Costs of Computers in Data Processing

When using a computer to produce information the costs incurred, as with any major piece of equipment, may be divided into two categories: fixed costs (i.e. those costs which stem directly from the equipment itself) and variable costs (i.e. those that vary depending on the amount that the equipment is used). In addition, in this case, there is a large portion of costs which are specific to the application for which the computer is used. The majority of these costs are associated with the development of these applications and thus development provides a third major area of cost.

The major elements included in each of these areas are:

Fixed costs
* the computer
* systems software costs
* the computer room
* operating staff
* overhead costs
* other fixed costs

Variable costs
* computer stationery
* storage media
* power
* other variable costs

Developmental costs
* development staff
* applications software costs
* other development costs.

(a) Fixed costs

(i) The computer
The first and most obvious cost element in the use of computers for data processing is the central processor itself and the peripheral equipment attached to it. The computer may be purchased, leased or rented by the organisation using it.

Historically, many organisations have declined to purchase computers because of the large investment required and the rapidity with which the equipment became obsolescent. Where computers are purchased, however, the acquisition is usually treated as a capital expenditure and the total cost (less the anticipated residual value) amortised over the expected life of the equipment in the organisation. To this direct cost must be added the cost of borrowing (or not investing) the money needed to finance the purchase.

Most organisations have found that any given computer rarely satisfies their information processing needs for longer than four years before requiring to be enhanced. This is largely due to the rate of technical development of computers, compounded by the fact that, once an organisation has access to the facilities that a computer can provide, the use of the equipment increases rapidly. The high rate of technical development also means that any assessment of the residual value of a computer is fraught with difficulty. Even though the equipment may be in perfect condition and operating without problems, there is generally little demand for second-hand computers. Occasionally, a combination of economic and market conditions will cause a thriving second-hand market to occur for a short duration. In general, however, the residual value of a computer after four or more years is usually a very small fraction of its original cost.

Where computers are purchased outright it is a matter of simple arithmetic to calculate the basic cost of a unit (say 1 hr) of computer time by dividing the net purchase price (including non-recoverable taxes), less residual value, plus financial charges, by the total number of hours for which the computer is expected to be used.

It is because of the factors mentioned above that alternative ways of acquiring computers have become popular.

Leasing is the arrangement whereby an intermediate financial organisation buys the computer (or other item of capital equipment) from the manufacturer or sales agent and lets out or leases the equipment to the organisation that wishes to use it. Ownership of the equipment is retained by the financial or leasing company and the using organisation pays them money on a regular basis throughout the period of the lease.

Leases invariably have a minimum contract period. Two types of lease have been widely used, financial and operating leases. Financial leases effectively ignore the potential residual value of the equipment so that the full cost of the computer and the lessor's profit are both recovered from the lessee during the period of the lease. From the lessor's point of view such a transaction is virtually without risk. For the lessee, the arrangement is usually only viable if the equipment is likely to be required for its full working life. Such leases are, therefore, an alternative to purchasing the equipment, but do not require the lessee to tie up large sums of capital in computing equipment.

Operating leases take into account the residual value of the equipment. The lessor, calculating that it will be possible to re-lease or sell the computer after the first lessee has finished with it, can offer competitive rates for leases covering only part of the estimated life of the equipment. Thus operating leases can be for shorter periods than are typical for *financial leases*. The nature of operating leases means, however, that they are normally only available for widely used machines manufactured by the leading manufacturers. The companies offering operating leases tend to be specialists in a particular type of capital equipment (in this case computers) because of the need to have well-developed industry contacts to re-lease the machines. Financial leases are available from regular finance houses. Some operating leases incorporate clauses enabling the lessor to terminate the agreement prematurely without onerous penalties provided that a new lease of equivalent or greater value is drawn up for the replacement equipment.

The third way in which a computer may be acquired and paid for is on a rental basis. In this case the organisation wishing to use the computer arranges with the owner (who is normally the manufacturer or his agent) to rent a machine and pays a regular fee for it. Separate rental agreements usually exist for the central processing unit and each of the peripheral items. Many rental agreements have a minimum cost for use of the equipment up to (say) 176 hours per month and impose additional charges for use in excess of that figure. Most rental agreements are for a specified minimum period (typically

1 year) and include maintenance services. Longer-term rental agreements are available for many types of equipment and may offer significant discounts compared with shorter-term agreements.

The decision by an organisation to purchase, lease or rent its computer capacity is a complex one. It requires not only a detailed evaluation of the costs of the various options, but also a clear idea of the medium- and long-term pattern of computer usage. When comparing costs it is essential to ensure that like is being compared with like. Do the different prices relate to identical machines? Do prices include maintenance and system software? Are there additional charges for insurance, carriage or installation? These are some of the obvious variations which need to be considered before a decision is made.

It is not uncommon to find organisations which have mixed financing for their computing needs. Different computers or even different parts of the same computer may be financed in different ways because of variations in the pattern of their present and expected usage. Thus, for example, a company may purchase computers used for dedicated purposes and with a long anticipated life because it is the cheapest option. At the same time it may lease the central processing unit of its main computer because it expects high usage of that equipment for (say) five years but does not want to invest too much capital. Finally it may rent the peripheral equipment on its main computer because it expects new requirements in a year or two which will require larger versions of this equipment.

(ii) System software costs

The computer, as it stands, is virtually unusable for most commercial purposes. Before it can be used on any convenient basis it is necessary to have some basic programs (called *system software*). The nature of these programs and what they do is discussed in Chapter 7. To all intents and purposes they are essential parts of the complete machine. Sometimes these programs are included in the price quoted for the computer itself, but often they have to be paid for separately.

Where systems software has to be paid for separately the usual options are outright purchase and a rental or licensing agreement. Systems software which is essential to the normal use of the computer is easy to account for, being effectively an addition to the costs of the equipment itself. More complicated is the case of system software which, whilst not essential, is highly desirable or is used only in conjunction with specific tasks performed on the computer. In this latter case it is probably better to consider the costs involved as part of the variable costs of computing considered below.

(iii) The computer room

Computers have differing requirements of the type of environment in which they can be readily operated. At the one extreme, many of the small microcomputers now available can be plugged into any domestic power supply and used in any normal conditions of temperature, humidity and pollution. If the operator is comfortable then the computer is usable! At the other extreme, some of the large conventional or mainframe computers (see Chapter 5) require a carefully controlled environment. This usually means the provision of a special computer room with air-conditioning, filtering and humidity control; a specially 'smoothed' power supply; a raised floor (so the connecting cables between the various units of the computer may be removed from the normal working area) and perhaps special cooling arrangements to dissipate the heat generated by the computer.

Clearly such elaborate provisions are not cheap and can add considerably to the total cost of computing. Most of these costs are 'one off' in that they are incurred when the computer is installed and can, therefore, be apportioned in the same way as the cost of the computer itself. The running costs associated with these facilities will be considered below as part of the variable costs.

(iv) Operating staff

For most data processing purposes computers require operators in constant attendance. To operate a large computer on a normal mixture of commercial work may require three or four staff operating the machine, changing the disks and tapes used on the peripherals (see Chapter 6) and loading stationery into printers. In addition to these operators (who will need to exist in sufficient numbers to permit the computer to be used for as many hours as required during the day), other staff will be needed to prepare input for the computer, schedule its use and to prepare and deliver the output produced. The tasks performed by these staff are discussed in detail in Chapter 13, but the point here is that these staff add to the cost of computing.

When considering staff costs, the direct salary or wage needs to be increased to take into account national insurance and pension contributions and any other direct staff charges.

It may be argued that operating staff are not fixed costs in the conventional way, but they will be needed whether the computer is used a little or a lot and it therefore seems appropriate to include them as fixed costs in this discussion.

(v) Overhead costs

In most organisations it is customary to allocate various central costs to each activity in that organisation. Costs treated in this way may include: rental for space occupied, rates, heat, light, cleaning, decorating, building insurance, security services, night porters, reception, telephone, canteen, personnel and accountancy services, etc. The basis on which these costs are allocated to the various activities vary, but floor space occupied and number of people employed on that activity are two which are commonly used. On either basis the computing department tends to absorb a significant proportion of the total costs. Data processing is, as has already been pointed out, inherently a labour-intensive activity. The provision of a specialised computer room, moreover, may mean that the computer department occupies more space than many others.

Whatever basis of apportionment is used the organisation will have to meet these costs, but such overheads are often forgotten in calculating the costs of computing.

(vi) Other fixed costs

In addition to the above elements of cost there are a few others which may be encountered. Examples would include: the leasing of telephone lines for data communications use (see Chapter 11), maintenance contracts for any equipment where these costs are not already included, and insurance premiums where these are specific to the installation of the computer.

(b) Variable costs

(i) Computer stationery

Computers tend to be voracious beasts consuming paper at an awesome speed. Computer stationery is not, however, cheap, needing to be prepared in continuous lengths of many yards and accurately cut. If specially printed with static information (e.g. company name, title, etc.) so that it can be used as a form it is, of course, even more expensive. In use, moreover, a considerable amount of paper is wasted. Several sheets may have to be used in lining up printing on preprinted stationery (such as invoices or payslips). More seriously, it is impractical to use small quantities of stationery which may be left from previous computer runs. Computer stationery is, therefore, a significant element of the variable costs incurred in running a computer.

(ii) Storage media
Another element of variable costs is that of *storage media*. This term includes such items as magnetic tapes and disks (see Chapter 6). Investment in these items may become very significant in a large installation.

(iii) Power
In many organisations power is regarded as an overhead cost in the same way as heat and light. Other organisations, however, recognising that a large computer may have a significant power consumption (especially when compared with other machines used in administration and data processing) treat power for the computer as a direct cost.

(iv) Other variable costs
Other variable costs of computing would include: operating staff overtime, the use of data preparation or other services from outside the organisation and the use of the public switched telephone network for data communications purposes (see Chapter 11).

(c) Development costs

(i) Development staff
The main cost element in developing a new computer application is almost invariably the direct cost of the staff employed for that purpose. Such staff, whose tasks are described in Chapter 13, may be either permanent employees of the organisation or contractors engaged for short periods (see Chapter 4). As with operating staff, the full cost of employment will be considerably greater than the direct salary.

Even staff employed specifically to develop new applications will not spend all their time on this activity. Sickness, holidays, training, etc., will all diminish the time actually available to develop systems. The staff costs which must be used when calculating the cost of developing a new application must, therefore, be obtained by dividing the total staff cost by the number of *effective* hours and multiplying the result by the actual time taken.

(ii) Application software costs
It is sometimes possible to buy applications software instead of developing it all within the organisation (see Chapter 7). Where software is purchased in this way its cost is clearly part of the cost of development.

(iii) Other development costs
A number of other costs may be incurred in the development process. These might include: travel costs (to other parts of the organisation or to other similar organisations, attendance at exhibitions, etc), costs incurred in demonstrating equipment to users and the cost of special training courses.

2.2 The Economic Benefits of Computers in Data Processing

In the preceding section the various costs associated with the use of computers in data processing have been itemised. The reader may be excused, at this stage, for thinking that this intimidating list means that computing costs outweigh any possible advantages! Notwithstanding this long list, computers can, of course, be extremely economic for data processing.

The economic benefits from computing are usually regarded as those financial savings which are clearly attributable to the introduction of the equipment. In Chapter 8 we shall consider how these are evaluated in the case of any single application or system. At this point, however, we should consider the ways in which direct economic benefits can arise from the use of computers. In essence these are the practical results of the key characteristics of computers considered in the previous chapter. The fact that computers are: fast; accurate and consistent; can store and access large volumes of data; and that they impose a formal approach to working methods means that they can perform certain tasks at lower cost than any other practical alternative.

The economic benefits from the use of computers in data processing normally result from one or more of the following:

* reducing the number of staff employed on routine data collection and manipulation
* improved control
* improvements in the speed with which the organisation can react to information
* improved customer service.

(a) Reducing the number of staff employed on routine data collection and manipulation
The classic reason for the early use of computers in data processing was that they 'saved staff'. Although there have been many instances

in which this is true it is almost certainly a fact that computers, like so much labour-saving technology before them, have been net creators of jobs. Nevertheless, within individual organisations or in particular applications, computers have either enabled savings to be made in the number of staff employed on routine data collection and manipulation or, more commonly, especially during the boom years of the sixties and early seventies, have enabled growth disproportionate to the increase in staff to occur.

An example will illustrate the way computers have been instrumental in saving staff.

Until the early 1960s, wage calculations were a labour-intensive activity in most medium to large organisations. Typically, time clerks were used to record the time individual employees were at work and large sheets summarising this data were produced weekly. This data was subsequently checked and in part processed by a pool of comptometer operators (a comptometer was a mechanical calculator widely used until the late 1960s; it required considerable dexterity on the part of the operator, who was usually employed full time on that activity). The partly processed data was then used as input for elaborate electro-mechanical machines (accounting machines) which were operated by skilled personnel. In addition to entering data produced by the comptometer operators, the accounting-machine operator also had to refer to printed tax tables and enter data from these. The accounting machines calculated the net pay, produced the payslips and various check or audit totals. A skilled operator could produce some sixty payslips per hour.

With the advent of computers, the initial move was often to substitute computer processing for the work of the comptometer and accounting-machine operators. Typically the work of the people in these groups would be performed by about a third of the number of data preparation staff (preparing punched paper tape or punched cards) and a small number of computer analysts, programmers and operators, all of the staff also being available to perform other tasks in addition to the calculation of wages. Moreover, the computer itself would typically produce payslips at a rate of several hundred per hour so that in a medium-sized company one half-day would usually be sufficient to carry out all the computer processing associated with payroll. Automating payroll and similar applications was, for many organisations, the first step taken in the introduction of computers for data processing.

Similarly impressive savings were also made in other labour-intensive administrative activities such as invoice preparation, costing and customer accounting; releasing staff for tasks in other parts of the organisation and, as pointed out above, enabling substantial growth with only limited increases in administrative staff.

In many cases, these savings alone were sufficient to justify the acquisition of computers.

(b) Improved control

A second category of economic benefit derives directly from the ability of computers to facilitate improved control within an organisation. By enabling management to exercise improved control direct cash savings can often be realised. Three examples will serve to illustrate this point.

The first example concerns stock control. If central management knows the quantity and location of stockholdings (whether of raw materials, work in progress or finished goods) accurately, it is often possible for stockholdings to be reduced. Thus if a company has, say, five warehouses for finished goods throughout the country and distribution management knows quickly and accurately what is available in each, then it is possible to provide the same level of customer service with less inventory than if only the stock in one warehouse is known. Since stockholding is expensive (costs include warehouse space, staff and financing the inventory itself), reduced inventory means a direct saving. As computers offer, in many cases, the practical means of providing such improved information these savings may be directly attributed to their use.

A second example of the benefits of improved control is to be found in the area of credit control. The use of computers makes it practical to check the credit status of each customer before any order is satisfied without delaying the delivery of goods. Consider the case of a food manufacturer supplying literally hundreds of small retail outlets from a chain of regional sales offices and distribution depots. Orders are placed by the customers weekly and payment is made direct to head office on recept of a monthly statement. If the sales offices know quickly when a customer exceeds his credit limit or delays payment then potentially bad debts can be avoided. Today, in many instances, credit limits are checked by referring to records held on a computer before the order is accepted.

The third example of improved control concerns monitoring salesmen's performance. The use of computers to analyse sales records and compare performance between different sales periods and over different periods of time (due to the computer's ability to store and access large quantities of data) makes it easy to identify any salesman whose performance is below average or is deteriorating. This information enables sales management to take action such as additional supervision, extra training or, in extreme cases, perhaps replacement of the salesman concerned. Thus improved control achieved through the use of computers can once again be converted into a directly identifiable benefit.

(c) Improvements in the speed with which the organisation can react to information

'Time is money' runs the old adage, and for many organisations this is true. It means, too, that in many cases the processing speed offered by computers can be translated directly into a financial benefit.

An example of the financial benefit to be realised from the speed of data processing lies in the computation of economic order quantities (EOQ). For many products – especially raw materials such as chemical feedstocks and primary goods (agricultural products, ores, mineral fuels etc.) – costs vary rapidly and are also highly sensitive to the volume ordered (the cost per unit of, say, palm-oil may be significantly cheaper if bought in lots of hundreds of thousands of gallons than by the five-gallon drum). For companies using such products, the timing and size of their orders can be a major factor in determining profitability.

The fact that detection of reorder point and calculation of EOQ (based on historical usage, market prices and requirement forecasts) is automatic, reduces the time needed to replenish stocks. This reduced lead time can itself enable the reorder level to be reduced and make further savings possible.

A second example concerns the computation of product costs. Only if companies know accurately the current cost of producing finished goods can they be sure that they are trading profitably. A good product-costing system is, therefore, a prerequisite of successful management. Changing costs of labour, raw materials and other direct and indirect costs makes this difficult to achieve. Until the advent of computers with their capacity for rapid calculation, standard costs were usually only computed at infrequent intervals (often annually). Rapid changes to labour and/or material costs could not be integrated into the costing system. The use of computers to calculate standard costs revised with each raw material invoice or labour rate change and to analyse variations between standard and actual costs can, however, materially assist in this process.

A third example concerns vehicle routing. If an organisation's delivery vehicles can be routed in the optimum fashion, the number of vehicles and drivers can be reduced and both time and (increasingly important) fuel saved. The calculation of optimum routings is, however, a complex mathematical task which was, using manual methods, impractical on a regular basis. Speed of computers enables this task to be completed speedily and in many cases leads to direct financial benefits.

(d) Improved customer service

Improved customer service can result in direct economic benefits not only because more custom arises, but also because more efficient operations are permitted. An example of this situation is provided by reservations systems of the type operated by airlines and, increasingly, hotel and package holiday companies. Reservation systems not only enable a better customer service to be offered (immediate confirmation of bookings, listing of alternatives if the first choice is fully booked, etc.), but also provide direct benefits to the companies using them.

Thus in the case of an airline, an extension to the basic reservation system gives accurate information on the payload for each flight thus reducing the need to carry extra fuel, while still preserving the full safety margins required. The reduced fuel load, by reducing the all-up weight of the aircraft, further reduces the need for fuel.

For a package-tour operator the facility to advise potential customers instantly of alternatives if the first choice is fully booked is likely to increase the overall level of reservations, and, moreover, reduce customer frustration due to overbookings, delay in booking holidays, etc. In both these cases, and in many more, improved customer service leads directly to financial rewards for the organisation.

2.3 The Changing Balance

No consideration of the economics of data processing would be complete without mention of the changing balance between hardware and software costs.

It is common knowledge that the 'electronic revolution' has led to cheaper and cheaper computer hardware.

Thanks to mass production and especially the development of the so-called 'chip', computing power, which twenty years ago cost millions of pounds and occupied a large room, is now available from High Street stores for a few hundred pounds and packaged in units about the size of a television set. Although this comparison is not strictly valid (raw computing power is only part of the value of a computer for data processing as we shall see in Chapter 5) it is nevertheless true that any given amount of data processing capacity is now likely to be cheaper in real money terms than ever before.

What is less commonly realised, however, is that the cost of *using* most computers is rising rapidly. To make use of the increased (and increasing) capabilities of computers ever more complex software (the instructions which the computer executes) is necessary. The amount of time that is required to develop software rises almost exponentially (or perhaps even more than exponentially) with its complexity. The major cost associated with software development is the cost of the staff employed for this task and thus the cost of software production is almost directly proportional to the salary levels and time taken. With wage inflation common to many of the countries of the western world throughout the past decade or so it follows that software costs have risen dramatically as salaries and the time taken to produce software (due to the increased complexity) have increased. It is this increase in software costs that has given much of the impetus to ever more powerful tools to enable users to have access directly to computers and to improve the efficiency of the systems development process (see Parts III and IV).

The rapid rise in software costs and the decline in hardware costs have reversed the situation of the early days of data processing when it was worthwhile economising on the use of expensive machine capacity by the use of (relatively) cheaper labour. This change is shown graphically in Figure 2.1.

Fig 2.1   *the changing balance of hardware and software costs*

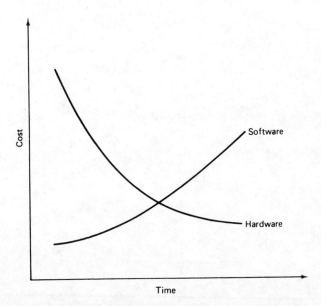

The inflation in wage rates has not only affected computer staff. Virtually all grades of staff now cost more in real money terms than they did in the early days of data processing. This, together with the reduced cost of computer hardware, means that it can be profitable to provide computer support to many more workers than ever before, despite increased software costs.

There is, therefore, a complex and constantly changing situation as computer equipment and software development costs move in opposite directions. As the potential benefits of computer usage increase, moreover, so too does the need of management to keep pace with a rapidly changing business environment. The net result of these changes tends to be a steady increase in the economic viability of computers for a wide variety of tasks.

3 The Impact of Data Processing on the Organisation

3.1 The Anticipated Impact

It is commonplace to state that computers have changed the world we live in. Indeed expressions such as the 'post-industrial society' and the 'information society' are, to a large extent, derived from visions of societies in which computers and computer power are ubiquitous. This realisation of the impact which computers have had and are having on our lives has not, however, always been evident. The initial forecasts for the use of computers were that they would be used for complex mathematical computation (it was widely assumed only scientific research establishments and universities would be the users). Indeed an extensive market research study predicted in the 1950s that the total world computer market would be about 1000 machines by the year 2000! Today no accurate count of the number of computers in the world is possible, but that they exist in millions and are used in every application from the originally envisaged mathematical computation for research through government and business administration to domestic use in consumer appliance control and 'home computers' is incontrovertible.

When it was realised that computers would be used extensively for administrative work the next prognosis was that middle management would become obsolete. Computers, it was believed, would eliminate most of the jobs that existed between the clerical staff (who would be producing input for the computer and using its output) and senior management (who would be taking strategic business decisions on the summarised data provided from the same computers). In practice the growth in the use of computers has almost exactly paralleled an explosive growth in the number of middle managers employed in government and industry around the world!

It was also widely assumed that once the 'computer revolution' was under way there would be a tremendous impact on business strategy, policy and planning; yet in the event these applications have proved among the most resistant to computer solutions.

3.2 **Changing Job Requirements**

So far we have indicated that the apparently reasonable forecasts of the impact that computers would make have not been fulfilled, but this is not to say that there has been no impact. Clearly, the advent of the computer has wrought significant (if largely unanticipated) changes on our organisations. One of the most significant changes has been in the types of white-collar skills that are needed in an organisation. Simultaneously, the advent of the computer has caused:

(a) the creation of new jobs,
(b) the elimination of certain jobs,
(c) the change of many jobs.

(a) The creation of new jobs
One of the paradoxes of automation through the use of computers is that it is a labour-intensive activity to introduce change! Modern, large-scale computers are surrounded by many skilled technicians who are necessary to analyse applications before the computer is used, to program the computer and maintain and operate the machines themselves. The list of jobs found in the typical computer installation of a medium-sized organisation is extensive and well over a hundred staff may be included within the computer department. Some of the jobs created (such as departmental management and the delivery of computer output) are recognisable as variations of tasks that are performed elsewhere within the organisation, but many (for example, computer programming) are completely new tasks which did not exist until the advent of the computer. In Chapter 13 the major tasks involved are explained and an outline of the human and educational requirements for each is provided.

In addition to the new jobs created in companies using computers, many new jobs have been created in the computer industry itself. The most obvious of these jobs are those involved in manufacturing, testing, selling and installing the computers themselves. In addition many new jobs in such fields as the writing of computer operating and generalised software and the production of such ancillary items as magnetic tape have also been created. As with an organisation's own computer department some of the jobs are recognisable variations of tasks found in many industries (for example, production control, electronics engineering and salesmanship), but others are unique to the computer industry.

The advent of the computer has, therefore, created new jobs in two ways. First, because it has been a growth area it has provided new openings for people with traditional or established skills. Second, and perhaps more importantly, it has created new tasks for which specific combinations of educational and personal characteristics are required.

(b) The elimination of certain tasks

As with most technological innovations, computers have been intermittently subjected to Luddite fears and opposition on the grounds that they 'eliminate jobs'. That they may eliminate specific jobs is undeniable but as we have seen they also create jobs. The balance between jobs lost and gained depends primarily on the growth of the economy concerned and is outside the scope of this book. It may, however, be observed that many jobs are created because computers make whole industries or projects feasible (the space research programme is an obvious example).

Nevertheless computers do eliminate certain jobs and, in mirror image of the way they create jobs, they both eliminate specific tasks and reduce the numbers employed on other tasks.

In Chapter 2 the work of the comptometer operator was briefly mentioned and this is one task which has been eliminated by the computer (aided and abetted by the pocket calculator). In the same way the job of the accounting-machine operator has disappeared (accounting machines were large electro-mechanical devices used for calculating wages, maintaining accounts and similar purposes). In most cases the people employed for their skills in using such machines were fairly readily absorbed into one of the new jobs created by the computer.

Where the computer has reduced the number of people needed to perform a certain task the adjustment has not always been so smooth and, as noted earlier, the opportunities for those displaced to find alternative employment have depended in large part on the growth (or otherwise) of the local economy. On the whole, however, the number of redundancies caused by the introduction of computers *per se* has been remarkably small. In many cases computers have been installed to cope with expansion, or to provide additional levels of management control or customer service. Where redundancy has occurred it has mainly been achieved by redeployment of the staff concerned or by natural wastage, for example employees retiring (perhaps earlier than anticipated) or otherwise leaving of their own volition.

One of the jobs where the computer has reduced numbers is work clerks and timekeepers where computer printouts and other ways of disseminating and, especially, collecting data at shop-floor level have eliminated many clerical positions.

(c) The change of many jobs

In addition to creating and eliminating jobs the computer has caused changes to the working lives of a great many people. The most visible manifestation of this is where the computer has been brought directly into the work routine.

A familiar example of this is found at the check-in counters for nearly every airline at nearly every airport. As soon as a passenger presents his ticket to the clerk he or she will type the name and flight number on to a convenient keyboard connected to a computer and almost instantaneously details of the flight (whether it is on time, which gate it will depart from, etc.) and confirmation of the passenger's reservation are displayed on a small screen. The clerk can then relate the information to the passenger (often also assigning a specific seat on the aircraft as well). The fact that the passenger has arrived, the weight of his baggage and his seat assignment can then all be stored in the computer and used to calculate operational and statistical information on the flight.

If for any reason it is necessary for the passenger to make any change to his itinerary (for example, to change a connecting flight because of the late departure of his first flight) this can often be achieved using the same computer system. Similar systems exist for hotel and package-tour reservations. In all cases the computer terminal becomes an integral part of the operator's work station and the use of it a part of most, if not all, of the tasks performed.

For many people the ubiquitous computer printout brings the computer into their daily work. Examples could easily fill the remainder of this book but a few will illustrate the enormous range of possibilities.

For many employed as materials controllers, production controllers, salesmen, inventory control clerks or in any other role which involves knowing how much of a particular item is available; a computer printout, replaced daily, obviates the need to maintain individual records. Similarly, a credit manager may use a short computer-produced list identifying 'bad risks' rather than maintain his own records. In these and many other cases the computer is releasing the individual from the necessity to spend time on routine record-keeping, thus freeing him or her to perform the task for which they are really employed. Moreover, in a properly designed system the records should be more accurate than those maintained manually and the total amount of paper circulating within the organisation should be reduced. Another use of computer printout is to provide work instructions. Thus in a complicated assembly process where many similar but different items are manufactured, a computer printout showing the materials to be used and the way they are to be assembled produced for each item may replace the complex manuals, each needing constant revision, which were previously necessary.

These are not the only ways in which computers have changed jobs. Consider the case of the design engineer who 'draws' a component on to a television-like screen using a light pen and then, when he is satisfied, presses a button and a drawing is automatically performed for him. Or the astronomer whose complex calculations might have taken years using log tables, but who can now have them performed on a computer in a few hours. Another example is the garage mechanic who, for some makes of car, now only has to link the vehicle to a small computer and run the engine for a few minutes to obtain a detailed diagnosis of the state of the engine tune.

For these jobs and for many more the computer has brought change: change in a way in which the work is performed and change in the amount of work that can be accomplished.

3.3 Centralisation and Formalisation

Early computers generally required a specialised environment in which they were installed. Air-conditioning, specially raised floors so that connecting cables could be buried and 'clean' power supplies were invariably necessary. Moreover, specialised staff were necessary to control and operate the computer. These factors combined with the high cost of acquiring (or even renting) a computer meant that for most organisations a single computer centre was established. Even for those organisations where there was sufficient work to justify more than one computer, computer centres were, of necessity, established in such a way that they were isolated from the rest of the organisation's staff and operations. This isolation, moreover, was reinforced by the need to institute formal procedures to process work through the computer centre and the attendant processes (data capture, the preparation of the continuous computer printout for office use, etc.).

Almost inevitably these factors, reinforced by the fact that working with computers was new and the staff involved used special jargon to describe their work, meant that in many organisations an alienation of the workforce from the centralisation epitomised by the computer was experienced. 'It's the computer's fault' became a standard explanation for many faults – whatever their real cause. (Computers, of course, rarely make mistakes; faults are almost invariably due to the computer being given instructions which are erroneous or incomplete or being fed with inaccurate data.)

This feeling of alienation from the main computer centre experienced in many organisations, coupled with the increasing realisation by staff at all levels that computers have, nevertheless, a major role to play in assisting people perform many types of activity has been one of the main thrusts towards the development and popularity of relatively small, robust and 'user friendly' computers. These machines, called mini, micro or personal computers, are cheap enough to be installed throughout an organisation and not just centralised in one location. Indeed, the economics of some of these machines is such that it is now becoming commonplace to see them in general offices or on individuals' desks, even though the individual or department does not have a sufficient workload to require the machine to be in use for more than an hour or two per day (such machines do not require air conditioning or special electrical supplies). At the same time, considerable effort has also been expended in trying to make the use of big, central computers less intimidating. To this end new software has been developed which in many cases is designed to enable the non-computer specialist to use the computer directly, and many organisations have also introduced special staff whose sole task it is to act as liaison personnel between those in line positions and the computer specialists.

For many jobs, therefore, computers have brought change: change in the way in which the work is performed and change in the way in which the work and ultimately the business itself is organised.

Although these technological and organisational developments, aided by the greatly increased familiarity of computers, have gone a considerable way towards overcoming the problems outlined above, the computer practitioner must, however, always be aware of the danger that he or she and their work can become remote from, or seem irrelevant to, the organisation that they exist to support.

4 The Data Processing Industry

4.1 **The Structure of the Industry**

The data processing industry covers a wide spectrum. As used in this chapter the term will be taken to mean any organisation, whether profit-making or not, which derives all, or a major part, of its revenues from the sale of goods or services provided to the users of data processing. Thus, at the one extreme it includes the large, multinational computer manufacturers whose names are household words, and, at the other extreme, it includes numerous one-man companies who offer freelance programming services.

In fact the industry comprises a few very large companies, mostly operating on an international basis, and a large number of small organisations whose staff is numbered in dozens or the low hundreds rather than in thousands.

For convenience the industry can be divided into three major segments: the computer manufacturers, software manufacturers and the data processing service industry.

4.2 **Computer Manufacturers**

The international market for large computers has long been dominated by International Business Machines (IBM) the American multinational corporation which is the major supplier of computers in most countries in the western worlk. Indeed at one time this sector of the industry was referred to as 'IBM and the Seven Dwarfs', the seven dwarfs being the other computer manufacturers (Honeywell, Unisys, CDC, NCR, etc.) – themselves large companies but having a much smaller share of the total market. In specific markets the dominance of IBM has sometimes been challenged. Thus in the market for the very largest machines Control Data Corporation (CDC) has held a significant position and in the United Kingdom, International Computers Limited (ICL) have competed with IBM throughout the range.

Nevertheless, IBM has become the dominant force in the market for a wide range of commercial and scientific computers. This has in turn produced a situation where a very large body of organisations throughout the western world have major investments in computer systems and software designed to operate on IBM computers. Converting such systems to other computers can be a time-consuming and expensive exercise which, moreover, takes resources away from other more productive work. There is thus a wide range of organisations which are effectively 'locked in' to IBM's technology. (This phenomenon does, of course, also tend to protect the market position of other computer manufacturers, but since this is smaller the effect is less significant.) One consequence is that other companies (NAS, Amdahl, etc.) have developed their own computers which are 'IBM compatible', i.e. designed to use software written for IBM systems with minimal changes. This approach is different from that pursued by ICL, Honeywell, Unisys, etc., who have developed their own technology in parallel with rather than in imitation of IBM.

In addition to computers which are designed to be IBM compatible, various peripheral items such as additional memory, magnetic tape and magnetic disk drives which are direct replacements for their IBM equivalents have been marketed and these are called '*plug-to-plug compatible*' devices, i.e. they can be used to replace the IBM equivalent simply by unplugging the latter and plugging in the replacement. Such devices can often be marketed more cheaply than the IBM equivalent because their manufacturers are not incurring the full costs of developing a whole range of machines and software. Competition has undoubtedly been stimulated by the development of compatible equipment.

One reason for IBM's continued dominance of the market for medium-sized and larger computers has been its ability to invest more on research and development (R & D) than other companies in the industry. Despite the fact that they are large companies in their own right (and in some cases backed by even larger companies) no other computer company has sustained the same level of expenditure on R & D or been active in such a wide range of hardware and software.

Although computers have been a growth industry, not all manufacturers have found them profitable. This has been due not only to the high R & D costs involved, but also the high costs of supporting customers' installations in many different places.

Some companies (e.g. RCA and Philips) have in fact withdrawn from the large general purpose computer market while others have experienced financial difficulties and/or have received Government assistance (e.g. ICL).

4.3 **Software Manufacturers**

It may at first sight seem strange to think of software being manufactured, but many companies now offer software as a product. The computer manufacturers are themselves very active as developers and suppliers of computer software, but there is also a group of specialist companies whose main business is the development and marketing of generalised software designed to be used by many organisations, and the largest of them are multi-million pound companies. Some of these companies concentrate on developing and marketing systems or utility software, while others specialise in productivity aids or application software (see Chapter 7). In some cases (especially where the software is intended to be used on a micro or personal computer) the software product is packaged in such a way that it can be sold by mail order or through retail shops. In this case the product (the computer programs being sold) is provided on a cassette or, more usually, a floppy disk (see Chapter 6) and supplied with information to the purchaser on how to install and use the product. In a commercial environment, data base management systems for personal computers, spreadsheets and word processing packages are among those most commonly sold in this manner. Hundreds of thousands of the most popular products have been sold.

At the other extreme, application software products, i.e. those computer programs which actually address the user's business problems (often called applications packages or simply packages) for major business functions to be used on a mainframe computer may have a price exceeding half a million pounds and require months of careful work by the supplier and purchaser working together to modify and implement on the purchaser's computer. Such packages may be designed for a specific industry, e.g. banking systems, hotel management systems, systems for travel agents, etc., or may be aimed at functions found in many organisations. Examples of packages available for specific functions include: payroll, general ledger, accounts receivable, accounts payable, fixed assets register, purchasing, inventory control, personnel records, manufacturing resource planning, maintenance engineering planning and computer aided design.

4.4 **The Data Processing Services Industry**

The third major element of the data processing industry identified above was the services element. This in turn consists of a number of distinct elements. The major sub-divisions are:

* service bureaux
* systems houses
* consultancies
* personnel recruitment and 'body shopping' agencies
* computer shops
* training organisations
* leasing companies
* other services

Some of the companies involved are active in more than one of these fields.

(a) Service bureaux

Historically probably the largest sector of the computer services industry, service bureaux were established to provide computing power to other organisations. Thus they offered the use of a computer (often with additional specialist software) to organisations which either didn't have or wanted to supplement their existing computing power. Both batch and on-line services (see Chapters 17–18) have been widely used. Increasingly, companies in this sector of the industry are supplementing the provision of basic computer with additional hardware, software and communications facilities to increase the value added to the basic services provided. A particular sub-division of this sector of the industry is facilities management. In this arrangement a service bureau contracts to do all the routine data processing operations (including the provision of staff and computers) for a client company, often on the client's premises and using those facilities exclusively for that client.

(b) Systems houses

Systems houses were mainly set up to develop bespoke (i.e. tailor-made) software for other organisations on a contract basis, which might be either a fixed price or time and materials (i.e. essentially cost plus) contract. From this base many systems houses have expanded their services to offer generalised software packages (see Section 4.3 above) or to be OEM (original equipment manufacturer) and/or turnkey suppliers. These latter two categories enable the customer to contract with a single source for a complete system, including both hardware and software, to meet some mutually agreed specification.

(c) Consultancies

Consultancies exist to provide a range of advisory services to users of computers. Typically advice covers such aspects as when to acquire a computer, what work should be put onto it, which computer should be selected, how the computer operations should be organised, etc. After a computer has been installed consultants may advise on the standards and methodologies to be adopted in developing systems, the policy for the development of data processing within the organisation, staffing and expenditure levels, security procedures, etc. Some consultancies specialise in a particular field, e.g. the use of computers in banking.

Consultancy services in data processing are offered by computer manufacturers, software houses, traditional management consultancies and consultancies attached to accountancy practices as well as specialist data processing consultancies. Since independence is the crux of a consultant's advice great care should be exercised in accepting such services from an organisation whose main objective is to sell some other product.

(d) Personnel recruitment and 'body shopping' agencies

As noted in Chapter 1, data processing is a labour-intensive activity. Moreover, rapid growth and technological change has meant that for considerable periods there has been a shortage of suitably qualified and experienced staff. Many of the staff available have also developed the desire to work on the most interesting applications from a technical viewpoint, using the latest hardware and software. These pressures and the desire to 'cash in' on the skills acquired have historically led to high turnover of computer staff. In consequence, specialist recruitment agencies have been developed to assist organisations in the recruitment of computing staff.

A further development has been the advent of the contractor. This phenomenon results in individuals (often incorporated as limited liability companies to secure beneficial tax treatment) offering their services on a body shop basis through an agency. Such agencies provide a marketing and commercial framework for many individuals and deduct a percentage of the fee provided by the user company in return for their services.

(e) Computer shops

A fairly recent development has been the emergence of computer shops in high streets up and down the country, either as separate shops or as departments in larger stores. These shops cater not only to the hobby computer market but also to a part of the commercial data processing market. Typically such companies are agents or dealers for personal computers from two or three manufacturers, a range of packaged software, computer supplies (paper, printer ribbons, floppy disks, etc.) and provide training, maintenance and other support services aimed at the non-specialist computer user. While perhaps aimed primarily at the smaller organisation without its own data processing department, such shops can and do also provide useful services for larger organisations.

(f) Training organisations

The rapid technological change in the field of data processing has created a large market for training. In part this need has been filled by the conventional academic education channels (universities, polytechnics, colleges of technology, etc.) and by the computer manufacturers who provide instruction on the use of their own equipment, but a large part of the need has been met by independent training organisations. In some cases these organisations are affiliated to a computer manufacturer or software house while in other cases they are completely independent. Some of these companies organise a wide range of courses while others offer only a single course which may be on a narrow and specialised topic.

The plethora of training sources makes it difficult to compare the training actually received by different individuals in the data processing industry.

(g) Leasing companies

The existence of leasing companies in connection with the acquisition of computers has already been discussed in Chapter 2. Those companies specialising in the leasing of computers and related equipment form an integral part of the computer services industry.

(h) Other services

In addition to the categories outlined above, there are numerous other service companies in the data processing industry. These include: independent maintenance companies (who offer an alternative to obtaining maintenance from the vendor of a computer or his agent); second-hand computer brokers (often associated with leasing companies); data entry services (which prepare computer input from the customer's own documents – see Chapter 6.5); companies which provide Computer Output on Microfilm (COM) services (COM is described in Chapter 6.3); printing companies specialising in computer stationery; and companies marketing a wide range of computer-related supplies ranging from magnetic media (see Chapter 6) through specialist office furniture to anti-static mats and fireproof safes for storing magnetic tapes.

4.5 **Related Organisations**

Data processing has not only created a whole new industry, but it has also spawned a complete community of interests. In this section some of the most important of these will be introduced. They are:

* professional bodies
* Government-sponsored organisations
* standards organisations
* trade press
* user groups
* telecommunication service organisations.

(a) Professional bodies

A number of professional bodies catering for the computer specialist and/or the data processing practitioner have been established. Some of these, such as the British Computer Society, conduct qualifying examinations of a high standard while others concentrate mainly on providing a forum in which experienced staff with common interests can pursue their aims and interests. Nearly all of these bodies publish magazines or journals and the best of these contain some of the most significant papers being published on the subject. In addition many of the professional bodies hold regular meetings at local or regional level as well as annual national meetings. Membership is typically by election (with or without qualifying examinations) and full membership usually requires several years' experience in the field although most bodies have student and/or less-experienced membership categories.

(b) Government-sponsored organisations

Recognising the importance of data processing to the national economy, many governments have sought to foster its development through direct intervention and/or the creation of schemes and bodies to encourage its growth. Direct intervention normally takes the form of involvement with the manufacturer or suppliers of computer equipment or services or through investment grants, etc.

Indirect intervention may take the form of positive government action to stimulate activity in the field or the creation of organisations to act as catalysts to development. One example of the former is the British Government's Grants for New Technology feasibility study programme aimed at stimulating the use of microprocessors, especially in manufacturing industry. This project provides grants to organisations establishing training programs or wishing to employ consultants to assess the potential of microprocessors in their organisation.

Another example of indirect Government intervention is the United Kingdom's National Computing Centre (NCC). The NCC is a hybrid software house, information centre, consultancy, publisher, standards and training organisation. Initially funded by both industry and Government, the NCC is now funded almost entirely by sales of its products.

In many countries governments also have regulatory functions relating to data processing. These may include registration or control of data relating to people, e.g. age, credit status, health, etc. (as with the UK's Data Registrar), controls over the import and export of data processing equipment and regulations governing data transmission.

(c) Standards organisations

The need for standards in data processing is vital if developments are to take place in such a way that the maximum benefit can be derived from them. Interface problems between equipment for example can become intolerable unless adequate standards exist. In many countries this has been recognised and although the rapid pace of technical development has made the task difficult, much progress has been made. The major national standard organisations (whose activities cover many fields in addition to data processing) have formulated many standards which have been widely adopted both nationally and internationally. These bodies include the American National Standards Institute (ANSI), the British Standards Institute (BSI) and Deutsche Industrie-Norm (DIN). In addition, the International Standards Organisation (ISO) has also been active in this field.

(d) Trade press

The data processing field has created its own literature. In addition to the wide range of book titles published by the reputable technical publishers and the journals of the professional bodies there is a wide range of other publications. Much of this is published by the computer manufacturers and covers not only their own equipment and software, but also a wide variety of related data processing topics (IBM has been described as the world's largest publisher).

In addition to the material provided by the computer manufacturers a number of independent companies produce comparative data on the equipment of several manufacturers. Among the best known of these evaluations, which are updated regularly, are those published by Datapro and Auerbach.

There is also a wide range of technical and industry newspapers and periodicals catering exclusively for the data processing community or sub-sections of it. Many of these are only available by direct mail subscription, but with the spread of personal computing a number are now available through the normal retail outlets.

(e) User groups

In many cases users of specific hardware and/or software have found it useful to form into user groups to discuss common problems and in some cases to exert combined pressure on the vendor of the hardware or software concerned. The biggest of these groups (those formed by users of the computers and/or software supplied by the major vendors) have regular national and international meetings and attract some of the leading speakers in the industry to address their conferences.

(f) Telecommunications service organisations

In Chapter 11 the links necessary to connect computer systems together are discussed. In most countries the provision of these links is a state-monopoly. In the United Kingdom the main provider of these links is British Telecom and in other countries they are normally provided by a division of the PTT.

Another type of service making use of computer and telecommunications technology is the *value added network* (VAN). The best known of these is probably PRESTEL, British Telecom's information dissemination service, which enables subscribers to browse through large quantities of information using a specially equipped television set. Other VANs offer such services as access to specialised databases of information and *electronic mail*, i.e. the transmission of 'written' messages via telecommunications to specific terminal destination(s) where they can be stored and 'read' when convenient.

Part II

The Tools of Data Processing

5 Computers – The Machines

5.1 **What is a Computer?**

The computers used in data processing are composed of one or more electronic machines using digital signals for recording and moving data and instructions.

Since the computer is an electronic device and works using electronic signals – electrical impulses – it follows that interfaces have to exist between the computer itself and the people using it:

(a) to provide it with instruction and 'raw material' or data, and
(b) to understand the information produced by processing the data.

Thus, at its simplest, a computer can be represented as consisting of three connected elements (Figure 5.1). All these elements are essential if the computer is to be of any practical use, but in many ways the most important element is the *central processor*. As shown in Figure 5.2 this is in turn composed of a number of different functional units. The exact *architecture* within the central processor varies considerably between computers and it is not unusual for several central processors to be linked together to form one more powerful central processor. Moreover, the arrangements of storage differ considerably between different computers. Nevertheless, the schematic in Figure 5.2 shows the essential functions and how they interrelate.

The *control unit* performs three main tasks: it accesses in sequence the instructions that the computer has been given, interprets them

Fig 5.1 *the elements of a computer*

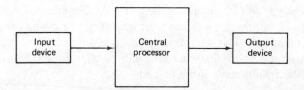

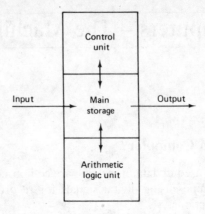

Fig 5.2   *schematic of the central processor unit (CPU) of a computer*

and initiates the appropriate action. The action taken will include moving the data from the input device to main storage and subsequently to the other parts of the computer as required, as well as performing arithmetic and logic operations. The actual list of operations that a computer can perform is known as its *instruction set*.

Clearly, the control unit has to be able to distinguish between the instructions which it is to follow and the data on which it is to perform them. It must, moreover, be able to deal with the first item of data or instruction that is presented to it! At this point the close interaction between the control unit and the control or systems software (see Chapter 7) becomes of vital importance.

Most computers perform operations on a cyclical basis, that is to say they perform a given instruction before proceeding with another. The time to process an average instruction is called the computer's *cycle time*.

The *main storage* also called *memory* is that part of the total storage of the computer from which instructions are executed and is therefore normally the fastest storage unit of the computer (i.e. data can more quickly be accessed and moved in this part of the computer than anywhere else).

The *arithmetic logic unit* (ALU) performs the actual manipulation of data taking its raw material from and replacing the answer to the main storage. As its name implies, the ALU performs both arithmetic (add, subtract, etc.) and logic operations (e.g. the comparison of two numbers). The ALU thus needs to be instructed by the control unit on what it has to do, where the data to be used is to be found and where the results have to be placed.

It has already been observed that the internal signals of a computer are electrical impulses which are, of course, unintelligible to human beings. These impulses may be either on or off and have only these two states. Using these two states, however, all the arithmetic and logic operations can be performed. This is achieved by using *binary arithmetic* and *Boolean algebra* (also called *Boolean logic*).

Binary arithmetic involves converting all conventional data (which is digital or uses a base of 10, i.e. the numbers 1–9 and 0) to binary or base 2 format (using only 1 and 0). The 0 and 1 are referred to as *binary digits* or '*bits*'. These two symbols can then be represented by an electrical current being ON or OFF.

Similarly, electrical impulses can be used to process Boolean algebra or logic operations. (George Boole was a nineteenth-century mathematician who devised an algebraic notation to express logical relationships.) It is used in computers because it reduces the number of variables resulting from a logic statement to either 'true' or 'false', and these states may therefore be expressed by the presence or absence of an electrical impulse.

The detailed operations of binary arithmetic and Boolean algebra are outside the scope of this book, but in any case they are transparent to most users of modern data processing computers. (The reader who wants to know more is referred to the works listed in the Bibliography.) It is usually sufficient to present data to the computer in conventional digital form and the results in due course will be in the same form, all the translation or conversion taking place automatically within the computer.

It will be realised that the paths along which data and information pass between and within the input, central processor and output devices are an important part of the total computer. These paths have various names, the terms '*bus*', '*data highway*', '*trunk*', '*channel*' and '*multiplexer*' all being used.

Before leaving this brief overview of the main elements and functions of a computer there is one more element that should be considered. In addition to the main storage nearly all computers have a significant amount of *backing store*. The high cost of main storage has meant that it has often been cost effective to supplement a relatively small amount of main store with much larger quantities of backing store which usually offers lower cost per unit of storage together with slower access times and larger capacities. Some types of backing store are external to the CPU and will be considered as peripheral devices (e.g. disk storage), whereas other types of backing store appear to the users to be part of the CPU itself and are distinguished only by their differenct cost/performance ratio and capacity; this approach is sometimes referred to as *cache memory* or *buffer storage*.

The speed of computer storage (both main and backing storage) is measured as the length of time it takes from the initiation of a transfer of data to or from that store to the time at which that transfer is complete. *Access time* is measured in minute fractions of a second, the most commonly used being milliseconds, microseconds, nanoseconds and picoseconds. The values associated with each of these terms is shown in Figure 5.3. Different computers access different amounts of data during an access and this must be taken into account as well as the access time itself when comparing data transfer rates.

Another technique which is used to extend the usable amount of storage with good price performance characteristics is the *virtual storage* (VS) technique. This technique enables the user to make use of large amounts of backing store as if it were main store. The control unit then 'rolls in' (i.e. reads) the appropriate sections of the backing store into the main store as they are needed, giving the illusion that the data or information is located in main store. Obviously this approach involves a more complex control system, but it is now widely used.

The storage capacity of a computer usually refers to the capacity of the main store and (usually) cache or buffer storage. Storage capacity is normally quoted in thousands (or K) of bytes or words. The *byte* is the smallest unit in which useful data is normally stored and usually consists of eight bits (i.e. eight zeros or ones). Thus each byte can

---

Fig 5.3   *measures of computer access and cycle times*

Term	Description	Value	Abbreviation
Millisecond	One thousandth of a second	$\frac{1}{1000}$ second	msec.
Microsecond	One millionth of a second	$\frac{1}{1000000}$ or 10^{-6} sec	μ sec.
Nanosecond	One thousand millionth of a second (one American billion)	10^{-9} sec	nsec
Picosecond	One billionth of a second (British)	10^{-12} sec	psec.

theoretically hold any one of 2^8 or 256 different combinations of zeros and ones. This is more than sufficient to represent the letters A–Z, the numbers 0–9 and necessary special characters and punctuation marks (e.g. $ £ * . , – / etc.).

For convenience of handling, bytes are sometimes grouped into *words* which range from 2–8 bytes. Because of the organisation of storage and the binary system used for addressing it, computer storage is almost invariably produced in multiples of 2^{10} (or 1024) bytes. Notwithstanding the slight inaccuracy, the term K is used (K is an abbreviation of kilo, meaning one thousand). Thus if the capacity of a computer is quoted as 512 K it means that it has 512 × 1024 (524 488) bytes of main storage. (Sometimes capacity is quoted as K words.) Increasingly the term *megabyte* (Mb, meaning literally one million or, in computer usage, 1024 × 1024 = 1 048 576 bytes) is necessary to describe computer capacity.

When comparing cars it is necessary to evaluate a number of features to get an accurate assessment of their relative performance. Thus not only engine power, but also body style and gearing, are relevant factors. Similarly, with computers there are a number of factors which must be considered when they are compared.

Among the most important of these factors are:

* storage capacity
* access speed
* cycle speed
* channel capacity
* instruction set
* available peripherals
* mips (millions of instructions per second).

It is the combination of these factors which gives an overall assessment of the performance of a computer, classifies it and determines its suitability (or otherwise) for a given application. In the following sections some broad categories of computers will be considered. The main characteristics of each category are summarised in Figure 5.4.

5.2 Supercomputers

Sometimes colloquially referred to as 'number crunchers', supercomputers are specially aimed at scientific and technical institutions which have a need for the largest amount of computer power available for use in such applications as astronomy, nuclear physics and meteorology. The true supercomputers embody a rather different architecture than that used in most commercially oriented

Fig 5.4 *typical characteristics for categories of computers*

Category	Cycle speed	No. of channels/ comm. lines	Typical word size (bits)	Typical memory size	Typical mips rate	Typical machines	Typical architecture
Supercomputer	16 Nsec	16–32	32, 64, or 128	up to 256 Mb	50+	AMDAHL mod 1200 CDC Cyber CRAY X-MP series	Designed for large-scale scientific and array calculations. Feature vector processing architecture
Mainframe	18.5–300 Nsec	6–48	32, 36, 48	1–256 Mb	1–25	ICL 2900 IBM 30xx IBM 43xx BURROUGHS B7900 HONEYWELL DPS8	Typically feature multiple channels
Supermini	75–810 Nsec	up to 512	32	512K to 32 Mb	Range overlaps with mainframe	HP 3000 VAX 11/xxx	Bus architecture
Minicomputer	6–13 MHz clock	up to 32	12, 16 or 24	32K to 4 Mb	1–4 up to 38 with array co-processor	HP 1000 PDP 11/xx	Single bus architecture
Micro or personal computer	3–14 MHz clock	—	8, 16 or 32	256K to 7 Mb	up to 20 with array co-processor	IMB PC XT HP 9000 Apple MacIntosh	Majority are stand alone, single-user systems.

machines (often using an approach called vector processing) and are designed to process arrays of data at very high speed (an array is a two or more dimensional table of cells). True supercomputers can process data at rates in excess of 50 million instructions per second (mips).

5.3 **Mainframe Computers**

Mainframe computers is a term which has come into use to describe data processing and large computers built to a conventional architecture. These machines are the logical descendants of the earliest computers and can trace their ancestry directly from machines like the LEO referred to in Chapter 1. As technology has advanced these machines have become larger (in terms of capacity) and faster and their cost performance ratio has improved greatly but their underlying philosophy has continued unchanged.

Mainframe computers are offered in a wide range of models, capacities and prices by a number of companies. The majority of the western world's mainframe computers are manufactured by American-owned companies. These companies offer a wide range of data-processing-related services as well as providing the equipment itself and provide significant support to users of their machines.

The major characteristics of mainframe computers are that they:

* are based on the philosophy that computing power should be concentrated. This implies that many people make use of the same machine with a consequent increase in organisational and especially software complexity
* normally require a specially protected environment (e.g. air-conditioning) as they are sensitive to variations in temperature, humidity, dust, etc.
* usually require specialist operators and programmers to support them
* usually have a wide range of peripherals
* incorporate large data-storage capabilities
* incorporate high-speed data channels to facilitate high through-put rates
* can make use of a wide variety of software including high-level languages and data-base handlers.

The combination of a wide range of peripheral devices (and the high performance of these devices), the large storage capacity, high channel capacity and wide range of software support makes these the machines used for most Government and commercial administrative purposes. It is, therefore, generally mainframe computers that prepare telephone bills, gas bills, electricity bills, create rate demands, prepare wage and salary slips, keep the accounts and personnel records for large organisations, keep records of driving licences, provide reservation systems for airlines and perform a multitude of other similar tasks.

In many cases these tasks are performed simultaneously or at least appear to be to the operator and user (a process known as *multiprogramming*). The common denominator of these applications is that they involve large quantities of data as input and usually large quantities of output. Moreover, these applications usually require the use of very large quantities of historical and static data. It is because of these requirements that the architecture of mainframe computers includes high-capacity data channels and their manufacturers provide a wide range of high-performance peripheral devices.

It is not uncommon with the large mainframes for two or more computers to be used in harness. This may take the form of using a relatively smaller machine as a '*front-end processor*' (see also Chapter 11) to carry out specific preliminary processing functions such as sorting and validating data received from different places, leaving the mainframe free to 'concentrate' on the actual applications themselves. Alternatively, two or more processors, called *multiprocessors* or *attached processors*, may be joined in such a way that they both are used in processing. Similarly, a specialised array processor may be added to a mainframe to offload repetitive computational tasks. Another arrangement is to use a second computer duplicating the work of the first. In this way either can go on working if the other fails. Although expensive, such a '*hot back-up*' arrangement may be necessary in some highly critical applications (see also Chapter 15).

A mainframe computer and its peripherals (the term 'mainframe computer' sometimes refers to both and sometimes only to the CPU) are put together in a *configuration* (also called a *computer* or *system*) to the customer's specification. A wide variety of combinations may, therefore, be encountered as different models and options of both the CPU and peripherals are selected to meet specific needs.

5.4 **Minicomputers and Superminis**

The term '*minicomputer*' began to be used in the 1960s to refer to those small computers that were then being developed for industrial and military control purposes. Because of their intended use these computers were built to operate in unprotected environments and to offer extremely high levels of reliability. This was achieved in part by making use of new developments in electronics – notably the integrated circuit – and this also helped provide extremely favourable cost/performance characteristics for the new machines. The use for which they were originally intended made the architecture of these machines noticeably different from that of mainframes and the range and performance of peripherals in general was somewhat limited. In particular minicomputers had rather less capacity to manipulate and store data. Moreover, the support provided by the manufacturers and the software available were both very limited by comparison with mainframe computers, factors which in turn helped keep the price of the new machines low.

It soon became realised, however, both by the manufacturers of these minicomputers and by the organisations with data processing problems to solve, that these machines had a valuable role to play in commercial data processing. This realisation was also assisted by the trend which became evident during the late 1960s and has continued ever since, of integrating industrial or manufacturing control computing with commercial data processing. Two manufacturers in particular (Digital Equipment Company, the makers of the PDP and VAX ranges of computers, and Hewlett Packard) have been especially active in developing and marketing what started as 'industrial' computers to the commercial or data processing markets.

The largest of the machines which stem from this line of development (sometimes called *superminis*) are now comparable in most respects to the conventional mainframes. As a class, however, they still show signs of their origins in such ways as:

* the lack of the need for air-conditioning, etc.
* the limited channel capacity offered in relation to their size and speed
* the relatively underdeveloped range of peripherals available (e.g. lack of really high-speed printers)
* the limited software available for such activities as data-base handling
* the relatively limited support offered by the manufacturers
* the ease of use which facilitates the direct operation of the machine by end-users rather than necessitating the employment of many layers of computer specialists
* favourable cost/performance ratios.

These machines have found a wide market both as data processing machines in organisations not large enough to justify a conventional mainframe computer and to handle specific data processing tasks (often related to industrial, manufacturing or operational needs) for organisations which are already users of mainframe computers.

Among the many applications of minicomputers which illustrate this latter type of use, the following example is typical.

A major manufacturing company uses a conventional mainframe computer for the standard accounting, personnel and statistical purposes. This machine also monitors sales and orders and arranges for the purchase of the necessary parts. Two large minicomputers (superminis) receive (via magnetic tape) details of the items to be manufactured and the parts ordered and when they are to be delivered. One of these machines is used to plan and track the workload in the factory whilst the other is used to control the flow of material into, through and out of the plant. This latter machine also provides instructions to a further minicomputer which directly controls an automated warehouse and its associated conveyor system.

5.5 Micro or Personal Computers

In the last few years the terms *microprocessors* and *microcomputers* have come into common use and with them they have brought such terms as LSI, VLSI, and, of course, 'the chip'. All these terms are the product of the miniaturisation of electronic components which has become possible through recent developments in technology.

Early computers used mercury delay lines, but these soon gave way to valves. In due course the semiconductor and transistor were developed and gave a major impetus to electronics in general and to computers in particular. The next development was integrated circuits, which are semiconductor devices containing circuit elements manufactured in a single piece of material and which are indivisibly connected to perform a specified function. As the technology developed it became possible to include more and more circuits on a single piece of material leading to LSI (*Large-scale Integration*) meaning up to 500 logic gates or 16 K memory bits on a single sliver of material (*the silicon chip*). VLSI (*Very Large-scale Integration*) refers to even higher densities of circuits on a chip.

These developments in the field of electronics have influenced data processing in two ways. First, they have enabled the performance of all computers to be improved and, second, they have enabled the microcomputer to be developed.

The microcomputer is a fully functional computing device combining the elements identified at the beginning of this chapter. A microprocessor, by contrast, is a LSI design that provides, on one or more chips, similar functions to those of the CPU identified in Figure

5.2 above. A microcomputer therefore includes a microprocessor, but not every microprocessor is a microcomputer.

For data processing purposes a microcomputer is necessary (although microprocessors find their way into many of the pieces of equipment used in full-scale computers). Microcomputers start at a very low threshold cost. These machines have very limited input and output capabilities, limited software and little storage capacity. On the other hand they are cheap and easy to use – many children have taught themselves to use this type of equipment, using only a manual for guidance.

For a price equal to a few months' salary for a middle-level manager, it is possible to purchase a personal computer (PC) with 512 K or 1 Mb of memory, a typewriter-like keyboard for input, a built-in hard disk and one or two floppy disk units (see Chapter 6) for backing store, a monitor like a television screen and a printer for output. Such a computer may be used on a stand-alone basis to perform many of the normal commercial functions for the smaller company or to meet particular application needs within larger organisations. Although these machines may be programmed in the same way as other computers, they are often used with software packages (see Chapter 7) supplied by the vendor or a specialist software house. Among the most popular such packages (and, therefore, the most common uses of PCs) are those which offer:

* word processing
* spreadsheet processing
* graphics applications

Other applications for which PCs are widely used include training (computer aided learning), monitoring industrial plant or equipment, and office automation.

Increasingly, PCs within a department or organisation are being linked together with a local area network (LAN) so that each PC can make use of all the programs and data within the network and is not limited only to the programs and data available on a single machine. For the same reason within larger organisations PCs are being linked to mainframes. In this case a typical application would entail downloading data from the mainframe to the PC where it might be subjected to some analysis, revision or the use of simulation techniques, or, through the use of a graphics package, be turned into a series of charts for incorporation into a report prepared on the PC using a word processing package.

Clearly these developments make extensive use of data communication technology, a subject to which we shall return in Chapter 11.

One further development in the PC market has been the introduction of portable machines which typically include keyboard, small monitor and a hard and/or floppy disk unit in a single unit the size of a large briefcase which can be used anywhere that has a standard, domestic power supply. Although the early machines earned the unfortunate sobriquet 'luggables', these machines have sold in large numbers to people whose jobs entail travelling and/or who want the convenience of being able to take the computer home to enable them to continue work in the evenings or at weekends.

A more recent development is the 'laptop' computer, a small computer with keyboard, flat screen display and some backing store. These machines are truly portable and many run on batteries as well as on mains supply, so the busy executive can continue computing even when travelling.

Obviously the microcomputer in no sense rivals the mainframe or minicomputer. The limitations on data storage, input and output capabilities are severe for most data processing uses. They do, nevertheless, further lower the threshold size of business for which computer data processing is a practical proposition and provide data processing support in a range of uses for which it had not hitherto been economic.

6 Computer Peripherals and Input Devices

6.1 Types of Computer Peripherals

In the previous chapter we have seen that input and output devices are essential parts of any computer used for data processing and also noted that computers make use of backing store to enhance their capability. Collectively input and output devices connected to the computer together with those types of backing store which are connected to but not fully integrated into the CPU are referred to as *peripheral units* or more simply *peripherals*.

In this chapter the main types of peripherals will be discussed and for convenience they will be grouped into four main categories. It should be noted, however, that these categories are not mutually exclusive. A magnetic tape drive can, for example, be used as a backing store and also for output and input purposes. A second word of caution concerns input devices. Some of these may be on-line to a computer in one application and off-line in another (i.e. in some cases they may be directly under the control of the CPU, whereas in others they may be used independently of the computer itself).

The categories of peripherals considered in this chapter are:

* data storage devices
* output devices
* interactive terminals
* input devices.

In view of the overlap between on-line and off-line devices for input both types will be considered in this section.

6.2 Data Storage Devices

As pointed out above, data storage devices may be used in many instances as input or output devices as well as or even instead of their main purpose of data storage. What makes them different from other input and output devices is, however, the fact that *the data or information on them is intelligible only when using a computer*.

The main types of data storage devices are:

* magnetic tapes
* magnetic disks
* mass storage devices.

With the exception of magnetic tapes these devices are known as *Direct Access Storage Devices* (DASDs) since each item of data on the device may (within certain limits) be referred to directly (see also Chapter 12). A comparison of the major characteristics of these devices is given in Figure 6.1.

(a) Magnetic tapes

Magnetic tape is a widely used technology for data storage.

As with magnetic disks the use of magnetic tape for data storage requires the use of both a *tape drive* (also known as a *tape transport* or *tape deck*) and media. In the case of magnetic tape the drive is a machine which is broadly analogous to a tape-recorder (indeed for home computers, ordinary commercially available sound tape-recorders may be used for this purpose). For mainframes and most minicomputers, however, specially developed drives are utilised and these often incorporate special arrangements (such as columns of air to buffer tape movement) to protect the tape itself from damage (including stretching) during the rapid movement and frequent starts and stops characteristic of data storage use.

The medium itself is a strip of flexible polyester tape mounted on a reel or cassette. The tape is covered on one side with a thin coating of magnetisable material upon which data may be recorded, using magnetised/unmagnetised 'spots' to represent binary zeros and ones.

Open reel tapes up to 2400 feet in length are in common use (the largest size is also probably the most widely used). On micro-computers and for some data-capture and data-entry purposes, cassette tapes to the same format as the familiar C60, C90 and C120 sound recording tapes are also in common use.

The tapes used on larger machines (tape or tapes is usually used instead of the term 'magnetic tape' in full) are most commonly half-inch in width, open reel tapes of 200, 600, 1200 or 2400 feet in length. The tape is subdivided into channels lengthwise (usually 7 or 9) and these channels are each used to record a single bit of information. A single line across the tape can therefore contain up to nine bits of information (more than enough to store one byte or character of information). One channel is commonly used for a check or *parity* bit to assist in checking that data has been read or written

Fig 6.1   a comparison of the main advantages and disadvantages of types of backing store

Magnetic tapes	Magnetic disks	Mass storage devices
Advantages		
* Any size record permissible	* Enables direct-access techniques to be used	* Enables direct-access techniques to be used
* Reusable	* Reusable	* Reusable
* Relatively inexpensive	* Easily transported between computers (floppy disks only)	* Very large storage capacity
* Easily transported between computers	* Enables on-line systems with fast response times to be developed	* Reduces need for handling of storage media (i.e. mounting and demounting tapes and disks)
* Provides good history of changes to file	* Interrelated files may be stored so as to facilitate data handling	
Disadvantages		
* Only permits sequential/serial files	* Not easily transportable (except floppy disks)	* Not readily transportable
* Inserting new records in sequence means copying entire file	* No automatic record of file updates	* High total cost (though cost/byte of storage is attractive)
* Relatively slow access to any specific record		

correctly. Figure 6.2 shows a schematic representation of the way data is recorded on tape.

The density of bits that can be recorded along each channel of the tape is obviously of crucial importance in determining the amount of data that may be recorded on a reel of tape. Densities of 556, 800, 1600 and 6250 bpi (bits per inch) have all been widely used with a continual movement towards the higher densities.

Data is recorded on to the tape in the form of records (see Chapter 12) or more usually blocks (blocks are groups of records). Between each record or block a gap called an *inter-record gap* or more accurately *inter-block gap* is left (see Figure 6.3). This gap provides a piece of vacant tape between records which must be read or written and is that portion of the tape which passes the read/write heads while the tape is accelerating to full working speed or while the tape is coming to rest. (If data were read or written during this time it would not be accurately spaced and could not therefore be interpreted correctly.)

The amount of data that can be contained on a tape is, therefore, dependent, not only on the length of tape and the density of recording, but also the length and frequency of the inter-block gaps.

Fig 6.2   *schematic showing the way data is held on magnetic tape*

Fig 6.3   *blocked records on magnetic tape showing inter-block gap*

The frequency of inter-block gaps is in turn dependent on the size of block adopted for a given use while the size of the gap depends on the design of the drive and speed of tape movement (which may be in the order of 200 in/sec.).

Tape transfer rates may be calculated by multiplying the tape speed by the recording density so a tape recorded at 6250 bpi (and because of the channel arrangement therefore recording 6250 bytes or characters per inch) and working at 200 inches per second has a transfer rate of 1 250 000 bytes per second (1250 Kb/sec.). This is, however, only the theoretical transfer speed since inter-block gaps clearly reduce the data rate actually obtained. Similarly, theoretical tape capacities may be calculated by multiplying the length of the tape by the recording density. Therefore, a 2400-ft reel of tape recorded at 6250 bpi can theoretically contain 180 million bytes of data (6250 × 12 × 2400), but in practice such capacities are not achieved because of the need to allow gaps between blocks of data.

The key characteristic of magnetic tape in data processing use is that it is a sequential medium. Each record stored is placed sequentially behind the one in front. As we shall see in Chapter 12, this arrangement has many limitations when it comes to developing data structures to support business use. Moreover, to add new records (or to remove those no longer required) to files on magnetic tape means that the whole tape must be read and copied inserting the (perhaps small number of) changes. This 'disadvantage' does incidentally have one corresponding benefit – historical records are easily provided (see Chapters 12 and 15).

Each tape contains a *header* and a *trailer* label written at the time the tape itself is written, containing its identity and information about the data stored on it.

Magnetic tape is a relatively inexpensive medium and this, together with the fact that reels can easily be changed and stored, means that it is in widespread use for high-volume, relatively low usage data, data that is required in sequential form and for archival, backup and security purposes. Moreover, magnetic tape is widely used to transfer data between computers.

(b) Magnetic disks

Magnetic disks exist in a wide variety of forms, but all share certain common characteristics in the way they store data. A magnetic disk unit consists of two major elements: the drive and the media. The *drive* (disk drive) contains the necessary equipment to receive and send signals to and from the CPU, and also a motor which serves to rotate the media at very high speed. The *medium* is one or more thin plates or *disks* of more or less rigid material the surfaces of which have a thin coating of magnetisable material. Data is recorded on the media in the form of minute magnetised or demagnetised spots which represent the zeros and ones of the binary system. Data is recorded onto and read from the disk by means of *read/write heads* which are positioned immediately next to the magnetised surface.

Magnetic disks may have single or multiple surfaces, be rigid or have some degree of flexibility (*floppy disks*) and be either permanently attached to the drive (*hard disk*) or be removable (*demountable*). Many disks are enclosed in a sealed container which also includes the read/write heads in one unit and these are called 'Winchester disks', but in other cases the read/write heads are part of the drive itself. The demountable part of the system is called a *disk pack* or *disk*.

Another development in magnetic disk technology has been the floppy disk or diskette. These are single, semi-flexible disks encased in a protective envelope with slots in it which enable the diskette to be read or written onto when inserted into a suitable drive unit with the protective cover still in place. These cheap, reliable, small disks have found ready acceptance as backing store for personal computers and also for data entry purposes. Their flexibility and robustness makes them a convenient medium for data transfer as they may be sent through the post. Diskettes come in a variety of formats, some recordable on one side only, some on both sides, and in a number of sizes ($3\frac{1}{2}$, $5\frac{1}{4}$ and 8 inches are used). Small, rigid diskettes are also used with personal computers.

Figure 6.4 shows a cross section of a typical multi-surface disk pack and the positioning of the read/write heads which, it will be noted, are all mounted on a single arm and moved together.

Data is stored on the magnetic surfaces in a series of concentric rings called *tracks*. On multi-surface disks, data which is likely to be required together (e.g. a single file) is not spread across a single surface, but located on the same track(s) of each of the surfaces to form a *cylinder*. This means that when the data is written or read the read/write heads do not have to move across the disk, but can access the data from a single position. The cylinder concept is illustrated graphically in Figure 6.5. To facilitate reading/writing and organising data each track is subdivided into *sectors* which are uniquely addressable. The layout of a typical track is shown in Figure 6.6.

To read data from a disk pack (or to write data on it) requires a certain amount of time. This is composed of a number of elements. These elements are:

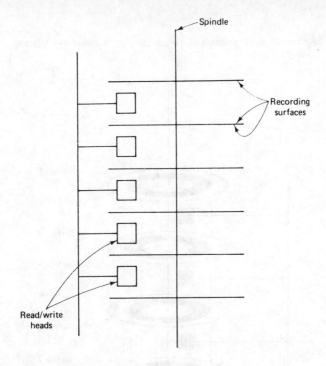

Fig 6.4 *side view of a disk pack*

* *seek time* or read/write head movement time (i.e. the time to position and read/write heads at the correct cylinder)
* *rotational delay* (while the correct sector(s) rotate to a position under the read/write heads)
* *transfer time* (while the data is actually read/written).

Obviously the first two elements of time are variable, depending on the distance of the movement and amount of rotation necessary, but for any given type of magnetic disk drive an average figure may be calculated. The actual transfer time is a function of the amount of data to be read/written and the rotational speed of the disk.

Magnetic disks have been built with *fixed heads* which eliminate the seek time but increase the cost per unit of data stored since, other things being equal, the number of read/write heads necessary for the storage of the same volume of data is increased.

The capacity of a disk depends not only on its physical size but also on the density with which data can be recorded on it. Capacities of up

Fig 6.5 *schematic representation of a magnetic disk showing the cylinder concept*

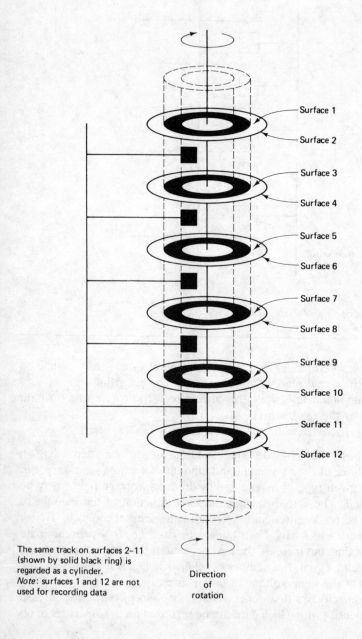

The same track on surfaces 2–11 (shown by solid black ring) is regarded as a cylinder.
Note: surfaces 1 and 12 are not used for recording data

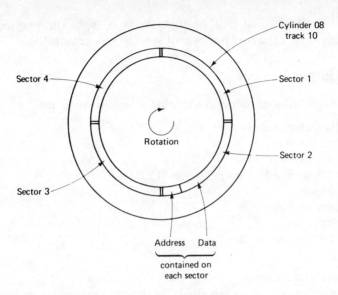

Fig 6.6 *the layout of data on a magnetic disk*

---

to 10 Mb are available on a single diskette, although most of those in use are of much more limited capacity. Transfer rates range from 20 up to 1500 Kb/second. Average access times of 6–130 msec are quoted. Multi-surface disks are available (6 disks of which the inside 10 surfaces are used for recording data, as shown in Figure 6.4, is a common arrangement) which store various quantities of data up to 5000 Mb and offer average access times of 17 msec and transfer rates of 3000 Kb.sec.

(c) Mass storage devices
In recent years some devices have been marketed which seek to combine the relatively low cost of magnetic tape technology without the disadvantages of only sequential access. These devices essentially consist of a large number of relatively short strips of tape contained in a single machine and with an index or indices to enable the correct strip or cartridge to be accessed. The strips are held in cells or cartridges and are often wound over a drum for read/write operations. Data may be 'staged' on to a conventional disk drive and then used by the computer from that device. This approach offers very high data storage capabilities with moderate access times (one such device enables over a trillion (1×10^{12}) bytes of data to be stored).

Although the capital cost of these units is high, the enormous capacity makes the cost per byte of storage very reasonable.

6.3 **Output Devices**

The major types of output devices for data processing are:

* character printers
* line printers
* page printers
* computer output on microfilm (COM)
* plotters
* card punches
* display units
* other output devices.

(a) Character printers

Character printers are closely similar to the conventional typewriter in that they produce printed output by consecutively printing each character necessary to produce a line of information. Indeed some of the computer output devices of this type are based on typewriters. Various modifications to the actual printing mechanisms, e.g. the use of '*golf balls*' or '*daisy wheels*' or the replacement of the traditional electro-mechanical mechanism by ink jet, dot matrix or electrostatic printing and the ability to print in both directions have not changed the underlying characteristics of these devices which are that they are slow and can only produce (with carbon paper) a few copies of a document (many of the newer devices can produce only one). Nevertheless, their low cost makes these devices highly suitable for low-volume printing applications (speeds are typically from 10–600 characters per second). In addition to their use as the main output for small computers and those with very low-output volumes, these printers may be used as auxiliary or *console printers* on larger machines providing a *hard copy* (i.e. printed record) of actions performed and/or printing messages to the operator. These printers are also used as terminals either alone or in conjunction with other devices.

(b) Line printers

Line printers, as their name implies, print a complete line (which may contain up to 160 characters) at a time. These printers are usually electro-mechanical devices and have the type characters mounted on a chain or barrel. The type characters are driven continuously and when the chosen character is positioned correctly near the paper a hammer behind the paper moves the paper against the print ribbon and type character. Using thin, one-time carbon paper or no-carbon-required (NCR) paper these machines can produce about six copies at a time on continuous stationery.

The stationery used usually has sprocket holes on both edges which are engaged by tractor drives mounted on either side of the print mechanism. Plain or preprinted stationery may be used.

Line printers with rated speeds of from 200 to 2000 lines per minute are commonly available. Vertical spacing is usually 6 or 8 lines per inch and horizontally 10 characters per inch is a widely used spacing.

As with character printers, newer technologies are being introduced to supplement, but not yet replace, the traditional electro-mechanical printing mechanism. These newer technologies generally offer high-quality printing, which makes them particularly useful in some applications.

In addition to producing output to be read by humans, many printers may be used to produce output which can be read by humans and subsequently by a computer. This is achieved using stylised characters such as those used in *Optical Character Recognition* (OCR). Similarly, printers may be used to produce a bar code (see Section 6.5 below).

Although usually attached directly to the computer, line printers can be used as stand-alone or off-line printers (also called *slave printers*). In this case the main computer produces a magnetic tape or disk containing the information to be printed, and this is then mounted on the stand-alone printer and the necessary output produced. Printers attached to a computer can also be used in a special mode by means of a technique called *spooling* (*S*imultaneous *P*eripheral *O*perations *O*n-*L*ine). This technique enables slow peripheral operations to take place concurrently with other processing, and thus makes more efficient use of the computer.

(c) Page printers

Page printers (also called *non-impact* or *laser* printers) use laser and electro-photographic technologies to assemble and print a page at a time. Machines in this category range from one offering 8 pages a minute through to machines offering speeds of up to 40 inches/second (equivalent to about 20 000 lines per minute). These machines provide print quality and a variety of characters, sizes and spacings unobtainable on other printers. Some machines allow a mask to be used during printing, thus enabling forms to be 'printed' at the time that the information is produced. Copies are produced on these machines by repeat printing. Like line printers, some page printers may be used as a stand-alone printing subsystem and may be used to produce bar code labels.

(d) Computer output on microfilm (COM)

COM is used where high volumes of computer output are produced but where reference to the data is relatively low, and also for those applications where the volume of the output is a major factor (e.g. some cataloguing applications). COM may also be used as an alternative to magnetic tape for long-term archival purposes.

COM may be produced either in the form of cassettes of microfilm or as microfiche. The COM unit is usually off-line. The computer output is in the form of a magnetic tape which is subsequently used as input to the COM machine. Because most installations want only a relatively small proportion of their own output on COM, the use of bureaux to provide a COM service using off-line equipment has been a feature of its use.

(e) Plotters

Although the primary requirement for output for data processing systems is, and is likely to remain, for hard copy printed characters, this is by no means the only type of output that is useful in a business environment. Another type of output which is of particular value is pictorial representation which covers a wide range from simple visual representation of statistical data (histograms, pie charts, etc.) to detailed isometric drawings.

To some extent this demand can be met using line or page printers. To meet the demand for high-quality presentation a special category of output devices has been developed. Often called *graph plotters* (a term which does not indicate their true value) these devices create a pictorial representation of the digitised data held in a computer. These devices are usually flat-bed printers (although drum plotters are also made) with contentional ink printers or '*pens*' under computer control. These 'pens' can draw continuous lines rather than the discrete points of characters printed by other types of computer printer. They are thus capable of 'drawing' complex shapes and patterns. Many of them have several pens so that multi-coloured output can be produced by using a different coloured ink for each pen. Compared with conventional printers these devices are slow, but there is no doubt about the effectiveness of the output produced. The software necessary to convert the digitised information into pictorial form is not simple (especially when isometric drawings are made) and constitutes an overhead when using this type of device. 'Computer Art' is produced on plotters.

Because of their slow speed, plotters are often used in an off-line mode.

(f) Card punches
When computer output devices are listed nowadays, card punches are not usually mentioned, yet they remain a useful form of output for certain applications. The punched card formed the basis of most automatic data processing systems from its original use in the American Census of 1890 until the 1960s. Punched cards existed in many formats, but each consisted of a flat piece of thin card (plasticised for some repeated-use applications) in which holes punched in vertical columns were used to represent individual characters of data. Cards with 40, 56, 80, 96 and other numbers of columns have been used with rectangular, circular and oblong holes being used to represent the data (the 80-column card with rectangular holes being the most widely used).

As an output device the attraction of the punched card is that it can contain both computer readable (holes) and human readable (printed characters) data. Thus, an output document can be produced which can be used to convey information to a person and subsequently used as input to a computer (for example, to confirm that a certain action has been performed). Applications of this type of *turn-around document* approach include the issue of work instructions in a manufacturing plant (the input of the card confirms that the work has been done) and credit card billing where the punched card is both the bill and the remittance advice accompanying payment.

(g) Display units
Display units exist in a wide variety of forms to meet the need for computer output which is transient and for which hard copy is not necessary. These devices are often associated with an input device and used in an 'interactive' manner (see Section 6.4 below). Display units are also used independently. Some display units are general-purpose screens, closely similar to television screens. These devices (also called *Visual Display Units* (VDUs) or, in American usage *cathode ray tubes* (CRTs or simply 'tubes') typically display 24 lines each containing 80 characters of information (numbers, letters, blanks or special characters) and may offer single or multi-coloured displays.

Typical uses of this type of device are to display flight departure and arrival information at airports, and to display instructions in automated factory environments.

Where the amount of information to be displayed is limited or the recipient is too far away to read the characters on a VDU (although several lines can be joined to make larger characters) special displays may be introduced. These may vary from simple coloured lights, via large LCD (liquid crystal display) or LED (light-emitting diode) displays of a limited range of numbers, to complex electro-mechanical display boards. Special devices of this nature are often custom built for a particular application.

(h) Other output devices
A number of other output devices exist for computers which are important in specific applications. Two of these are *digital/analog converters* and voice or speech units.

Digital/analog converters are used to change the digital output from a computer into an analog (i.e. continuous) signal which can be used to control a scientific or technical process or piece of equipment.

Voice or speech units enable the computer to 'speak' and may either use pre-recorded messages or generate specific messages as required. Although not yet in widespread use, it seems likely that this technique will be the subject of significant developments.

A final class of output devices which should be mentioned is that of special-purpose printers. Numerous devices exist to print labels and special codes (such as those used in bar code applications – see Section 6.5).

6.4 **Interactive Terminals**

Interactive terminals are computer peripherals which permit a human operator to conduct a *dialogue* with a program in the computer. This process is also called *conversational computing*. As such they incorporate both an output function (providing the computer with a channel of communication to the human user) and an input function (enabling the user to communicate instructions or data to the computer).

The most commonly encountered type of interactive terminal is a VDU with a typewriter keyboard attached to provide the input function. There are, however, a range of other devices which may be used in an interactive manner. One alternative is to substitute a *light pen* for the keyboard (some devices incorporate both). The light pen is a photoelectric device similar in shape and size to a conventional pen, which the operator can pass over the screen of a VDU to 'mark' positions. Thus it can be used to select options displayed by the computer by pointing it to the desired location. In most cases the display on the screen of a VDU includes an indicator (the *cursor*) which may be positioned either by the computer or the operator and indicates the position on the screen at which the next piece of data will be input.

The cursor may be moved by the operator using special keys on the keyboard, by program (as when the computer expects a response in an interactive computing environment) or by means of a 'mouse'. A mouse is a roller device which is moved across a surface (usually the desk adjacent to the terminal) and is connected to the terminal in such a way that as it moves in two dimensions it causes the cursor to move over the screen. A button on the top of the mouse enables action to be taken when the cursor is in the correct location (e.g. selecting an option from a displayed list or 'menu'). Using a mouse and specially designed software, interactive use of a computer can be achieved by people with little or no familiarity with a keyboard.

A further way in which data may be captured on a VDU or personal computer without the use of a keyboard is by use of a *touchscreen*. In devices equipped in this way the display screen is surrounded by a series of photoelectric cells. When the operator touches the screen the computer 'reads' the coordinates intercepted.

Interactive terminals are often described as being *dumb* or *intelligent*. A dumb terminal has no processing capability built into it and merely acts as a channel of communication or interface between the user and the computer. An intelligent terminal incorporates its own microprocessor or minicomputer and is capable of carrying out some processing on its own. Typically this processing includes some validation and formatting of the data to be input into the main computer and reduces the workload of the mainframe. The advent of inexpensive personal computers which may be used as terminals means that an increasing proportion of terminals are 'intelligent'.

The majority of terminals are *buffered*, i.e. they store a complete message which is only released to the computer when the operator is satisfied that the information entered is correct.

Interactive terminals may be permanently connected to one computer or may be connected to any suitable computer via standard telephone line connections (see Chapter 11). Some interactive terminals are portable. One example of a portable terminal closely resembles a portable electric typewriter and can be used anywhere a normal electric socket and telephone are available. The terminal is simply plugged into the electrical outlet and after the computer has been 'dialled up' on the telephone, the telephone handset is positioned in a cradle (called an acoustic coupler) on the terminal, providing truly portable access to a mainframe computer. Increasingly, devices which incorporate PC, terminal and telephone facilities are being used as multipurpose workstations.

6.5 Input Devices

Input devices exhibit as much variety as output devices. Three main types may, however, be distinguished. These are:

* keyboard devices
* character and code recognition devices
* other input devices.

(a) Keyboard devices

Keyboard devices include a whole range of equipment which shares certain common characteristics. In all cases the data to be entered into the computer is 'typed' on to a keyboard (usually by a specialist data preparation clerk working from a form or other documentation) and the data is stored on an intermediate storage media before it is read into the computer, using a special 'reader'. (This 'reader' is the actual computer peripheral.) The storage media in use include: punched cards, paper tape, floppy disks, magnetic tape (both reels and cassettes) and magnetic disks. Most keyboards are similar to the standard keyboard and have the keys laid out in the familiar QWERTY sequence, but abbreviated keyboards or *keypads* containing only numbers, limited character sets or alternative layouts are in use for special purposes.

The simplest of these devices are the basic electro-mechanical (or even purely mechanical) card and paper tape punches where a key depression leads directly to the recording of data on the media (in these cases by cutting a hole in it). This procedure is wasteful inasmuch as it means that, if an error is made, correction entails repunching the media (including, in the case of punched cards, the data on that card which had already been correctly entered).

To overcome this disadvantage, and therefore to increase operator productivity, *buffered punches* were developed which enabled the operator to correct any errors of which he or she was aware by storing them in a buffer until a discrete portion of work (for example, a record or a card full of data) was completed and released by the operator.

The devices which read such media as punched cards and paper tape into the computer are slow and there has been a steady move away from punched cards and paper tape as input media (except for such applications as those mentioned in Section 6.3, where punched cards created by a computer are later used as input on a turnaround document basis).

Keyboard devices using cassette tapes are basically analogous to the machines already described, but using cassette tapes as the storage media.

The advancing technology of electronics, and especially the development of microprocessors, has meant that it is now practicable to 'pool' the output from several keyboards on to a single storage unit (floppy disk, magnetic tape or magnetic disk), and this approach is now in widespread use. A number of operators all working independently using their own keyboards enter data which is stored on a common storage unit. The use of microprocessors in these devices has also made it possible for some (often extensive) data validation or checking routines to be built into the data preparation process. Many data-entry devices of this type also store some master records or information for comparison purposes (e.g. is the customer name just entered already on our list of clients? Erroneous or unmatched information being displayed back to the operator on a VDU). At this point the data-entry device has become *de facto* a separate computer system configured especially for data input. On some of these devices it is necessary to demount the storage media from the data-entry system and read it into the mainframe or other computer, but the devices themselves may also be linked on-line to the computer which merely reads the data from the intermediate storage at intervals.

Operating speeds for operators using keyboard data-entry devices range from about 8000 key depressions per hour on unbuffered card punches to over 20 000 key depressions per hour on intelligent key to disk devices. In addition to operator skill the rates achieved depend on the layout of the source document, the legibility of the entries, the nature of the data (all numeric or mixed alpha numeric) and the environment (lighting, the ergonomic design of the operator's working position, etc.).

Before leaving keyboards, brief mention should be made of the portable input devices now obtainable. Looking like a large pocket calculator and often having only numeric and a few command keys, these devices can record data (usually on to cassette tape) which is later used as computer input. Such devices can, for example, be used by travelling salesmen to record orders in computer readable form at the time of sale, thereby eliminating much intermediate paper handling and error-prone data transcription.

(b) Character and code recognition devices

The need to provide easy ways to capture data for computer use and in many cases to provide data in ways which can be understood by humans and computers has led to the development of a number of character- and code-recognition devices.

These devices are all readers which may be attached directly to a computer (on-line peripherals) or may be used off-line to create an intermediate storage medium (usually a magnetic tape) which is actually used for computer input.

Each device reads only data presented to it in the form of a special code. The four most commonly encountered codes used in this way are:

* mark reading
* magnetic ink character recognition (MICR)
* optical character recognition (OCR)
* bar coding.

(i) *Mark reading*. Mark reading is the automatic sensing or reading of marks made in predetermined positions of a form or other document (e.g. punched cards). The marks made (so-called 'lead' pencils which in fact deposit a graphite mark are most widely used) are read electrically or optically and create data on a magnetic tape or directly into the computer. The form or document on which the marks are made has to be printed to fine tolerances and the reading mechanism has to be carefully aligned. Smudging of the marks after they have been made and careless positioning of the marks on the form are ever-present risks and can lead to high reject rates. A part of a typical mark-reading input document is shown in Figure 6.7.

One of the widest applications of this approach is by Britain's Open University, which uses mark reading as one means of testing students on the progress they are making through a course. The student enters a reference number, the test number and the selected answers to multiple-choice questions in 'cells' on a standard form and sends it back to the university, where the computer (by reference to a table of correct answers supplied by the university's teaching staff) 'marks' the student's work and prints out the results.

(ii) *Magnetic ink character recognition* (MICR). Information to be read on a MICR device has to be printed to a special format using stylised characters and special ink. This combination enables the data which has been preprinted to be easily and accurately read at a later date for computer input purposes.

The most widely used application of MICR is in the banking field,

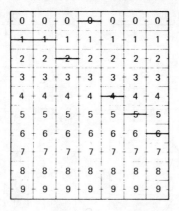

Fig 6.7   *part of a mark reading input document showing a grid which enables a seven-digit reference number to be entered. The marks to represent the number 1120456 are shown*

where data such as bank code, account number and a reference number are printed on cheques and other documents.

Some characters printed in MICR format are shown in Figure 6.8. MICR is only of use in applications where the reader of the document has control of the format in which it is produced.

(iii) *Optical character recognition* (OCR). OCR readers have the capability of reading optically a range of stylised letters, numbers and special characters which can also be read more or less easily by human beings. These characters may be either printed on the document to be read or, in some cases, written by hand. The form of the character, its size and its positioning on the document are all, however, critical if error-free reading is to be achieved. Devices which read standard typewriter founts allow OCR to be used in a wider variety of applications than when special founts are required.

(iv) *Bar coding*. Bar-code reading devices are specialised character readers for data coded in a series of lines or bars. These codes (over a hundred different ones are in use) cannot be written or directly interpreted by human beings (human readable digits are, however, often printed below the bar code). Moves to standardise and reduce

Fig 6.8   *magnetic ink character recognition (MICR) characters*

OCR–A

Space	0		P		
|	1	A	Q		
▼▼	2	B	R		
£	3	C	S		
$	4	D	T		
%	5	E	U		
&	6	F	V		
'	7	G	W		
{	8	H	X		
}	9	I	Y		
*	:	J	Z		
+	;	K			
¬	♪	L			
−	=	M			
.	⌐	N			
/	?	0			

OCR–B

Space	0	@	P	`	p
!	1	A	Q	a	q
..	2	B	R	b	r
£ #	3	C	S	c	s
$ ¤	4	D	T	d	t
%	5	E	U	e	u
&	6	F	V	f	v
'	7	G	W	g	w
(	8	H	X	h	x
)	9	I	Y	i	y
★	:	J	Z	j	z
+	;	K	[	k	{
	<	L	\	l	|
−	=	M	]	mm	}
.	>	N	^	n	~
/	?	O	_		o

Fig 6.9   *optical character recognition (OCR) founts*

the number of codes in use are under way and should assist the spread of this technique.

A bar code is a group of parallel dark bars of varying widths separated by white spaces. Variations in widths of the bars and the spaces between them are used to encode different information. '*Guard bars*' are often included at the beginning and end of the code to prevent other printing being accidentally interpreted as part of the code. These guard bars can also indicate the direction in which the code should be read. Some examples of bar codes are shown in Figure 6.10.

In a bar-code reading system optical code sensors or readers (which may be either on-line to a computer or off-line – in which case the data is read to an intermediate storage such as a cassette tape) scan the code. The reader senses the variation between the spaces and the bars by the presence or absence of reflections.

Readers are produced in both hand-held (called *light pens* or

The principle that makes a bar code work is that light is reflected from a white (or other light-coloured) surface and absorbed by black (or other dark-coloured) surface.

One typical code called '2 or 5' is illustrated. In this code each digit is represented by two wide and three narrow bars. Spaces between bars convey no information. Wide bars are three times the width of both narrow bars and spaces.

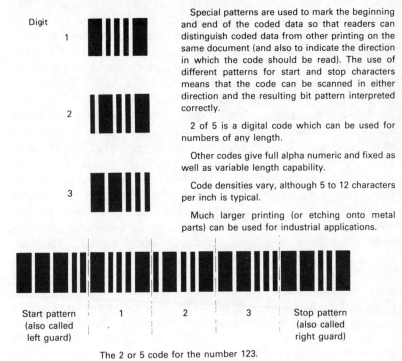

Digit

1

2

3

Special patterns are used to mark the beginning and end of the coded data so that readers can distinguish coded data from other printing on the same document (and also to indicate the direction in which the code should be read). The use of different patterns for start and stop characters means that the code can be scanned in either direction and the resulting bit pattern interpreted correctly.

2 of 5 is a digital code which can be used for numbers of any length.

Other codes give full alpha numeric and fixed as well as variable length capability.

Code densities vary, although 5 to 12 characters per inch is typical.

Much larger printing (or etching onto metal parts) can be used for industrial applications.

Start pattern (also called left guard) 1 2 3 Stop pattern (also called right guard)

The 2 or 5 code for the number 123.

Fig 6.10   *bar coding*

wands) and fixed versions and suitable for use in different applications (e.g. where the code is close to or remote from the reading head).

All readers have four main components: a light source which is focused on to the code, a photoelectric cell which senses the presence or absence of reflected light (the white spaces reflect light while the dark, usually black lines, absorb light), a circuit which amplifies this signal and an analog digital converter which interprets the signal into digital form.

As with other optical code readers, bar-code readers are sensitive to the small differences in the code format (printing must be accurate) and the degree of contrast achieved between bar and space.

Black bars on a white ground are usually used, although other colours may be accepted by some readers. The black or coloured ink used should have a low reflectivity if good results are to be obtained (glossy ink can cause reflections which are misinterpreted as spaces).

Bar codes and readers are used to speed data entry since the data can be captured as quickly as the code can be passed across the reader. Such codes also improve the accuracy of data capture.

The most widely used application of bar coding is probably in the grocery industry where the voluntary 10-digit *Universal Product Code* (UPC) and the European version – European Article Numbering system (EAN) – are now widely accepted. This code has 5 digits to identify the manufacturer and 5 digits to identify the product and package combination (a 6-digit version is used in some instances).

In the grocery industry light pens are increasingly being incorporated in check out or *point-of-sale* (POS) terminals. When the shopper presents his/her selections taken from the supermarket shelf to the cashier the latter uses a light pen to read the UPC on each item (a soft 'beep' indicating a successful read). The terminal uses this data to obtain the current sales price of the product (by reference to a master file) to bill the customer and also records the sale of the item. At convenient periods (often when the shop is closed) all the sales information is collated and analysed by computer and orders raised for those items which have fallen below the minimum level required.

Hand-held light pens attached to portable data recorders can also be used for stock-checking purposes, by scanning the UPC of items on the shelves.

Other applications of bar coding include part and stores recording in industrial environments and in libraries for keeping track of the issue and return of books.

(c) Other input devices
In addition to the input devices described above there are a number of other types of equipment which may be used for computer input.

One such type of input device is a *badge reader*. This type of equipment 'reads' data coded on to a simple plastic card (like a credit card). The data may be recorded on the card by means of holes punched in it, characters embossed on it or data encoded on a magnetic strip on the back of the card.

If precoded badges are associated with particular units of work and readers are located in various places within a factory, the movement of raw materials, work in progress and finished stock throughout the factory may be monitored (punched cards and punched card readers have also been used in this manner).

Voice recognition is another technology which is used to a limited extent for data input. It can be a practical approach when a small number of people have to communicate a limited amount of information to a computer. These restrictions apply since most current systems can only identify a limited vocabulary – about 40 words – and each individual has to be treated separately because accents and voice patterns vary. The individual speaks the necessary data into a microphone and the analog signal is converted to digital form to enable the computer to compare the information received with its pre-recorded library and take the appropriate action. It seems likely that with improving technology voice recognition will gain in importance.

Voice recognition uses an *analog-to-digital converter* and these units are also used in other ways to capture data. These devices may be used to convert such continuously variable data as temperature, flow rates, etc. (which are often measured on analog devices in scientific and technical applications) into digital form for computer input.

7 Software

7.1 **What is Software?**

As we have seen a computer is an electronic machine which consists of a number of discrete elements. In addition to the electronic components there are electro-mechanical units (such as printers) and of course, the metal and plastic frames and covers which are used to support and enclose the complete assembly. Also necessary are the cables and connections which join the various parts together. Collectively all these physical units are referred to as *hardware*. Hardware alone, however, is not sufficient to make a practical computer for data processing purposes. To make a computer perform it needs instructions. Collectively all the things necessary to make the computer hardware operational are called *software* and it includes, therefore, such items as instruction manuals and documentation as well as programs. The trend, however, is to reserve the term 'software' for the various types of instructions which are actually put into the computer, and it is in this sense it will be used in this chapter.

The terms *liveware* and *middleware* (or *firmware*) to descibe the human elements of a computing system and those elements of a computer which, although 'hardware' perform 'software' functions, may also be encountered.

Computer software exists in a number of different forms, and three categories may be identified. These are:

* programming languages
* systems software
* applications software.

Each of these categories in turn can be subdivided and further subdivided. The schematic in Figure 7.1 shows the 'family tree' of computer software. It should be noted, however, that not all the forms shown in Figure 7.1 and discussed in this chapter apply to all computers. Although not universally accepted (some might combine the first two, for example) these categories offer a useful basis for descriptive purposes.

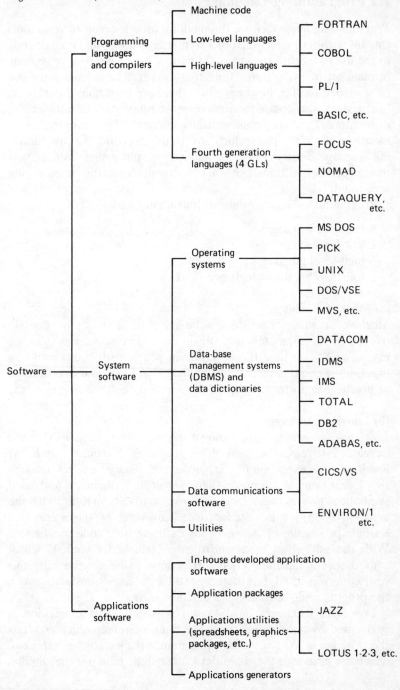

Fig 7.1 *the 'family tree' of computer software*

7.2 **Programming Languages**

Programming languages are the medium used for man to communicate his wishes (instructions) to a computer in a way that is analogous to the use of English (or any other natural language) by a supervisor or manager in giving instructions to a worker. The analogy must not be stretched too far, however, since there are important differences. For a start, the computer (unlike most humans) will only accept instructions that are 'grammatically correct'. The term *syntax* is usually used for the rules which govern the structure of a programming language. Furthermore, a computer will not assume information or interpret instructions, but will carry them out literally even if they are stupid.

Programming languages are of four main types:

* machine languages
* low-level languages
* high-level languages
* fourth generation languages (4GLs).

(a) Machine language
Machine language is written in binary code and can be directly obeyed by the computer since it is in the code used internally in the machine. At one time the only way in which instructions could be input into a computer, machine language has long since ceased to be of practical importance to users of general data processing systems.

(b) Low-level languages
Low-level languages (also known as *assembler languages*) were developed to ease the task of programming computers. Initially, low-level languages simply replaced the binary instruction with simple *mnemonics* to make them easier to remember and used symbolic *addresses* (i.e. a label or representative term rather than the actual location) for the data locations. Low-level languages provided a single *programming statement* for each machine code instruction. With the advent of *macro instructions* (single instructions which caused several machine code instructions to be carried out) this restriction was lifted, but there was still a close relationship between the programming language and machine code.

Low-level languages have to be translated. This translation is performed by another program called an *assembler* which converts the statements written by the programmer (called *source code*) and which are read into the computer on magnetic tape or other media, into machine processible form (*the object program*). The object program can be stored and used at any time.

Low-level languages are time-consuming to write and errors are easily made. With the changing balance between the cost of hardware and computer staff, low-level languages are used less and less for general data processing.

(c) High-level languages
High-level languages were developed for two basic reasons: first, to improve the productivity of programmers by making one programme instruction generate a considerable amount of machine code. Second, to enable programs to be used on different types of computers without the need to rewrite them completely. (With low-level languages this is necessary because the machine code of computers is different and the close relationship between low-level languages and machine code means that the former are specific to one type of family of computers.)

High-level languages also have to be translated into machine code and this is achieved using a *compiler* program, the process being known as *compilation*. (In some cases, particularly in microcomputers, an *interpreter* may be used instead of a compiler. An interpreter is usually a hard coded or firmware device which interprets the source statements into machine code as they are needed. Functionally the effect as far as the user is concerned is the same as using a compiler.) The result of compilation is executable code (object code), which, as with low-level languages, may be stored (usually on disk) and used at any time it is *called* (i.e. selected for use). In microcomputers, the interpreter is usually held on a special chip called a *Read Only Memory* (ROM). This approach (which is an example of the use of firmware) can also be used on microcomputers for other types of system 'software'.

Among the high-level languages currently in widespread use are:

* BASIC (*B*eginners *A*ll-Purpose *S*ymbolic *I*nstruction *C*ode)   An easily learned language especially popular on microcomputers
* COBOL (*CO*mmon *B*usiness *O*riented *L*anguage)   As its name implies a standardised language widely used on commercial applications
* FORTRAN (*For*mula *Tran*slator)   Developed for mathematical and scientific purposes
* PL/1 (*P*rogramming *L*anguage/One)   Developed to provide the facilities of COBOL and FORTRAN in one language.

The languages identified above are all general-purpose in that they are designed to address a wide variety of problems, albeit being in some cases directed to a particular approach to problem-solving. In addition to these general purpose languages there are a number of specialised statistical and simulation languages such as GPSS (*G*eneral *P*urpose *S*ystems *S*imulator).

(d) Fourth generation languages (4GLs)

Fourth generation languages have been developed to speed the process of application development. Like many terms in data processing, 4GL is widely used but rarely defined. 4GLs are oriented towards the retrieval, formatting (including basic processing) and reporting (by screen or by printer) of data from an established data base or data bases. Most 4GLs may be used interactively to produce an instant report or in batch mode (see Chapter 17) to produce larger reports. Although designed for ease of use and ease of learning (several are aimed at end users rather than data processing professionals), 4GLs often include additional facilities to enable more complex tasks to be performed. Many 4GLs are based on a relational data-base concept (see Chapter 12).

7.3 System Software

System software is a portmanteau term and as used in this chapter will be taken to mean all the programs used within a computer installation which are neither assemblers or compilers (although some definitions include this group) nor applications programs (i.e. those that produce directly useful output for the user of the computer). This broad definition embraces programs which are almost essential and are in constant use, through to software which is only used in support of specific applications.

The main categories of systems software are:

* operating systems
* utility programs
* data-base management systems
* data communications software.

(a) Operating systems

An operating system is the program, programs or ROM that manage the computer's internal resources. The size and complexity of operating systems differ a great deal and tend to vary directly with the size of the computer concerned. These programs supervise the operations of the CPU, control the input and output functions (I/O) and, where multiple user programs are run on the computer at the same time (*multiprogramming*), control the allocation of resources (CPU cycles, primary storage, I/O channels and space on peripherals). Similarly, in computers using the virtual storage concept, it is the operating system which controls the paging of data between the CPU and storage. The operating system may also monitor the queue of jobs waiting to be processed so that the most suitable jobs can be selected when resources become available. Another function included in the operating system is the *initial program loader* (a program that loads the operating system itself from its resident position (usually on a disk) into the computer itself when it is started). This program is sometimes called a *bootstrap* program. A library function to control programs stored on the computer may also be included.

The terms *control program*, *executive* and *supervisor* are sometimes used to refer to simple operating systems or central portions of a more comprehensive operating system.

A *job-control language* is provided with many operating systems to enable the programmer or operator to inform the system about the resources that will be necessary to execute the program efficiently (e.g. files to be loaded, space to be reserved on disks for output, routing of output to be printed remotely, etc.).

A list of the functions of an operating system for a typical medium-sized mainframe is shown in Figure 7.2. It will be noted that some of these functions supplement or replace functions shown elsewhere in this chapter.

(b) Utility programs

Utility programs, also known as *utility routines*, are general-purpose programs which carry out a given function on whatever data is presented to them. They are used to carry a wide variety of functions which are regularly used in data processing work. The programs have often been optimised and perform more efficiently than a program written by an average programmer. More importantly, they avoid the need to 'reinvent the wheel'. Utilities exist for a wide range of functions including:

* *Sorting* taking data in one sequence and reordering it on the basis of another key (see Chapter 12) into a different sequence
* *Merging* mixing two streams of data into a single stream whilst maintaining its sequence
* *Dumping* moving the contents of a file, a backing storage device or primary storage to another location – e.g. dumping the

* Initial program loading
  — starts the operation of the computer under the control of the operating system

* Resource management
  – controls the use of the computer's resources (including main, virtual and backing storage and processing cycles). This function, therefore, controls both virtual storage and multiprogramming operations

* Job control
  – allocates systems resources to individual programs

* Linkage editing
    arranges the output of compilation and assembly processes in usable form

* Library maintenance
  – maintains a catalogue of available programs and routines

* Data management
  – provides input and output functions and basic file organisation routines to obviate the need for these to be coded into every program

* Operator communications
  – provides the operator of the computer with information to enable work to be monitored and with instructions on human intervention, e.g. mounting of tapes and disks when required

* Utility functions
  – provides some of the utility routines or programs needed for the effective use of the computer

* Serviceability and debugging aids
  – provide information to maintenance personnel

* Assembler function
  – assembles programs written in a particular low-level language

* Paging management
  – controls the paging of data between storage and CPU

Fig 7.2   *functions included in an operating system for a typical medium-sized mainframe*

---

contents of a magnetic disk on to a magnetic tape for security or back-up purposes (see also Chapter 15)
* *Software or performance monitors*   programs designed to check the activity of specific aspects of the computer system to ascertain where bottlenecks exist.

(c) Data-base management systems

A *data-base management system* (DBMS) is the software system used to manage large quantities of data in a way that is more or less independent of the specific applications for which they are used (see also Chapter 12).

DBMSs are supplied by both computer manufacturers and also software houses (see Chapter 4). Depending on the particular DBMS chosen, some or all of the following features may be included:

* handling of the data stored
* allocation of space to data
* maintenance of the pointers and chains used to access the data (see Chapter 12)
* logging of changes to the data stored
* logging of accesses to the data stored
* password or security access control (see Chapter 15)
* a special high-level language to manipulate the data
* data dictionary facility to help track what data is contained in the data base and how it is used.

(These last two features may be supplied as stand alone items or in conjunction with the DBMS.)

(d) Data communications software

Data communications software is necessary whenever computing is conducted across telephone lines or other telecommunications links (see Chapter 11). This software, which in some respects may be thought of as an extension of the operating system in that it is concerned with I/O and control functions, varies considerably depending on the type and speed of communication devices and links used.

As with DBMSs, data communications software may be obtained from equipment vendors or software houses.

7.4 Applications Software

Applications software is the program(s) used to solve the user's problems. Thus the programs written to compute pay, to create invoices, to calculate reorder quantities for a warehouse, to analyse sales data for a chain store and many other examples are all applications software. This term may be contrasted with system software, which is used to control or enhance the facilities of the computer as a machine or to perform general 'housekeeping' functions for the computer user.

Applications software may be written specifically to solve a given problem (e.g. to calculate and print invoices for company X). In this case the applications software is described as being an *in-house* development (even though it may actually be written by a software house or contractors (see Chapter 4) rather than company *X*'s own staff). The majority of applications software is, in fact, written in-house.

A further development in the field of applications software is what might be called the *applications utility*. This is a form of generalised program which may be used for a variety of processing needs. The most popular of these are the ubiquitous *spreadsheets*, which provide what is effectively an applications skeleton which may be used for many purposes when data needs to be tabulated and subjected to relatively simple manipulation. Applications may also be developed using an *applications generator*. An applications generator is a software package developed with the aim of improving systems development productivity. Essentially it offers a series of processing 'skeletons' which may be tailored to fit specific requirements by the use of parameters and/or by responses to a series of prompts or questions from the system. In many ways, applications generators may be considered functionally equivalent to 4GLs.

The alternative to in-house development is the acquisition of a suitable *applications package*. An applications package is a generalised system which has been developed to obviate the need to design and code the same system in each installation. The need to consider application packages as one of the alternatives when developing systems is discussed in Chapter 10. Such packages are available for a wide range of common applications such as payroll, capital asset registers, bought ledger, sales ledger and inventory management. These packages may be used 'as is' or added to or amended to meet the specific requirements of the organisation concerned. The principal sources of applications packages are the computer vendors and software houses. Larger organisations may also develop packages 'in-house' to use at their own computer centres.

Part III

Developing Systems

8 Systems Analysis

8.1 Systems Analysis and the Systems Analyst

Systems analysis is a structured process of analysing the ways in which things are done and designing and implementing new and better methods. This process has, of course, been practised for many years, but it is only in recent years that the procedures of analysis have been developed to a sufficient degree to merit their description as a distinct discipline or area of study. Modern industry has a number of analytical disciplines which it can use to improve its efficiency. These include: work study, organisation-and-methods study and operational research as well as systems analysis.

The term 'systems analysis' is usually reserved for the process of analysing business procedures with a view to using a computer as a tool for improving efficiency and effectiveness. This description would seem, at first sight, to imply that systems analysis is a highly technical activity. In fact, although the discipline does have a very significant, and rapidly changing, technical content, the techniques used also require a high level of skills in human communication.

As defined above, systems analysis includes the functions of design and implementation as well as analysis *per se*. This complete set of functions is sometimes called 'systems development'.

The systems analyst is the person who applies the process of systems analysis within an organisation. As a result he or she has a key role to play in the application of computers. In practice the tasks of the systems analyst rarely stop at the analysis of the problem or even the design of an improved solution. Above all the systems analyst is an agent for change and an important aspect of the work is the implementation of new or revised systems. This involves training staff in the operation of the system and maintaining close liaison with user staff throughout the early days of its use.

In this chapter we will concentrate on the analysis tasks that are carried out by the systems analyst and introduce a methodology for systems development. In following this methodology the non-technical aspects of the work must always be borne in mind. Organisations are composed of people and it is only by paying careful attention to the human relations aspect of his or her work that the systems analyst will experience the satisfaction of seeing a system, for which he or she is responsible, operating successfully.

8.2 **The Approach to Systems Analysis**

It has already been stated that systems analysis is a structured process and that implies that there is a *process* that can be followed in carrying out the function of systems analysis. That process (usually called a *methodology*) exists in a number of different forms depending on the particular circumstances of the organisation concerned, but most follow a number of set principles. These principles are:

* there are a number of discrete sequential phases in the methodology
* each phase or step consists of a number of set tasks and may be supported by a formal checklist
* the phases are divided by decision points at which explicit GO/NO GO decisions are taken
* tasks are performed from the 'top down', i.e. the subject is studied in a number of iterations, each of which examines a smaller portion of the whole in greater depth.

The systems development methodology outlined below adopts these principles, but, before considering it in detail, it is necessary to examine some of the reasons why a methodology is important.

The basic purpose of a methodology is to increase the probability that the project being undertaken will be successful. Systems analysis is often applied to a function; for example, production control, personnel, stock control or accounting with which the analyst has only a limited familiarity. In these circumstances it is particularly important that there is an established procedure to use which ensures that essential factors are not overlooked. A methodology also serves to help avoid mistakes when, as so often is the case, the project being conducted is under severe pressure (usually critical deadlines).

A further, vital, reason for using a formal methodology is that it forces re-examination of the project at intervals. This enables projects which are going seriously off course either in terms of unexpectedly high costs, extended timescales or reduced benefits to be reassessed and, if they are no longer viable, discontinued in favour of more promising projects. Any organisation has only limited resources for developing new projects and it is clearly important that these are deployed in the most advantageous way.

The basic systems development methodology consists of six phases:

* the feasibility study
* the detailed analysis phase
* the buy/build analysis
* the design phase
* the system building phase
* the implementation phase.

These six phases of the methodology proper are preceded by a preliminary stage in which potential projects are identified, either on the basis of systematic investigation or to satisfy an *ad hoc* requirement. If the projects identified at this stage do not have the potential to realise substantial advantages to the organisation, no amount of skilful analysis or technical ingenuity can introduce it. For this reason system project selection should be part of an on-going activity designed to identify a continuing series of projects which are individually profitable and collectively provide a coherent pattern of support to the organisation's activities. Many organisations develop systems plans on the basis of the data that they will use, the objective being to build applications on a coherent data base (see Chapter 12).

The six phases of the basic methodology should be followed by a post-implementation review stage immediately after operational use of the system begins. During this review all aspects of the project are critically examined so that the lessons learned may be fed back into the design and management of subsequent systems. Ideally each operational system should also be reviewed periodically (say every two or three years) during its lifetime to ensure that it is still operating both effectively (that is, doing what the organisation wants of it) and efficiently (that is, doing it in a cost effective manner).

Although the systems development methodology has six main phases these fall readily into three main groups: group one (the feasibility study and detailed analysis phases) can be called Analysis, group two (the buy/build analysis, design and systems building phases) Design and Progamming and group three concerns Implementation. For convenience these groups are discussed in separate chapters are shown in Figure 8.1 but it is important to remember that they form part of a continuous procedure.

8.3 The Feasibility Study

The feasibility study starts with either the outline of a problem which is thought to be susceptible to solution by the use of systems analysis or an idea for systems development and ends with either a concrete

Fig 8.1 *a methodology for systems development*

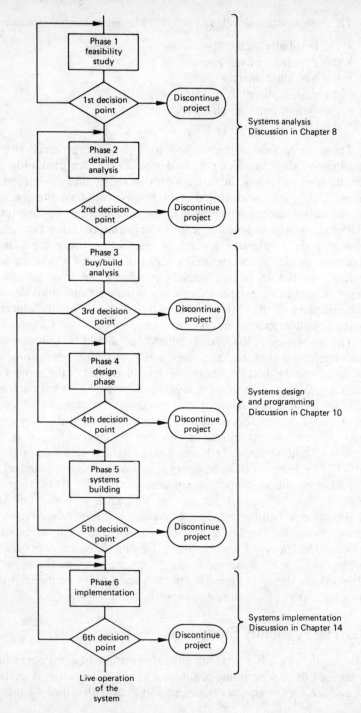

proposal to proceed with the development of the system (whether or not it makes use of computing technology) or the recommendation not to proceed.

Essentially the object is to establish whether the idea or suggestion is technically, humanly and economically practical. That is, to answer the questions:

* can the project be done? (is it within the state of the art?)
* can we carry out the project? (does the organisation have or can it obtain human resources – both quantitatively and qualitatively – to develop and operate the system?)
* is the project economically worthwhile? (do the benefits exceed the costs – and is it therefore worth doing?).

The amount of time and effort spent on a feasibility study will obviously depend not only on the scope of the suggested system, but also on the degree to which the basic idea has been investigated before the feasibility study is started. Where there is a detailed systems plan prepared by a team which includes adequate technical as well as business knowledge, the feasibility study is likely to be short. Similarly, where the scope of the project is limited, and it falls within the range of existing projects from a technical viewpoint, the feasibility study is also likely to be of short duration (perhaps the order of one or two man-weeks). Conversely, where the suggested project is large in scale (by comparison with previous systems developments performed by the organisation) and/or has a significant innovative element in it (whether in terms of techniques or equipment to be used), then the feasibility study should be a major effort which may require months of work from a team of people. What is always important is that the feasibility study is carried out and that no further development occurs until satisfactory answers have been provided to the three major questions listed above.

Clearly, no meaningful answers can be provided to these questions until the analyst has at least a broad concept of the sort of system that will be developed and this immediately highlights the key problem of the feasibility study: some preliminary design work must be done before the viability of the project can be assessed, yet design should not start until the feasibility of the system has been established! The answer to this dilemma is to prepare a conceptual design or outline with just sufficient detail to enable the technical content and economics of the proposed system to be assessed. It is important to note that these assessments are not expected to be exact, they are estimates which should be accurate enough for planning purposes and to enable decisions to be taken on the basis of reasonable data.

The other main point to note about the feasibility study is the danger that the first idea or suggestion which gave rise to the feasibility study will be the only one to be considered and, although this may well be established as a viable approach, it is not necessarily the best available alternative. The feasibility study should, therefore, consider a number of alternatives and answer the basic questions for each. The number of alternatives considered will vary with circumstances, but should be kept to a relatively small number to avoid the other risk of spending large amounts of time on investigating possibilities which will never be developed. Two to four alternatives will be sufficient in most cases.

The actual work of the feasibility study may be divided into four parts:

* establishing the objectives for the proposed system
* preparing outline designs for alternative approaches to meet the objectives
* collecting the evidence to establish the technical, human and economic viability of each alternative
* reporting the outcome of the feasibility study.

(a) Establish the objectives for the proposed system
It might be thought that by the time the systems analyst becomes involved with a potential project by being asked to carry out a feasibility study that the objectives have been firmly established. This is not always the case however, and the first task must be to establish what the real objectives are. Not infrequently the stated objectives will not be the real ones. Moreover, objectives such as 'improving efficiency' or 'providing more information' rarely lead to satisfactory systems since they really hinge on the idea that if things are not satisfactory then change must bring improvement. In these cases it is easy for money to be spent without solving the underlying problem. It is therefore necessary for the analyst to try to identify the real objective and to express it in quantifiable terms. This will necessitate considerable discussion with senior members of user management and, where the function exists, information systems planners. A request for 'more' or 'quicker'' information in a proposed cash management system, for example, might be translated, after discussion, into the objective of producing forecasts for the organisation's cash requirements for the following working day by 3 p.m. so that any surplus funds can be placed immediately on deposit and generate interest. The benefits from meeting such objectives can then be estimated in a way that those of 'quicker information' cannot. Unless

this part of the investigation is carried out it will prove impossible to take subsequent decisions; for example, which of two alternative proposals is to be adopted, on any rational basis.

As soon as the objective has been agreed between user management and the department providing the systems analysis function it should be recorded and signed by both parties. It is also most beneficial if terms of reference for the feasibility study can be established at the same time. These should set out the scope of the study and indicate approximate time and cost involved. Such terms of reference go a long way towards preventing the sort of misunderstandings which all too often mar relationships between users of systems and those providing such systems. At this stage the analyst should also identify the shortcomings of the present system.

The final point to be considered under this heading is how the proposed system relates to the organisation's long-term plan for information systems development. Clearly there is no point in developing a major new system if the longer-term plans either eliminate the need for it or envisage its early replacement by a larger, more comprehensive system.

(b) Preparing conceptual or outline designs for alternative approaches to meet the objectives

Having established the objectives of the proposed system the analyst can turn his attention to preparing in outline alternative systems designs which would meet those objectives. As has already been noted, more than one possible solution should be evaluated and if possible the alternatives should cover a wide spectrum. Nor should it be taken for granted that all alternative solutions should be based on the use of computers. Obviously the scope which an analyst has to consider alternatives depends on the environment within which he is working and the scope of the project upon which he is working, but, at this stage, the advice is always to think as broadly as possible.

Depending on the circumstances the alternatives that may need to be considered might include:

* continuing with the present system (with or without modification)
* manual systems
* manual systems using time-sharing computing services for some functions
* automated systems using dedicated personal computers
* automated systems using on-line access to a general-purpose mini or mainframe computer

* developing an in-house computer system (either batch or on-line) using custom-built programs
* software packages purchased for use on the organisation's own computer(s)
* batch computer systems using the services of a computer bureau.

(c) Collecting the evidence to establish the technical, human and economic viability of each alternative

In collecting this evidence the analyst will be using many of the same fact-gathering and recording techniques that are used in the later detailed analysis phase, and are described in Chapter 9. The analyst will need to find out:

* what are the main outputs required from the system?
* when are the main outputs required? (immediately, daily, weekly, monthly, etc.)
* what are the main sources of input into the system?
* what volume of data will have to be processed by the system?
* what volumes of data will have to be stored within the system for reference purposes? (e.g. files of master data)
* what volumes of data will need to be retained for archival purposes?
* how many people will be involved in using the system, where are they located and who are they?
* what is the anticipated life of the system?
* what are the audit trail and security requirements of the system?
* are there any planned changes to the business or organisation which will affect the proposed system?
* what are the estimated development and running costs associated with each alternative?
* what are the estimated benefits associated with each alternative?
* what are the technical problems associated with each alternative?
* what are the human problems associated with each alternative?
* what is the effect of each alternative on the organisation?
* what resources would be needed to develop each alternative?
* what is the estimated elapsed time needed to develop each alternative?
* what is the degree of risk associated with each alternative?

Once all the necessary facts have been assembled the analyst can analyse them to provide the answers to the basic questions about the technical, human and economic feasibility of each alternative considered.

Technical feasibility is usually the easiest to establish as most proposed systems either fit within the framework of equipment and procedures already in use within the organisation or require only minor extensions to that framework. Sometimes, however, proposed projects require a major change to that framework; for example, the introduction of data-base or distributed processing based systems (discussed in Chapters 12 and 19 respectively), and such proposals should receive very careful attention.

Human feasibility refers to the capabilities of both systems' development and user staff. In the former case the situation is usually closely related to the technical environment. If the proposed system is within the existing technical framework it is likely that the organisation will have the human capability to develop the system. Moreover, if the assessment is that the proposed system is beyond the capabilities of the organisation's own systems development staff it is possible to recruit staff with the requisite experience or to employ specialist staff from a software house or agency for a short period. With regard to user staff the capabilities of operational personnel have to be considered as well as those of managerial staff.

Establishing economic feasibility requires an evaluation of the costs and benefits of the proposed system. Costs include both those of developing the system and also the running costs associated with the system after it is in use. The costs involved in developing a system are drawn from the full list of the costs incurred in the use of computers for data processing given in Chapter 2 and may include: staff costs of systems personnel, staff costs of user staff, equipment costs (for example, cost of computer time for program testing) and any other costs (for example, costs for buying or installing new equipment). Estimating the time and therefore costs that will be incurred in developing a system is extremely difficult. A number of formulae have been developed for this purpose, but in reality there is little alternative to educated guesses based on experience. This is no excuse for avoiding the exercise however, if anything the reverse, since it is only by making estimates (and comparing them with the eventual outcome) that the accuracy of future estimates may be improved.

Running costs will include: operating staff costs, equipment hire or rental costs, stationery costs and any other direct costs that may be incurred.

Benefits are typically of two types, *tangible* and *intangible*. Tangible benefits are all those that may be directly measured in financial terms. Depending on the application concerned these benfits might include: reduced labour costs, reduced stock-holding costs due to improved ordering procedures, reduction in bad debts due to improved credit control, etc. (see also Chapter 2).

Intangible benefits are those that cannot be measured *directly* in financial terms. The most common intangible benefit is probably 'improved information'. Although improved information does often allow the organisation to reap substantial benefits it is notoriously difficult to quantify. Where it proves impossible for the analyst to quantify a benefit of this kind the most appropriate course is to identify it clearly, together with the marginal cost of producing it, and to make the inclusion (or otherwise) of this item a specific item in the proposal submitted at the end of the feasibility study.

A straight comparison of costs and benefits is rarely sufficient to enable the respective merits of two or more alternative solutions to a problem to be evaluated properly. Costs are incurred at different times in the development cycle and the benefits accruing from the implementation of each of the alternatives might be realised at different times. This coupled with the time effect of money (a pound in a year's time is not worth the same as a pound today) means that some notice must be taken of when costs are incurred and benefits realised. Financial techniques to take account of the time effect of money are well established and many organisations have adopted a specific variant of one of these techniques for use in assessing potential projects. The analyst should be thoroughly familiar with the technique in use within his own organisation or, if there is no prescribed technique, use a basic form of discounted cash flow (DCF), details of which may be found in many standard management texts. A formal examination of the costs and benefits of a proposed system is called a *cost–benefit analysis*.

(d) Reporting the outcome of the feasibility study

The final task in a feasibility study is to report the facts obtained. In practice the tasks outlined above will not be completely sequential and a certain amount of reiteration will occur. As the analyst proceeds with analysis further alternatives for evaluation may be identified and most commonly, when it comes to reporting findings, gaps in the analysis will be revealed, necessitating further work. For this reason many analysts find it convenient to prepare an outline of the feasibility study report very early in the study and add the facts as the study proceeds.

This discussion already assumes that a written report on the feasibility study is to be prepared. This is certainly to be recommended but may not be the only report that the analyst is required to provide. Oral reports or presentations are also frequently used. In all cases the content is substantially the same and should involve discussion of each of the following points:

* an outline of the problem or business opportunity including the limitations of the present system
* a description of the organisation or business environment in which it occurs
* a statement of the objectives of the proposed system
* a list of the alternative solutions considered
* a statement of why those alternatives not fully evaluated were discarded
* an evaluation of the technical, human and economic feasibility of each alternative considered seriously, including details of any assumptions made when evaluating them
* a proposed plan for the implementation of the favoured alternative
* a recommendation on the proposed course of action.

8.4 **The First Decision Point**

The feasibility study report is the major input to the first decision point shown in Figure 8.1. At this stage the analyst's recommendation as contained in that report may well come into competition with other projects which could potentially make use of the same development resources.

Depending on the organisation the decision to be taken at this point will be made by a steering committee, a senior manager or perhaps by the management services or data processing manager. In making this decision other considerations beyond those considered by the analyst during the study may be relevant. Such factors as the performance of the organisation as a whole (for example, the availability or otherwise of investment funds) may have a major bearing on the decision actually taken.

The decision taken at this point will be: to continue with the proposed project, to discontinue the project or to re-do the feasibility study in total or in part. Even if the decision is to proceed it may not be exactly along the lines proposed in the report. Indeed an alternative other than the solution recommended by the analyst may be selected. However, if the feasibility study has been carefully prepared and presented this will be an unusual occurrence. More frequent would be a decision to proceed, but after a time delay imposed by a shortage of resources to carry out the project.

What is important is that a clear decision does emerge from this stage so that the future workload of the system development staff can be planned.

8.5 The Detailed Analysis Phase

The detailed analysis phase (also called the 'system definition phase') continues the development of the proposed system from the feasibility study to the point of a design specification. If a considerable time has elapsed since the completion of the feasibility study it may be necessary to rework some of the information contained in the report to ascertain that the basic factors are unchanged.

The final results of the detailed analysis are a design specification and a short report. The design specification will include an outline of the proposed system (taken from the feasibility study and amplified or amended as a result of the activities performed during this phase) and a number of detailed documents arising from the activities in this phase. The formal report is described below.

In conducting the detailed analysis phase the analyst is concerned both with the opportunities for the new system and the constraints within which it must operate. The basic activities of this phase are:

* to establish the detailed objectives of the proposed system
* to establish the definitive facts about the functions to be performed by the proposed system
* to identify and define the interfaces between the proposed system and other systems whether in use or proposed
* to identify and define the interface between the proposed system and the supporting data base(s) and/or the necessary data files
* to identify constraints on the design of the proposed system
* to specify the user's responsibilities in operating the proposed system
* to update the cost–benefit analysis and time estimates for the development of the proposed system
* to update the plan for the further development of the proposed system
* to prepare a report for management approval.

(a) To establish the detailed objectives of the proposed system
The objectives of the proposed system have already been established in broad terms during the feasibility study. In this phase these broad objectives should be quantified and turned into specific design objectives. Often, the analyst will find that this exercise presents a

serious problem, since the principal users of the proposed system do not have a clear understanding of their detailed requirements. This is natural since many systems are born more out of a sense of dissatisfaction with the status quo than a clear picture of what things should be like. It is at this point that the *prototyping* approach becomes valuable (although it may also be used during large-scale feasibility studies). Prototyping requires the quick and inexpensive construction of at least a workable subset of the total system which can be readily modified or replaced if it proves unsuitable or if an improved approach is identified. If, on the other hand, it proves successful, it becomes a working model of the system that is to be developed (or if efficient and comprehensive enough, may become the actual system). Prototyping is usually only practical where much of the data required is already in established data bases, and tools like 4GLs are available for rapid systems development or where a reasonable approximation of the system may be constructed on a PC.

The detailed analysis phase may require a study of the existing system to identify the functions being performed by the system and its practical limitations. Where this is the case, it is strongly recommended that the technique of data flow diagramming, in conjunction with hierarchical decomposition (see Chapter 9), be used.

(b) To establish the definitive facts about the functions to be performed by the proposed system

This activity will involve the analyst in verifying and supplementing all the data collected during the feasibility study. All the basic data on which the proposed system will operate must be identified and projections made about anticipated volumes of data.

(c) To identify and define the interfaces between the proposed system and other systems whether in use or proposed

Few systems exist completely in isolation from other systems and the way in which the proposed system relates to other systems requires careful study. The interfaces must be looked at in terms of both data exchanged between systems and the timing of operations.

(d) To identify and define the interface between the proposed system and the supporting data base(s) and/or the necessary data files

The data requirements for the proposed system may be met by use of a data base common to a number of systems or individual files. Where the proposed system is based on the use of computer technology this data will also be held on a computer. During the detailed analysis phase the analyst will specify the data requirements of the proposed system. In the case of a system using a computerised data base this will involve preparing a representation (often called a user view or 'sub-schema') of data that the proposed system will require from the data base and in the case of a system that is to be based on conventional files will normally involve the specification of the data to be held in each file. In both cases the arrangements to collect and verify any data that is not already captured must be identified. The subject of data management and the techniques used in development of data bases are discussed in detail in Chapters 9 and 12.

(e) To identify constraints on the design of the proposed system
All systems are, in practice, designed within certain constraints and it is the duty of the analyst to identify these constraints during this phase. The constraints may be financial (the system must not cost more than £x), technical (the capacity of the installed computing facility) or operational (the system must be implemented by a specified date). Constraints which emerge later in the development cycle could lead to expensive re-design work and delay.

(f) To specify the user's responsibilities in operating the proposed system
The analyst should indicate clearly the broad area of operational responsibility that the user staff will be expected to perform.

(g) To update the cost–benefit analysis and time estimates for the development of the proposed system
Towards the end of the detailed analysis phase a clearer picture of the proposed system will have emerged and both the analyst and user will have a much better understanding of the work that will be necessary to develop and implement the system and the benefits that may be expected. This improved understanding should be used to update the cost–benefit analysis and time estimates as input to the next decision point.

(h) To update the plan for the further development of the proposed system
As with the cost–benefit analysis and time estimates the plan showing resources to be used, when and for how long they will be needed and when implementation may be anticipated, should be updated.

(i) To prepare a report for management approval
The final activity in the detailed analysis phase is to prepare a report for management. This report should be brief and set out the changes that have been made to the system concepts since the adoption of the feasibility study and any changes to the cost–benefit analysis or time estimate. The objective of this report is to provide the basis upon which a decision to proceed with the project can realistically be taken.

As with all systems reports it is important that as much as possible of the content is drawn directly from the documentation (e.g. data flow diagrams) produced during the phase.

It is desirable that the principal user and the analyst are jointly responsible for presenting the report in order to demonstrate that the user is both involved and in agreement with the development to date.

8.6 The Second Decision Point

The detailed analysis phase is followed by a second decision point. This point is somewhat different from the one that followed the feasibility study inasmuch as it provides the first opportunity at which actual development work (as opposed to preliminary investigation) may be halted.

There is a tendency, once a project, be it systems development or of any other kind, has started to let it continue unchecked even when it has become obvious to many that the basic objectives cannot be met or can only be met at a cost quite disproportionate to the benefits that will be obtained. This tendency must be resisted. Not only does it mean that undesirable projects are completed when they should have been discontinued, but it also means that the resources that have been used have not been available for other, potentially more profitable uses.

It is important, therefore, that formal decision points are included in the systems development methodology in order that the project may be reviewed periodically to ensure that its continued development makes the most use of the resources involved. As before, the decision point offers the option of discontinuing the project, proceeding with development or repeating some of the previous phase. No further development work should be undertaken until the steering committee or other decision-maker has performed this evaluation.

9 The Techniques of Systems Analysis

9.1 Introduction

Before continuing with the chronological description of the systems development methodology it is necessary to step aside and look at some of the techniques that the systems analyst will be using.

In addition to their obvious value in helping to meet immediate objectives during the analysis and design phases of the system development process, many of these techniques have a vital extra role in promoting communications. That is to say they are tools for communication, between analyst and user, analyst and management, analyst and programmer. Moreover, these techniques and the documentation resulting from their application provide communication between the people developing the system and those who will subsequently have to maintain it in operational use.

At the end of each phase of the systems development process all the documentation produced during that phase should be examined and sorted into two types. Working documentation (which can generally be archived and in due course discarded) and permanent documentation. Permanent documentation will include all the formal outputs produced during the phase, essential correspondence concerning the extent of the system and other relevant letters, memoranda, minutes of meetings, records of walk-throughs, formal reports and the principal supporting documents. Supporting documentation will include many of the charts and diagrams produced in applying the techniques described in this chapter. Permanent documentation should be checked to ensure that it meets the basic requirements of clarity, has a descriptive title, is dated and bears the originator's name and that the material recorded in it is prepared in accordance with the standards in use within the organisation. All permanent documentation should be indexed and included in the master project file. A security copy of all documentation should also be made and filed in a separate place for safe-keeping to avoid problems if the master copy is lost or damaged. It is important that this 'back-up copy' is amended in the same way as the original throughout the life of the system.

In this chapter the following techniques will be described:

* procedure charting
* flowcharting
* decision tables
* HIPO charting
* data-flow diagramming
* structured English, tight English and pseudo code
* interviewing
* data analysis or bubble charting
* normalisation.

9.2 Procedure Charting

Procedure charting is a family of well-established techniques which have been extensively used for many years by Work Study and Organisation and Methods (O & M) practitioners. They had also been a valuable asset to the data processing profession especially for recording and describing existing systems and in defining manual procedures to be used in conjunction with new computer systems. Procedure charts are also a useful way of analysing a procedure to find bottlenecks.

One of the more widely used procedure-charting techniques is based on five symbols originally promulgated by the American Society of Mechanical Engineers (ASME) and shown in Figure 9.1 These symbols (often supplemented by the input and output symbols used in flowcharting and shown in Figure 9.3) can be used in a sequential flow manner or in a horizontal format. An example of one of the main formats will be found in Figure 9.2 overleaf.

9.3 Flowcharting

Flowcharting has been one of the most widely used data processing techniques being used to plan the flow through a program, show a sequence of events in a system (including both computer and non-computer activities) and to show the interaction of systems. Moreover, the symbols are widely used by computer staff as a form of 'shorthand'. Thus, for example, computer configuration charts (i.e. charts showing the combination of peripheral devices attached to a central processing unit) are commonly drawn using flowcharting symbols.

Flowcharting is thus a flexible and versatile technique. At various times different organisations (computer manufacturers, user groups,

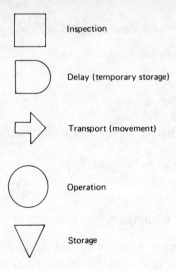

☐	Inspection
D	Delay (temporary storage)
⇨	Transport (movement)
◯	Operation
▽	Storage

Fig 9.1 *procedure charting symbols (based on those recommended by ASME)*

Fig 9.2 *a procedure chart (the symbols are preprinted and inked in as appropriate)*

Procedure: Processing Suppliers Invoices (present system)		
Prepared by: A.N. Analyst	Sheet: 1 of 2	Date: 4 March 1982

No.	Activity	Description
1	☐ D ⇨ ● ▽	Invoice received in Mail Room and sorted to Accounts Department mail bag.
2	☐ D ➡ ◯ ▽	Mail bag sent to Accounts Department
3	☐ D ⇨ ● ▽	Invoices sorted into supplier groups
4	☐ D ➡ ◯ ▽	Invoices passed to clerks dealing with appropriate Supplier
5	☐ ◗ ⇨ ◯ ▽	Filed pending end of present cycle
6	■ D ⇨ ◯ ▽	Invoices checked
7	☐ D ➡ ◯ ▽	Sent to Head of Section for approval
8	☐ D ⇨ ● ▽	Approved
9	☐ D ➡ ◯ ▽	Sent to Data Control Clerk
10	☐ D ⇨ ● ▽	Entered into 'Invoices Received' log
11	☐ ◗ ⇨ ◯ ▽	Filed pending data preparation
12	☐ D ⇨ ● ▽	Batch totals calculated and batch slip (Form 1234) prepared
13	☐ D ➡ ◯ ▽	Invoices & batch slip passed to data preparation
14	☐ D ⇨ ● ▽	Keyed and verified
15	☐ D ➡ ◯ ▽	Invoices returned to Accounts Department (mail receipt clerk)
16	☐ D ⇨ ◯ ▼	Filed in Supplier's File

standard organisations, etc.) have published differing suggestions about the symbols that should be used, and the meaning to be attached thereto. In practice a fairly small subset of the total range of symbols is sufficient for most purposes and those most widely used are shown in Figure 9.3.

The conventions of flowcharting (based on those recommended by the International Standards Organisation) are shown in Figure 9.4

When drawing any flowchart the steps to be followed are:

Step 1   Decide on the purpose of the chart, e.g. to record data, to communicate to an audience, to help design a program or process.

Step 2   Decide the extent of the activity to be charted.

Step 3   Collect or develop the data to be charted.

Step 4   Select the starting-point for the flowchart.

Fig 9.3   *a limited range of flowcharting symbols for general use*

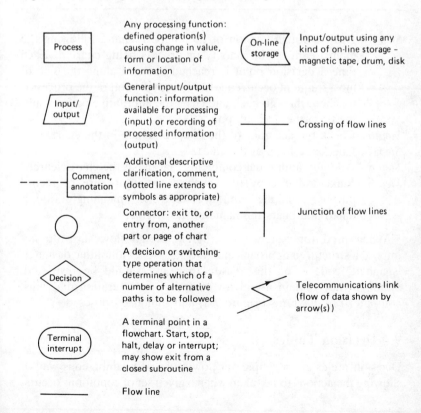

1. The general direction of flow in any flowchart is:
   From top to bottom
   From left to right

2. Arrowheads will be used whenever the flow of information or *sequence of events* is not as indicated in 1 above *and* whenever necessary to improve the clarity of the flowchart

3. Flowlines crossing shall imply no logical connection between those lines

4. Two or more flowlines may join without any explanatory note. Two or more flowlines may only diverge at a symbol, which is annotated to show under what conditions divergence occurs

5. Flowchart symbols may be drawn any size, but the ratio between dimensions should be maintained within reasonable limites in order to facilitate recognition

6. Any flowchart should be identified with a title, date and the name of the author

7. Annotation and cross-references should be made when the meaning is not apparent from the symbol(s) used

Fig 9.4   *conventions for the use of flowcharting in data processing*

Step 5   Draw a rough version of the chart freehand following the mainstream of the activity or process being charted. Each time a decision point is reached proceed along the line of most frequent occurrence until the end-point of the process is reached, then go back and chart the alternative paths resulting from the decision points.

Step 6   Check the accuracy of the data contained in the chart.

Step 7   Check the logic of the chart.

Step 8   Add any additional comments that make the chart clearer.

Step 9   Make a fair copy of the chart for future use or record purposes, making sure that it has a clear, meaningful title, is dated and bears the name of the originator.

When used for systems or program design flowcharts do not impose a structured approach and may lead to a monolithic design or 'spaghetti code'. For this reason their use should be restricted, although they remain useful for computer configuration diagrams, computer run diagrams (Figure 9.5) and similar purposes.

9.4 Decision Tables

Decision tables are a simple yet powerful and unambiguous way of showing the actions to be taken when a given set of conditions occurs.

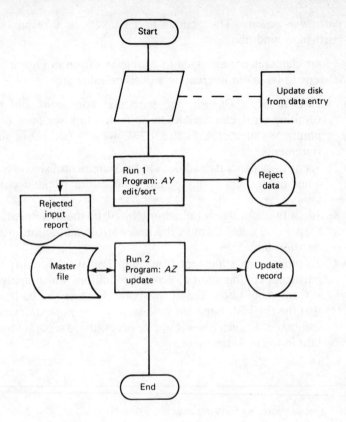

Fig 9.5   *flowcharting symbols used to show the interaction of computer runs (for use in computer operations documentation) for a cyclical procedure to update a master file*

Moreover, they can be used to verify that all combinations of the conditions have been properly catered for. In this way they can reduce the possibility that rare or unforeseen combinations of conditions will result in confusion about the action to be taken.

A decision table brings together four elements:

* *general conditions*. The individual events or situations that may occur.
* *particular conditions*. Combinations of one or more general conditions.
* *general actions*. The actions or events that should follow from the general conditions.

* *particular actions*. The actions to be taken as a result of a particular condition.

These four elements are arranged in a table as shown in Figure 9.6. The steps to be taken in creating a decision table are:

Step 1 List, in plain English, the particular conditions and the resulting particular actions to be tabled in a series of brief points or statements. Figure 9.7 shows a typical list of such statements.

Step 2 Identify all general conditions in the statements listed in Step 1 and enter them in the top left-hand section of the decision table.

Step 3 Identify all the general actions listed in the statements in Step 1 and enter them in the lower left-hand section of the decision table.

Step 4 Examine each statement from Step 1 in turn. Identify the particular combination of general conditions which apply.

Care should be taken at this point as it may be be found that the original statement is, in fact, two or more statements combined. In such cases it will be necessary to separate these into individual statements.

Fig 9.6   *general structure of a decision table*

	Rules							
	1	2	3	4	5	6	7	8
General conditions				Particular conditions				
General actions				Particular actions				

1. If parcel weighs less than 20 kg. and destination is more than 300 km. from factory send by air (unaccompanied baggage)

2. If parcel weighs over 20 kg. but less than 150 kg. and destination is more than 300 km. from factory send by air freight

3. If parcel weight is greater than 150 kg. and destination is more than 300 km. from factory send by haulage contractor

4. If destination is less than 300 km. from factory send by own transport

Fig 9.7   *statements to be used to produce a decision table*

Step 5   Treat each statement separately and apply Steps 6 and 7, matching the particular conditions in the statement with the particular actions which also apply to it. Each statement will occupy one column (or rule) in the table with at least one entry against the conditions and at least one entry against the actions.

Step 6   The general conditions applicable to each statement are marked Y (for Yes) in the next free vertical column (or rule) in the particular conditions section of the decision table. All other general conditions in that column may be marked N (for No).

Step 7   The general action(s) applicable to the specific combination of general conditions should be marked X in the same vertical column as the appropriate Ys and Ns have been entered.

Step 8   Check that no combination of Ys and Ns occurs more than once, eliminating any duplicate rules found.

At the completion of this process the left-hand side of the decision tables lists all the conditions and actions covered in the statements and the vertical columns on the right-hand side of the decision table (usually called rules) show specific combinations of conditions and the resultant actions. Figure 9.8 shows the statements from Figure 9.7 translated into a decision table.

At this level the decision table is a valuable communication tool facilitating communication, for example between user and analyst ('Are these the rules that apply now?' or 'Are these the rules you want to apply in the new system?') or between analyst and programmer ('These are the rules to be applied in processing this data'). However, as mentioned above, the decision table can also be used to verify that all conditions or combinations of them have been catered

	Rules							
	1	2	3	4	5	6	7	8
Weight < 20 kg.?	Y	Y	Y	Y	N	N	N	N
Weight > 150 kg.?	N	N	Y	Y	Y	Y	N	N
Distance < 300 km.?	N	Y	Y	N	N	Y	Y	N
Ship by air freight								X
Send by air (unaccompanied baggage)		X	Impossible rule	Impossible rule				
Send by sea freight								
Dispatch by own transport	X					X	X	
Send by haulage contractor					X			

Fig 9.8   *a decision table – the statements in Figure 9.11 translated into decision-table form*

for. This can be achieved because there is a strict mathematical relationship between the number of general conditions and the number of possible rules. Where each condition is answerable by the question Yes or No the number of rules is 2^n where n is the number of conditions. Thus if there are three conditions the number of rules is $2^3 = 8$. Clearly, with more than a few general conditions the number of possible permutations leads to a very large table (called an extended table), and quickly becomes unmanageable. In practice it is often sufficient to introduce an ELSE rule, i.e. for any combination of conditions not previously covered a specific default action should be carried out, e.g. refer to supervisor for instructions or reject the input data.

Preparing decision tables takes a little practice, but when mastered they are a useful technique for many purposes in data processing particularly when it is necessary to provide an unambiguous statement of a complex set of rules. They can thus play a key role in ensuring that computer programs apply user policies accurately. To make use of this power of decision tables directly, some compilers have been written which use decision tables to specify program logic. For some applications such tools can be extremely valuable. As with all documentation, decision tables should be titled, dated and bear the originator's name.

9.5 **HIPO Charting**

Unlike the other charting techniques considered so far, the *H*ierarchy plus *I*nput *P*rocess *O*utput (HIPO) technique aims to provide a complete documentation set for data processing rather than providing tools to help in specific aspects of the work. HIPO charts are of two basic types, the *Visual Tables of Contents* (VTOC) and the *overview* and *detail diagrams*.

(a) Visual table of contents

The visual table of contents is a schematic representation of a complete system or of part of it, and as its name implies it serves as a contents list for the rest of the package. The way in which it is drawn reflects the structure of the complete system and is thus most commonly used in conjunction with top-down design principles, i.e. the successive decomposition of a complete entity into discrete elements which collectively serve to achieve the objectives to be met.

As the system is being designed from the top down so then should the VTOC be prepared in a similar manner as work on the system (or that part of it being documented using this approach) proceeds.

By convention the box at the top of the hierarchy is the complete entity being represented and is numbered 1. The first-level decompositions (i.e. major subentities) are the next level in the chart and are numbered 2, 3, 4, 5, . . ., *n* sequentially across the chart from left to right. Further decompositions (which need not be symmetrical) result in additional levels in the hierarchy and are numbered by adding a numerical suffix to the number of the box of which it is a decomposition, e.g. the decomposition of box two into two boxes results in their being numbered 2.1 and 2.2. An example of a visual table of contents is shown in Figure 9.9.

All documents relating to the system (which may include not only other HIPO charts, but also other charts and documentation) are indexed according to the visual table of contents.

(b) Overview and detail diagrams

An overview or detail diagram is a simple model of a system or process at any level showing on one sheet of paper the inputs to that system or process, the process itself and the resultant output. These elements are presented in a stylised manner to facilitate interpretation.

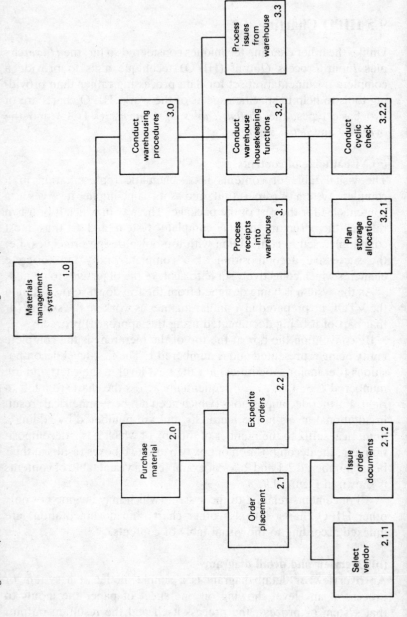

Fig 9.9 a partial visual time of contents for a materials management system

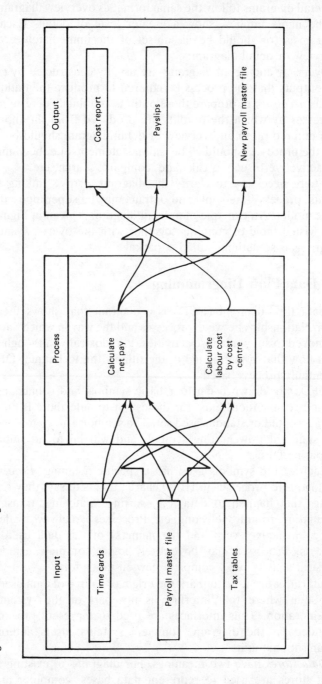

Fig 9.10 *a HIPO overview diagram*

Detail diagrams follow the same format as overview diagrams, but, as the name implies, show a greater level of detail. Each detail diagram is (or should be) a sub-set of the immediately preceding overview or detail diagram.

Overview and detail diagrams are usually constructed by entering the outputs that the process is required to produce then adding the inputs *necessary* to prepare those outputs and finally determining the processes by which the outputs are produced from the inputs. All data entered on to an overview or detail diagram should be concise and the processes should all be action statements, i.e. beginning with an 'active' verb such as calculate, compare, search, etc.

Where necessary to clarify the diagram, arrows linking specific inputs, process statements and outputs may be superimposed on the basic model. An example of a detail diagram is given in Figure 9.10.

A visual table of contents together with the overview and detail diagrams is sometimes called 'a package'.

9.6 Data Flow Diagramming

A data flow diagram (DFD) is a diagram that shows the logical interrelationships between processes and the way in which data has to be moved to support those activities. Paradoxically, although it is the data flow that is mentioned in the title of the technique, DFDs are essentially process based.

DFDs are drawn using four basic symbols and connecting lines. Various conventions exist for these, but to date there is no universally accepted or standardised set. The symbols shown in Figure 9.11 are standard flowcharting symbols and will be found suitable for preparing DFDs.

Each of the symbols used has a specific meaning. *Processes* are analogous to processes in HIPO charts; that is to say, they represent things that happen to data, e.g. sorting, matching, transforming, calculating, routing, selecting, etc. Processes can always be described using an 'active' verb and the name(s) of the data used in that process. Processes may be entirely logical or may include some physical activity, e.g. 'complete new entrant's form'.

Interfaces are used to mark the origin or source of data used within a system where that interface is not part of the system under consideration. Thus interfaces are used to represent processes not included on the diagram, complete systems, users and/or other organisational units.

Data stores have two meanings. For diagrams of existing systems data stores are used to represent data bases, computer and non-

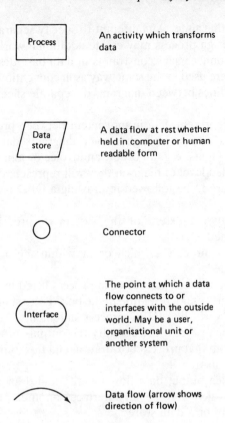

Process — An activity which transforms data

Data store — A data flow at rest whether held in computer or human readable form

Connector

Interface — The point at which a data flow connects to or interfaces with the outside world. May be a user, organisational unit or another system

Data flow (arrow shows direction of flow)

Fig 9.11   *data-flow diagramming symbols*

computer files. For diagrams of proposed systems data stores are either points of origin for data flows that do not arise from other processes or interfaces or, similarly, the destination for data which is to be saved for later processing, future reference or archival purposes. Data stores for proposed systems are *not* equivalent to files or data bases – they are merely logical collections of data. In fact in the early stages of design it is only necessary to have a single data store which represents the complete collection of data for which manual files and data base(s) will subsequently be designed. The techniques of data analysis described below will subsequently be used to associate those elements of the data to be stored on the computer into data base(s) or files. Those elements of data which are to be stored in conventional hard copy files may similarly be grouped as may be most convenient at that time. Any attempt to specify separate data stores early in the design process may create additional work later on and can introduce unnecessary constraints in data base design.

Connectors are used in the same way as in conventional flowcharts; that is, to join lines between diagrams or separate sheets of the same diagram.

Data flows represent data in movement between processes, interfaces and data stores. In higher-lever diagrams data flows often represent documents, e.g. an order, an invoice or a payslip, while at the most detailed level of diagram they will represent data elements.

The procedure to be followed in drawing a DFD is as follows:

Step 1   Identify the extent of the system or process to be diagrammed.

Step 2   List the processes which occur within the area being diagrammed.

Step 3   Draw a process box for each process listed in the preceding step and enter a brief title in the box. Titles should begin with action verbs like HIPO process statements.

Step 4   For each process box identify the outputs produced from it and from that process box draw a data flow representing that output in transit.

Step 5   For each output data flow identify and draw in its destination, which may be an interface, another process on the diagram or a data store.

Step 6   For each process box identify the inputs necessary to the process and draw a data flow into the process box representing that input in transit.

Step 7   For each input data flow identify and draw in its point of origin (the options are as for output destinations).

Step 8   Give each data flow and interface an appropriate title.

As noted above, the data flow names will often equate to document names at the higher levels and will be data element names at the detailed level of diagram. When the system has been fully designed and the data base and files defined they should be entered on to the diagram, replacing the composite data store used during the design phase. Data stores in diagrams of existing systems should bear the name of the data base or file they represent.

Step 9   Restructure the diagram to provide the clearest possible graphical representation.

Step 10 If the DFD is too cluttered, combine processes or eliminate exception routines and include them in a lower level of diagram.

Step 11 Validate the accuracy of the DFD by checking that the outputs from each process can indeed be produced from the inputs to it and that the inputs can be derived from the data stores or other sources as specified. For detailed diagrams of proposed systems the data elements obtained from the data stores must be the same as the data elements deposited into the data stores for that system.

Step 12 Prepare a 'fair copy' of the DFD ensuring that it is properly identified.

Step 13 Conduct a 'walkthrough' of the DFD with user staff, analysts and programmers as appropriate (a description of a walkthrough will be found in Section 9.11 below).

An example of a completed DFD is shown in Figure 9.12.

It will not have escaped notice that the process box of a DFD is very similar to the overview diagram in HIPO charting. In the same way as overview diagrams, DFDs can be decomposed; each process in the original DFD can become the subject-matter of a further DFD at a more detailed level. This process can, if carefully carried out and with the introduction of physical constraints, e.g. geographical dispersion of processes, result in decomposition to the point where each process represents either a module of computer code or a brief manual task description.

At this level, the data elements (see Chapter 12) contained in each data flow should be identified. The data stores therefore represent a collection of elements. In fact the data elements form the input for the data analysis process and the data stores are, *de facto*, sub-schemas as described in Chapter 12.

A decomposition of process box 1 in Figure 9.12 is given in Figure 9.13. The convention for numbering process is the same as for HIPO charts (see Section 9.5).

In addition to their use in building logical models as outlined above, DFDs may be used to document an existing system or process. Secondly, because the overall DFD of a proposed system is a logical model it may be used in a feasibility study to outline possible alternative systems approaches with greater or lesser amount of automation. Figure 9.14 shows a decomposition of process box 1.1 in Figure 9.13 with the superimposition of two possible alternative computer system boundaries.

As with all techniques, DFDs have disadvantages as well as

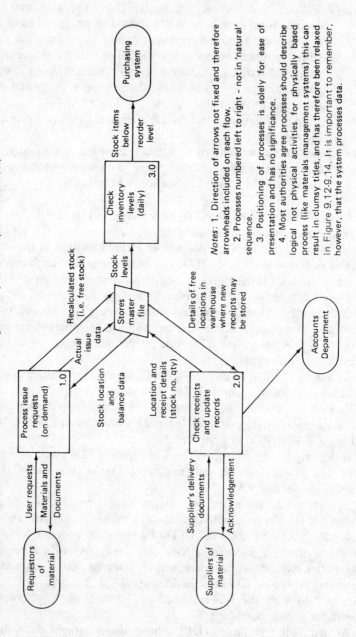

Fig 9.12 a data flow diagram showing a materials management system (simplified overview)

Notes: 1. Direction of arrows not fixed and therefore arrowheads included on each flow.

2. Processes numbered left to right – not in 'natural' sequence.

3. Positioning of processes is solely for ease of presentation and has no significance.

4. Most authorities agree processes should describe logical not physical activities for physically based process (like materials management systems) this can result in Figure 9.12-9.14. It is important to remember, however, that the system processes data.

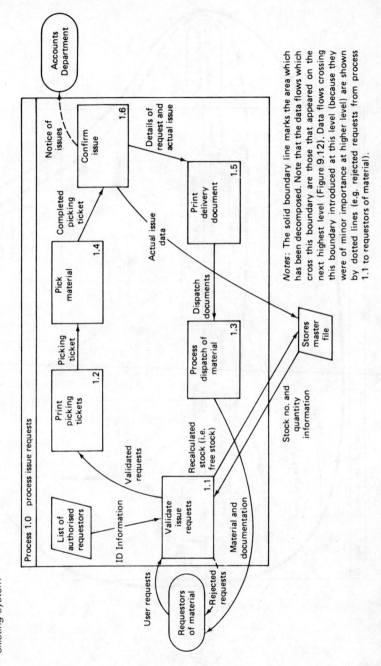

Fig 9.13 a data flow diagram. This diagram shows the first decomposition of process 1.0 in Figure 9.12. It depicts an existing system

Notes: The solid boundary line marks the area which has been decomposed. Note that the data flows which cross this boundary are those that appeared on the next highest level (Figure 9.12). Data flows crossing this boundary introduced at this level (because they were of minor importance at higher level) are shown by dotted lines (e.g. rejected requests from process 1.1 to requestors of material).

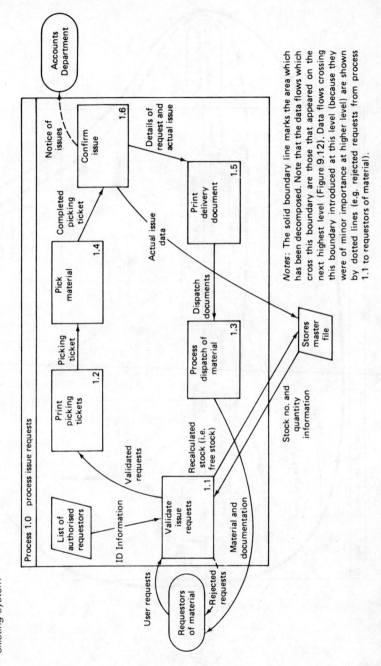

Process 1.0   process issue requests

List of authorised requestors

ID Information

Validate issue requests
1.1

Validated requests

Print picking tickets
1.2

Picking ticket

Pick material
1.4

Completed picking ticket

Confirm issue
1.6

Notice of issues

Accounts Department

Details of request and actual issue

Print delivery document
1.5

Actual issue data

Dispatch documents

Process dispatch of material
1.3

Recalculated stock (i.e. free stock)

Material and documentation

Stock no. and quantity information

Stores master file

User requests

Rejected requests

Requestors of material

124

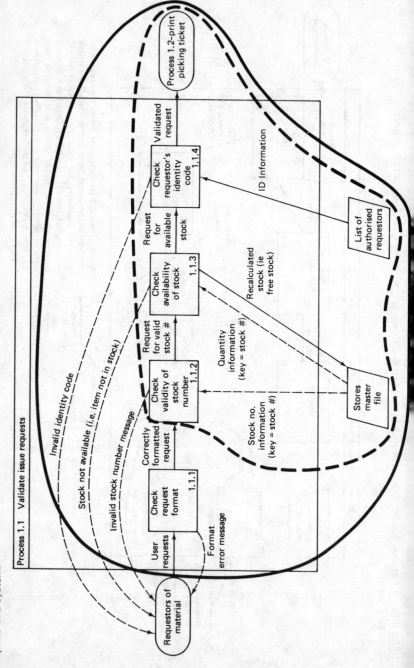

Fig 9.14 a data flow diagram. The thick lines (solid and broken) show two possible boundaries for the computer-based parts of a system.

advantages and it is as well to be aware of these before use. The major disadvantages of DFDs are:

* the tendency to confuse logical data stores with physical data files
* the risk that the first decomposition of a proposed system into processes (or process into sub-process) will be the only one seriously considered
* it is difficult to represent systems which will be implemented on a distributed network of computers
* it is difficult to represent *ad hoc* reports and inquiries effectively since they are by their very nature divorced from routine processing, yet may nevertheless be a vital part of the total system
* it is difficult to identify the important data flows from those which are relatively unimportant.

With care, however, DFDs can be a powerful tool for documenting and helping to design systems.

Various computer programs exist to help the analyst prepare DFDs, and some of these also create a skeleton data dictionary (see Chapter 12) for the system being documented.

9.7 Structured English, Tight English and Pseudo Code

These three techniques will be described together since they are basically similar. In all cases the aim is to produce a descriptive with the power and flexibility of standard English, but one which is more concise and avoids the ambiguity of much written work.

The basic approach is to reduce a standard narrative to a series of concise statements, each of which begins with an active verb followed by the subject then the object. The basic mathematical operands: add, subtract, multiply and divide as well as such well-known symbols as the equals sign are all allowed in these techniques. Thus an ordinary statement such as:

'Net pay is calculated by subtracting deductions from gross pay'

would become:

SUBTRACT DEDUCTIONS from GROSS PAY

Any additional information required can then be added in brackets after the statement.

Equations may be used in place of statements so the example above could also be written as:

NET PAY = GROSS PAY — DEDUCTIONS

The similarity of such statements to high-level programming language instructions is immediately obvious. It must be stressed, however, that despite this similarity in appearance (and as we shall see in the way these reduced forms of English are set out), neither structured English nor tight English nor pseudo code is a programming language, although they can be made very like fourth generation languages. For a start they lack all the instructions necessary to specify the data being used. Reduced English can be used to describe clerical procedures as well as computer procedures and is a useful form of communication between users, systems designers and programmers.

These forms of reduced English can be made even more powerful if a few simple rules are observed. These rules are:

* start each statement on a separate line
* put appropriate explanations in brackets after statements (comments) to explain or clarify the statement
* use a limited range of active verbs, e.g. CALCULATE, GET, MOVE, ADD, MATCH, etc.
* group statements dealing with a particular topic, e.g. calculate net pay into paragraphs each of which may then be labelled
* use statements reflecting the basic processing structures shown in Figure 10.3 (p. 148).
  These statements are:
  (a) Sequential
      DO (a)
      DO (b)
      DO (c)
      DO (d)
  (b) DO while
      DO (e)
      WHILE (condition x applies)
      THEN
      DO (f)
  (c) DO until
      DO (g)
      UNTIL (condition y is reached)
      THEN
      DO (h)

(d) IF then else
     IF (condition *z* applies)
     THEN
     DO (i)
     ELSE (i.e. otherwise)
     DO (j)
* use END and START statements to mark the limits of particular sections.

The differences between structured English, tight English and pseudo code are really a matter of degree. There is, however, a tendency to reserve the first two terms for forms of reduced English which, whilst concise and freed of the ambiguities common in normal written text, are nevertheless still recognisable as English and to use the term pseudo code to refer to those forms of reduced English most nearly approximating high-level program languages. Thus the examples in Figures 9.15 and 9.16 would probably be called structured English and pseudo code respectively.

As with any tool used for communications purposes, attention should be paid to the audience to which it is to be addressed and the form of reduced English selected which is likely to be most easily accepted.

Fig 9.15   *example of reduced English for process 1.1 of Figure 9.14*

For each Request to Withdraw Stock from Stores, do the following things:

1. Check that the Request contains: stock number, quantity required, requestor's identity number and date.

2. If data incorrectly formatted, annotate Request and return to requestor. Otherwise:

3. Check that the requested stock number is included in the master file of stock numbers.

4. If there is no match, annotate Request and return and return to requestor. Otherwise:

5. Check quantity required is less than available stock on hand in master file of stock balances.

6. If there is no match, annotate Request and return to requestor. Otherwise:

7. Check requestor's identity is on master file of authorised requestors.

8. If there is no match, annotate Request and return to requestor. Otherwise:

9. Endorse request, Request Validated and pass to Warehouse Foreman.

For each CORRECTLY FORMATTED REQUEST

SEEK	STOCK NO INFORMATION FROM STORES MASTER FILE USING STOCK # AS KEY
IF	NO MATCH IS FOUND (i.e. Request is for an invalid stock number)
THEN	SEND INVALID STOCK MESSAGE TO REQUESTOR OF MATERIAL
ELSE	(i.e. request is for valid stock number) CONTINUE WITH AVAILABILITY CHECK

AVAILABILITY CHECK

For each REQUEST FOR VALID STOCK #

SEEK	QUANTITY INFORMATION FROM STORES MASTER FILE USING STOCK # AS KEY
IF	STOCK < ONE UNIT (i.e. there is no stock)
THEN	SEND STOCK NOT AVAILABLE MESSAGE TO REQUESTOR OF MATERIAL
ELSE	(i.e. stock is available) COMPUTE RECALCULATED STOCK (QUANTITY INFORMATION − REQUESTED QUANTITY)
	IF RECALCULATED STOCK < ZERO (i.e. request is for more than balance on hand)
	THEN AMEND REQUEST QUANTITY TO EQUAL QUANTITY INFORMATION
	LET RECALCULATED STOCK =- ZERO
	CONTINUE
	ELSE WRITE RECALCULATED STOCK TO STORES MASTER FILE
PASS	REQUEST FOR AVAILABLE STOCK TO PROCESS 1.1.4

Fig 9.16   *an example of reduced English for processes 1.1.2 and 1.1.3 of Figure 9.14*

9.8 Interviewing

At first sight interviewing one or a small number of people may not sound like a technique to be compared with decision tables or flowcharts. A moment's reflection, however, will indicate that it is a major way in which information is obtained in a data processing (or indeed any other) environment. Moreover, interviewing requires a particular approach if it is to be successful and as a technique it can be learned. The successful analyst is almost entirely dependent on information and data obtained from other people. A poor interviewing technique will adversely affect the quality of information obtained (because it is incomplete or not properly qualified) and this in turn will be reflected in inadequate analysis and poor systems.

The key to successful interviewing is preparation. Decide what information is required and whenever possible let the interviewee know in advance what is required. That will give him/her a chance to marshal thoughts and collect any necessary evidence or supporting documentation. It may also lead to the suggestion that other people should be present as well. Interviews should therefore be arranged in advance and a mutually convenient time and venue arranged. In practice data processing staff will often find themselves interviewing busy operational staff and it is common sense to avoid the most active periods in the interviewee's work-cycle if possible.

During the interview the aim should be to establish a co-operative working relationship, and attention should be paid to the social niceties to help in this process. Thus the interviewer should, for example, refrain from critical comment about the interviewee's work, and only start smoking after asking (and being granted) permission.

Few people have a total recall on facts and whenever possible the interviewer should obtain evidence to support statements made by the interviewee, especially if these are likely to influence the work being done. Similarly, opinions should be carefully noted, but verified with others before being accepted as more than a particular interviewee's viewpoint.

Any formal interview should be recorded and the main points summarised. Notes to facilitate this may be taken during the interview (providing this does not make the interviewee nervous) and written up as soon as possible afterwards. It is always prudent to let the interviewee see a copy of the summary so that it can be confirmed as an accurate record of fact and opinion. After confirmation the record, which should meet all the usual requirements of documentation, should become part of the formal documentation of the process in question.

9.9 Bubble or Data Analysis Charts

The analyst is not only concerned with 'what happens' but also with 'what it happens to'. To help in studying the data itself (as opposed to the processes that use the data) a number of graphical techniques have been developed. One of these is the technique of *bubble* or *data analysis charting*. These charts (from now on called simply bubble charts) are used to represent data and especially the associations between different items of data. (For a discussion on the nature of data see Chapter 12.)

In bubble charts each piece of data is represented by an elipse which contains the name of that item of data, and the association between data items are shown by the way in which these elipses (bubbles) are joined together.

An association is a logical connection between two items of data; for example, employee name and employee address are clearly connected data items. In this case the relationship (association) will normally be one to one (i.e. for every employee there will be a single address). In bubble charting this association is represented by a single-headed arrow going from the employee bubble to the employee address bubble. Sometimes, if a one-to-one relationship is optional, e.g. an employee may or may not have a spouse, then a 0 is placed on the shaft of the arrow just behind the head. Similarly there is clearly a connection between employee and dependants, but in this case an employee may have zero, one or several dependants. This is a one-to-many relationship and is represented by a double-headed arrow from the employee bubble to the dependants bubble. (The sleight of hand in this particular technique is that 'many' really means an unknown number including zero and one, whereas one, as in one-to-one, means one and only one – although as we have seen a qualifier may make this optional.) The examples described above are shown in Figure 9.17.

Sometimes it is useful to include the reverse associations, since if there is a relationship between A and B there is at least an implied relationship between B and A. Thus a single or double arrowhead may be added to the 'originating' end of the arrow. The four possible combinations are shown in Figure 9.18. In this example drawn from a purchasing application, Figure 9.18(a) shows a true one-to-one

Fig 9.17   *bubble chart notation*

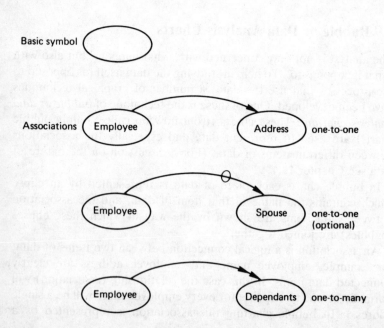

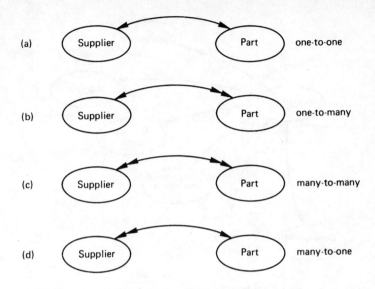

Fig 9.18   *bubble charting: reverse associations*

relationship between the data items' supplier and part. It means that each supplier supplies one part and each part is supplied by only one supplier. Figure 9.18(b) shows a more likely situation, where each supplier may supply many parts but each part is supplied by only one supplier. Figure 9.18(c) shows what is probably the typical situation in manufacturing industry, where one supplier may supply many parts and each part may be obtained from multiple suppliers (a many-to-many relationship). Figure 9.18(d) shows an odd situation in which each supplier provides only one part but each part may be obtained from many suppliers.

In practice, bubble charts are used to develop user views of data (i.e. a graphical representation of the way in which data appear to be logically related for one or more users of that data) and will normally consist of several, perhaps many, data items. An example of a user view of data for a personnel officer is shown in Figure 9.19. Notice that in this example only some of the reverse associations are shown. It is usual only to include those reverse associations that are considered meaningful in that particular user's view. Thus in Figure 9.19 the reverse association between employee and address is not shown (the personnel officer is not likely to be interested in questions like 'Who lives at 24 Ayston Road, Uppingham?' unless, that is, the

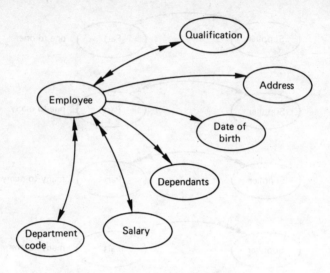

Fig 9.19   *user view of data (simplified personnel example)*

organisation provides housing for its employees). Similarly, no reverse association is shown between dependant and employee, although again this might be included if the organisation concerned was in the habit of holding Christmas parties for its employees' children. On the other hand, the reverse association is shown between employee and department code and between employee and qualification since it is highly likely that a personnel officer will be interested in such questions as 'Who works in Department X?' and 'Who has an MSc in chemical engineering?' Where reverse associations are concerned, the analyst is advised to include them if there is any doubt as to whether or not they are useful.

User views are prepared by interviewing the relevant personnel and/or by a study of the documents in use (data items may be readily extracted from forms and reports and the probable associations identified). Many users quickly become adept at using this technique to produce their own 'user views'.

Different user views may be synthesised to produce a logical data model by combining two or more user views which include common data items. This process is shown in Figure 9.20. At this stage it will be necessary to eliminate the many-to-many relationships found in the majority of user views. A many-to-many association essentially means that a single occurrence of a data item relating to the items joined by such a relationship, i.e. its value at any given time, cannot

First user view

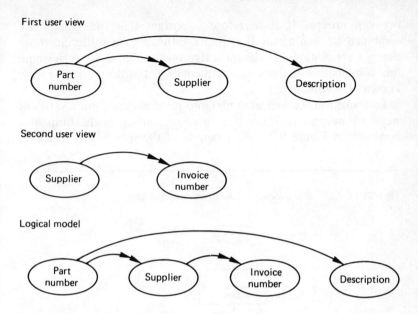

Fig 9.20   *synthesising user views into a logical model*

be found by using either of the data items alone as the key to finding that piece of data. Thus, for example, if the many-to-many relationship between supplier and part is not removed, it would be impossible to associate price with part except in the unlikely situation where all suppliers charge the same price. Many-to-many relationships can be eliminated by adding an additional data item consisting of the two data items concerned. Such a data item is called a *concatenated key* (concatenated is derived from the Latin words meaning 'joined together'). In practice concatenated keys may be constructed which consist of multiple data items.

Data items associated into bubble charts are a convenient input for the process of normalisation (see Section 9.10) as well as being a valuable analytical tool in their own right.

9.10 **Normalisation**

An important technique in data analysis is the synthesis of groups into records for data storage purposes. Since organisations are dynamic the data they use is likely to change over a period of time with the addition of new groups and the need for new relationships between groups. It is therefore important that the groups are combined in such a way that future difficulties in reflecting those changes are minimised. The most rigorous technique for performing this combination is the quasi-mathematical transformation process known as *normalisation*.

To transform the logical model into third normal form a series of steps are necessary. These steps are summarised in the form of a flowchart in Figure 9.21. An example of the way in which data is

Fig 9.21 *transforming a logical model to third normal form*

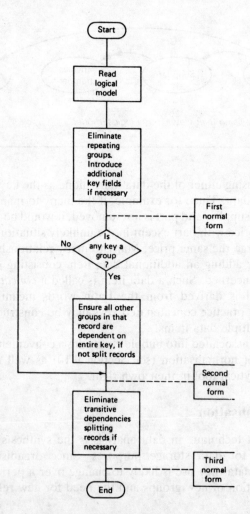

transformed is given in Figure 9.22. When the transformation into third normal form (often abbreviated to TNF or 3NF) has been completed a structure for the data has been achieved which will support the user requirements and may be implemented physically. Performance considerations may occasionally cause the physical implementation to differ slightly, but these cases should be reduced to a minimum in order to preserve the logical framework of the data base.

9.11 Other Techniques

The techniques outlined above do not exhaust those available. There are many others which are also of use to the analyst. They include:

* formal observation techniques
* procedure analysis, procedure flow, movement and X charts
* critical path, network and Gantt chart planning methods
* narrative report writing
* procedure writing
* questionnaire design and analysis
* forms design
* statistical sampling and analysis
* operations research methods
* simulation.

Although not perhaps strictly a technique, this is also an appropriate time to introduce 'walkthroughs'. These are a formalised evaluation process during which an analyst or other originator explains or *walks through* a data flow diagram, flowchart or other document in a systematic manner with an actively participating audience of users, peers and/or other interested parties. Comments and suggestions are formally recorded by a secretary. The outcome of a walkthrough may be formal acceptance of the document 'as is', acceptance subject to specified alterations, or rejection coupled to an agreed date for a further walkthrough of a revised document. (A more detailed explanation of walkthroughs will be found in Chapter 14.) With so many techniques available it is important that the analyst has a good working knowledge of the strengths and weaknesses of each of them to know when they are appropriate to the work being undertaken. Figure 9.23 provides a guideline for the principal techniques discussed in this chapter.

Fig 9.22   *normalisation of data*

1. The unnormalised logical model shown is for a
   vendor's invoicing application. The group
   'invoice line data' includes: date of sale,
   product reference, line number, description,
   size, quantity, unit price and value (i.e.
   quantity multiplied by price).
2. The first stage is to eliminate repeating groups.
   This produces two sets from the logical model
   called here 'invoice' and 'line item'. Note that
   each 'line item' must be identified by the
   concatenated key invoice number and line
   number.

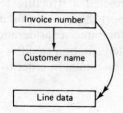

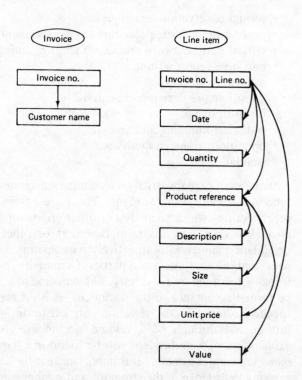

Notes: (1) It is necessary to add 'invoice no.' to 'line item'.
       (2) The group 'line data' has been expanded into its constituent elements for
          clarity.

THE MODEL IS NOW IN FIRST NORMAL FORM

3. The second stage of transformation is to remove elements not dependent on the whole of a concatenated key. This step removes 'date' (dependent only on 'invoice no.' not on 'invoice no.' and 'line no.').

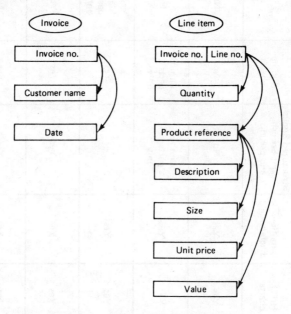

THE MODEL IS NOW IN SECOND NORMAL FORM

4. The third stage of transformation is to remove elements dependent on data items other than the primary key (i.e. eliminate transitive dependencies). This leaves three sets, called here 'invoice', 'line item' and 'product'.

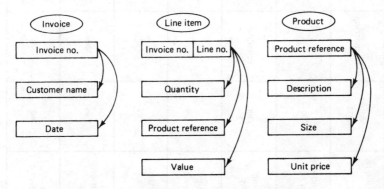

THE MODEL IS NOW IN THIRD NORMAL FORM

Note: It is probable that in most cases unit price would be dependent on description and/or size rather than solely on product reference as shown here. This illustrates the necessity of user input to data analysis specifying the real relationships of the data involved.

Fig 9.23   *the use of data processing techniques*

Technique / Use	Procedure charts	Flowcharting	Decision tables	HIPO charts	Data flow diagramming	Structured English tight English, and pseudo code	Bubble charts	Normalisation
As basis of complete documentation system	No	No	No	Yes	Yes	No	No	No
For documenting existing systems	Yes	Possibly	Limited parts only	Yes	Yes	Limited parts only	Limited parts only	No
As systems design aid	–	–	–	Yes	Yes	–	Yes	Yes (data base only)
As communication tool within data processing	Yes	Yes	Yes	Yes	Yes	Yes	Yes	Yes
As communication tool with users	Yes	No	Possibly	No	Yes	Yes	Yes	No
For explaining complex processing rules	No	No	Yes	Yes	No	Possibly	No	No

10 Systems Design and Programming

10.1 Designing Computer-Based Systems

In Chapter 8 the design specification for a new system was described. After approval to proceed has been granted (which should include specific approval by the users of the proposed system as well as technical approval by management services and resource allocation approval by senior management) it is the analyst's responsibility to produce the detailed design for a workable system.

In producing the design there are a number of considerations that must be borne in mind if the system is to be successful. In addition to the obvious characteristics of meeting the design objectives, being cost effective and operating reliably, four specific attributes of successful systems may be noted which should be in the forefront of the designer's mind during this phase. These four attributes are:

* user friendliness
* flexibility
* maintainability
* system security.

(a) User friendliness

A system is an integrated set of computer programs and operational procedures. The systems analyst is responsible for the design of both, especially the crucial interface between man and machine. This interface may be direct (as, for example, where a clerk sits down at a computer terminal and types information directly into the computer) or indirect as where a supervisor or operator collects information on a special form which is later prepared for input into the computer by another person or process. In either case the analyst's objective should be the same: to design the interface in such a way that the computer is seen to be a useful adjunct to what the individual is trying to do rather than a voracious beast that has to be fed with data at regular intervals. Designing this level of user friendliness into a system is not always easy. Care must be taken over forms design and the design of man–machine dialogues using terminals. Particularly important here is the amount of data on a screen, the way in which it is presented, how the operator has to respond, and the availability of HELP screens on-line (instructions which can be displayed at the touch of a button without the operator losing his or her place), the provision and content of error messages, the handling of rejected data and the layout of output documents. Other important considerations are office layout (the choice, number and location of input devices can be important factors in on-line systems) and timing (response times, input deadlines and output availability). It is vital that attention is paid to all these points because they are highly influential in determining the user's reactions to the system and therefore its acceptability to them.

It is probably true to say that up to the present insufficient attention has been paid to this aspect of systems design. The result has all too often been systems to which users develop negative attitudes and the best results are therefore not obtained.

(b) Flexibility

A second key feature of successful systems design is flexibility. A new system is, in many cases, a major capital investment and as such must be expected to have a life of several years.

Almost any organisation is constantly subject to change, either because of the operational requirements of the organisation itself or the requirements imposed by Government or other external bodies. No matter how adamant the user may be that 'This will never change', the systems designer must design on the assumption that it may! Many quite unnecessary constraints get built into systems simply because the analyst takes the users' statements at face value or simply does not think of the possibility of change. An example will serve to illustrate the point.

A materials management system was designed on the assumption that no storage location would ever be required to store more than one part number at a time. Yet within weeks of implementation the system had to be modified to cater for parts which naturally occurred together yet retained their separate identities, e.g. ball bearings and their ball race.

This constraint, imposed by the systems designer, was not functional in that it did not improve the system at all. It was just the way that he or she had chosen to design it. To be fair, the system met the immediate requirements, but a little more care could have eliminated the constraints at the design stage and thereby the need for expensive and time-consuming changes at a later date.

One way in which a system may be designed to be as flexible as possible is to make it *parameter driven*. That is to say, the important semi-constant data items, e.g. the number and organisation of the warehouses in an inventory control application, are held in a separate file of values rather than embedded in the applications programs themselves.

(c) Maintainability

Closely related to flexibility is maintainability. Maintenance as here defined may be necessary to a system for one of three basic reasons:

* to eliminate errors revealed in operational use
* to incorporate changes imposed from outside the organisation, e.g. a change in tax rates or procedures
* to make minor changes requested by users of the system, e.g. changes in the layout of reports.

In many companies these three tasks account for the majority of the effort of systems analysts and especially programmers. Looked at another way, more money is spent maintaining many systems than was spent on their original development. It is clear, therefore, that attention should be given from the outset to making the system design as maintainable as possible. The two key elements in ensuring maintainability are good documentation and a well-structured design.

The principles of good documentation have already been stated in Chapter 9, and here we are seeing one of the prime uses of that documentation: providing the technical manual which the maintenance 'engineer' can use to 'repair' the system. Even if the engineer was also the original designer or programmer of the system (and with staff turnover and the demands of other projects that cannot be assumed) it is highly unlikely that he will retain the detailed knowledge to make alterations to the system for more than a few weeks. This is especially true if he is working on other projects. Thus good documentation has an essential role in ensuring the maintainability of the system.

The second key element in ensuring maintainability is a well-structured design. A structured design is one in which functions of the system are segregated into separate elements or modules and the interfaces between these modules are kept as simple as possible. This technique, which has been widely adopted at the programming level, should also be applied at the systems design level. Thus the system should not been seen as a single monolithic whole, but rather as a series of logically interconnected modules or building blocks which collectively form the complete system.

Various techniques exist for breaking a system into such elements including the HIPO and data flow diagramming techniques described in the preceding chapter. Using these techniques, the objectives of good design and documentation can be brought together so that, to a large extent, the design process becomes self-documenting.

(d) System security

Security is a theme to which we will return in Chapter 15, but at this stage it is as well to remember that good security can and must be designed into a system. Security is not something that can be 'added on' at a late stage of development. It is an integral part of the whole design process and must be considered from the outset.

10.2 Buy/Build Analysis and Third Decision Point

Before proceeding with detailed analysis the analyst should always consider the possibility of using a software package or applications utility. The basic factors that need to be taken into account in deciding whether to buy or to build are:

* the degree to which the available packages meet the users' requirements
* the compatibility of the most suitable package(s) to the organisation's hardware and software environment
* the support from the package vendor
* the flexibility and maintainability of the package
* the price of the package and the cost of in-house development
* the availability of in-house resources to do the development
* the opportunity cost associated with performing the work in-house (while resources are used on one project they cannot be used on other potentially profitable projects)
* the different timescales within which a package or in-house development can be implemented and benefits be realised.

The buy/build analysis is followed by a formal decision to purchase a package (which may need to be modified or supplemented by in-house development) proceed to detailed design, or discontinue the project.

10.3 The Design Process

Having outlined some of the considerations the systems analyst must bear in mind during the design process, and having stressed the advantages of a modular or structured design, we can now turn our attention to the specific functions to be carried out during the design process if the decision is to build the system in-house.

The major activities are:

* data definition
* specification of system logic
* design of system modules
* detailed definition of interfaces
* design of input and output
* specification of control procedures
* development of test requirements
* preparation of conversion plans.

(a) Data definition

The identification of the data elements to be used in the system, how they will be captured, stored and maintained. This will entail development of user views (see Chapter 9). This activity will require the volumes and growth rate of data to be forecast to enable data storage requirements to be planned.

(b) Specification of system logic

This will include the logic of the complete system showing how the elements combine to produce the results required and is a development of the outline of the proposed system prepared during the analysis phase. In practice the complete specification will be a collection of diagrams or charts supported by a number of narrative descriptions (preferably in the form of reduced English) of the processes shown in the charts. Two points to remember are: the need for a clear, concise overview of the complete system, and adequate cross-references between various documents.

(c) Design of system modules

The point has already been made that the procedures used by people in conjunction with the computer are an integral part of the system design. This activity will therefore include the design of associated clerical and operating procedures as well as the computer parts of the system. For the latter the design will consist of:

* identification of all processing to be carried out, including the specification of all formulae and processing rules
* identification of procedures to be followed for all error conditions
* identification of timing constraints. The response time requirements and/or output deadlines.

(d) Detailed definition of interfaces

Building on the work performed in the previous phase, the interfaces between the proposed system and existing systems have to be defined in detail. This includes specifying the what, when and how of data transfers. Thus it is necessary to define the format, timing, volume and method (e.g. via temporary data storage or direct program to program) of all interfaces.

(e) Design of input and output

This activity includes the design of all input and output document layouts and all terminal dialogues. In addition the volumes, frequency, source and/or distribution of all inputs and outputs will need to be defined.

(f) Specification of control procedures

The nature of the control procedures will depend on both the type of system under consideration – accounting systems, for example, are normally subject to more stringent control procedures than routine statistical or computational systems – and on the type of technology used. Thus on-line or real-time systems require a different approach to control than a batch system.

(g) Development of test requirements

At first sight it might appear that testing has little to do with design. A moment's reflection, however, will indicate that no one is in a better position to know which are the crucial parts of a system than the designer and these areas are clearly ones that need particular attention during the testing phase. This is not to say that it is the designer who should test the system, still less that he or she should create all the test data and examine all the test results. Rather it means that the designer has an important role to play in specifying what sort of testing will be needed and what resources (both qualitative and quantitative) will be needed for this process.

(h) Preparation of conversion plans

In many, if not most, cases the systems analyst will be designing systems to replace an existing system. It therefore follows that there will be a need to convert from the existing system to the proposed system. Although this is not strictly a design task it requires detailed attention at this stage. Prominent among the factors to be considered is the preparation of the data base(s) to enable the new system to be introduced while maintaining the existing system until it is no longer needed. Further discussion on implementing systems will be found in Chapter 14.

10.4 The Fourth Decision Point

At the completion of the design phase there is another decision point at which the status of the project is formally reviewed. It is convenient at this point to carry out a technical quality-control review as well as the management review concerned primarily with economics and meeting systems objectives. The inputs to both reviews are basically the same: a complete set of the formal design documentation assembled and indexed in such a way that it is a coherent whole and not just a mass of papers. For the management review this will need to be supplemented by a detailed implementation plan specifying the resources required (people, machines, money), the elapsed time necessary and an updated version of the cost–benefit analysis prepared in the preceding phase.

10.5 Programming

The precise point at which the design phase stops and the programming phase begins is not always clear. Depending on the organisation and the job descriptions, experience and availability of the individuals concerned the border may move in one direction or the other. Indeed, where staff are organised into project teams which are charged with complete responsibility for designing and implementing systems the boundary may almost disappear. Although there will always be a point at which the first line of programming code is written for any project, programming actually commences well in advance of that point. In essence programming entails all the steps necessary to turn the design of the computer part of the system into tested instructions in a form that can be used by the computer. These steps are:

* program design
* coding and compilation
* program testing.

(a) Program design
For convenience it will be assumed in this section that the design process ends at the point where the logic of all the processes to be performed has been specified, but before these processes have been arranged into programs. Thus the first step in program design is to

group or subdivide processes into appropriate units. The size of the groups chosen will depend on a number of factors of which the two most important are intended mode of operation, i.e. on-line, real time or batch, and the capacity of the computer that will be used for processing. The next stage in program development is to outline the processes for each program. The key concept here is that of *modularity*, which is used for the same reasons as outlined in respect of systems design. If anything modularity is even more vital at the program design stage, being perhaps the most important single determinant of the maintainability of programs and indeed the system as a whole. Modularity in the programming context means that the program consists of a series of smaller sub-programs each of which is initiated, when required, by an instruction within the main program. It is common practice to have one control module from which and to which data is passed as the functions performed by a given module are started and completed. A modular program may be a simple one-level hierarchy or may have several levels as processing modules initiate subsidiary modules for specific functions (see Figures 10.1 and 10.2).

Not every module will necessarily be called for each use of the program; indeed some modules will only rarely be used. Moreover, modules at the lowest level may be initiated by more than one module at a higher level. As with systems design the key to successful modularity is in keeping the interfaces simple. Where the contents of any single module are limited to one of the simple logical constructions of SEQUENCE, DO WHILE or DO UNTIL or IF THEN ELSE (see Figure 10.3), or simple combinations or variations of them, the program may be said to be a *structured program*.

One way of dividing a program into modules therefore is to

Fig 10.1　*a simple modular program structure*

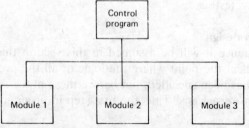

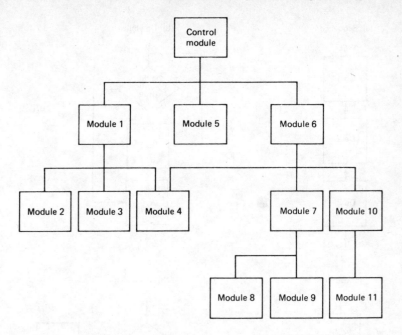

Fig 10.2 *a more complex modular program structure*

---

decompose the process to be achieved into a series of these simple logical structures. This process (called *functional decomposition*) provides a process-based program design. Alternatively, a data-based programming design may be adopted in which the key for the division of the program into modules is the structure of the data to be processed.

After the program design has been completed and documented it is important to check the program logic by testing it with data.

It is only when this stage has been reached that the task of coding – i.e. the task that in most people's minds is associated with programming – can actually begin.

(b) Coding and compilation
Coding is carried out using a computer language. The main languages used in data processing are identified in Chapter 7.

Which language is actually used to program a system will depend on a number of factors. The most important of these are:

* the compilers which exist and are in use for the computer to be used

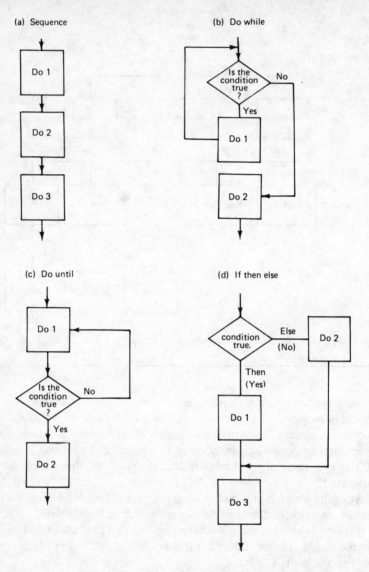

Fig 10.3   *basic logical structures*

* the standards relating to the languages to be used within the computer installation concerned
* the languages with which the programmer concerned is familiar
* the nature of the system to be coded.

The economics of modern data processing and the tight deadlines imposed on most projects mean that the highest level language available should generally be used for programming.

Good coding requires considerable self-discipline. Almost always under time pressure, the programmer faces the twin temptations to take short cuts and to exploit the capabilities of the computer to the full through the use of 'clever' programming. Short cuts include the use of abbreviations or codes for data names and omitting comments. Neither causes any problems in the short run, but add immeasurably to the difficulties of maintaining the program later. Similarly 'clever' coding, i.e. doing things with the minimum amount of coding rather than with the maximum clarity, may save a few milliseconds of processing time, but the time saved is usually irrelevant. Such coding may, moreover, take extra hours to achieve and maintain.

It is important that all coding is prepared in accordance with clear, well-thought-out standards and subjected to thorough quality control by competent reviewers.

(c) Program testing

Coding is of little use until it has been thoroughly tested and found to be capable of performing the tasks for which it was designed. The testing of programs normally has at least three levels. The first level is the testing of the module to see that it functions correctly. This stage (often called *debugging*) is usually the responsibility of the programmer responsible for writing the code concerned. The second stage is to test the coding in conjunction with other programs which would normally work with it (for example, all the modules from a complete program or suite of software). Rigorous testing at both these levels requires testing unexpected as well as expected error conditions and testing with operational and greater than expected operational volumes as well as special test data of limited range and volume.

The third and final level of testing (which may in turn be subdivided into system testing and user acceptance testing) is part of the Implementation Process and will be discussed in Chapter 14.

10.6 The Fifth Decision Point

Cancellation of a project or system is perhaps rarer at this tage than at any other, yet this does not obviate the need to carry out a review. Indeed it is all too often at this stage when the abstract concepts and design result in tangible and testable programs that basic difficulties of a technical or operational nature are first evident. Such difficulties may make the system uneconomic or even impractical. In such cases it is better to go back and reconsider the objectives, structure and economics of the system rather than to try and force the implementation of an unworkable system which will only alienate users and frustrate data processing staff.

Moreover, the programming stage is itself prone to difficulty. This is frequently the stage that gets 'squeezed' to enable preset deadlines to be met even after the preceding stages have overrun their own deadlines. In such cases impossible combinations of time deadlines and quality/efficiency criteria could be, and very often are, imposed on the programming staff.

The review at the end of this stage of the development process must therefore be carried out with especial care and include careful technical evaluation of the programs developed.

11 Data Communications

Data communications systems bring together the technologies of data processing and communications engineering. As such these systems require representatives from both disciplines to construct them and make them work. In this chapter a brief overview of the concepts of data communications of most interest to the data processing practitioner is given, and for further details the reader is referred to the appropriate works listed in the Bibliography.

11.1 The Need for Data Communications Systems

When modern data processing equipment first became available it offered the opportunity to process data much more rapidly than had ever been possible before. On the other hand, to be used efficiently, such equipment required work to be presented to it in batches whether or not that was the way in which it occurred. Moreover, because of the expense of the equipment, its need for special air-conditioned accommodation and specialised staff to attend it, it was located in a central position. This in turn created organisational (and often geographical) distance between the users and originators of data and the processors of that data. The result was that, all too often, the processing of data was speeded up, but the elapsed time between the origin of data and the availability of information derived from it was unchanged or even extended. For many people bank statements provided a good example of this phenomenon. Before computers were introduced, many banks could provide a statement of the customer's account within a few minutes and without prior notice. The advent of computers meant that in many cases it was not possible to obtain a printed statement until at least the following business day. For some applications such delays did not cause any significant problems, but for many more it led to the search for ways to shorten the data processing cycle. In part this search resulted in the development of smaller data processing machines which could be dedicated to one use or user and located at his or her work station (see Chapter 5). This search also led to the realisation that data for processing and the results obtained from the processing could be transmitted from place to place using telephone lines and similar communication links.

11.2 Elements of a Data Communications System

Any data communications system requires four distinct elements before it can start to support any data processing applications. These elements are:

* a host processor
* communications links
* terminals
* communications software.

(a) A host processor

Host processor is the name given to the central computer performing the bulk of the applications work in a data communications system. Depending on the computer equipment in use it may be 'assisted' in this role by a second computer dedicated to controlling the data communications traffic. Such a subsidiary data communications computer is called a *front end processor*. Depending on the nature of the data communications system it is possible to have multiple host processors arranged in a network but in the majority of commercial data processing environments there is a single, identifiable host processor. The host processor may or may not control the transfer of data to and from remote locations.

(b) Communications links

Communications link is the name given to the path between the host computer and the point or points at which data originates or to which it is dispatched. This path may be a matter of a few yards or metres, a few miles or kilometres or halfway round the world. Where the path is short (say up to about one kilometre) it is often possible to connect the computer and the remote point using extended computer cables. In this case the system is not really a communications system at all, but rather a single location system in which the directly attached computer peripherals are unusually widely dispersed. *Local area networks* (LANs), which are for communications within a small geographical area (say a factory or office complex) normally used exclusively by one organisation and which can be used to link multiple computers (PCs, minis and mainframes) to each other and/or shared peripherals and data also fall into this category. It is when the remote points exceed this critical distance and it is necessary to use a communications link provided by someone other than the supplier or user of the computer that real communications systems begin.

In a sense the term 'link' is a misnomer since it might be taken to imply physical connection. In fact communications links may be by cables, conventional radio wave, satellite transmission or optical fibre. The term 'path' is also open to objection in that it may convey the impression that data between two points always follow the same route. Links can be either dedicated (i.e. reserved for the exclusive use of one organisation) or provided on a commercial basis either by a state monopoly or by a common carrier (*public switched networks*) and used for short periods when required in the same way as the domestic use of the telephone. Only in the case of a dedicated hard-wire (i.e. cable) link is the path likely to be fixed.

For data processing purposes communications links are commonly rated by their capacity to transmit data. This is usually quoted in *bits per second* (bps), or thousands of bps (*kilobits* or *kbits*). The term 'Baud' is also used as a measure of the capacity of a link to transmit data. In most cases 1 Baud is equivalent to 1 bps.

When translating this capacity into the time necessary to transmit a given volume of data it should be noted that 1 character is equivalent to 5 to 8 bits (depending on the code used) and there is an overhead in the order of 30 per cent transmitting data (i.e. the amount of data actually transmitted is approximately 30 per cent more than the data it is desired to transmit).

The capacity to transmit data varies considerably between different types of communications links. Public switched networks commonly offer facilities varying between telegraph and telex lines offering capacities in the order of 50–200 bps and special data communications services with much higher capacities.

The capacity of dedicated or leased lines varies between countries, but data transfer rates of 4800 or 9600 bps are widely available. So-called wideband or broadband facilities are also available offering data transfer rates in the range of 50 000–72 000 bps (usually referred to as 50–72 kbps or kiloHertz (kHz)) and maximum speeds available in the UK range up to 140 megabps (i.e. 140 000 000 bps). Public switched network services are paid for according to the time and distance over which they are used, whereas dedicated or leased lines are generally charged on a fixed-price basis. There is thus a balance to be struck between: volume of data to be transmitted (currently and planned), the time it takes to transmit that volume of data and the costs of the various types of communications links available. Figure 11.1 illustrates graphically how leased lines are normally more economic for large volumes of data whereas for lower volumes the public switched network is generally cheaper. In Figure 11.2 the calculation of the transmission requirements for a particular application is shown.

In addition to the links themselves the term 'communications link' is usually taken to include the various items of hardware necessary to enable the computer to make use of the link. The major items of hardware of this type are:

* modems
* concentrators and multiplexers
* control units.

(i) Modems. The term 'modem' is a contraction of *mo*dulator – *dem*odulator. Computers use digital signals while most communications links use analog signals for transmitting data. There is thus a 'translation' process necessary at both ends of the link to interface that link to the computer equipment. This process is transparent to the users at both ends, but the need to provide modems is an element of cost which can easily be overlooked.

(ii) Concentrators and multiplexers. *Concentrators* and *multiplexers* are also 'black boxes', the operation of which is transparent to the user. Their purpose is to improve the economics and performance

---

Fig 11.1   *comparison of public switched network and leased line charges showing break-even point*

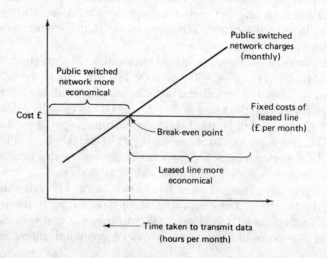

A. Volume of data to be transmitted
(i) From remote location to computer centre:

Estimated number of terminals   = 20
Estimated number of inquiries per
terminal per day   = 15
Estimated number of characters per enquiry:
  – from terminal to computer   =   100
  – from computer to terminal   = 1200
  – number of bits per character   =   8
Volume of data from remote location to computer
= 20 × 15 × 100 × 8 = 240 000 bits per day

Volume of data from computer to remote location
= 20 × 15 × 1200 × 8 = 2 880 000 bits per day

Giving a total of (2 880 000 + 240 000) = 3 120 000 bits per day

Assume 8 hours per working day and that peak load is expected to be 2.5
average workload
  required transmission capacity

including 30 per
cent overhead

Note: This calculation makes no allowance for future growth.

Fig 11.2   *calculation of transmission requirements*

---

of data communications links by a 'main line' and 'branch line' structure. Imagine a system for a large retail store chain which required data to be collected at each branch and transmitted to the Head Office in (say) London. Imagine too that for economic or technical reasons it is necessary to use dedicated links for this data traffic. Each branch may generate only a small volume of data and although it may be convenient to link all the London branches direct to the host computer site this may not be the case for other branches. Consider the case of Lancashire. Suppose our hypothetical retail store has branches in Wigan, Bolton, Blackburn, Preston, Rochdale, Oldham, Bury and Manchester. Here there may be a case for routing all the data traffic along relatively slow 'branch lines' to (say) Manchester, where a concentrator or multiplexer 'loads' it on to a higher-speed 'main line' to London.

Although functionally equivalent for this purpose, concentrators and multiplexers are based on different approaches to the same problem. Concentrators have some built-in processing capability and may be programmed whereas multiplexers are basically unintelligent units.

(iii) Control units. While the modem is used to 'translate' between the codes used by the computer and on the communications links, *control units* provide a similar role in *buffering* the speed differences of the two parts of the system. Even high-speed communications links are generally slow by comparison with a computer's internal data transfer rate and thus there is a need for a buffer between the two. Control units also commonly carry out a code conversion process. (Data is usually transmitted in bit serial form, i.e. in a sequential pattern of binary characters, whereas processing is typically carried out on parallel characters.) Control units can often support a small group or cluster of terminals or may be built into the terminal itself.

(c) Terminals

The term 'terminals' is used in data communications systems to refer to the computer equipment that is at the end of the link from the host processor. The terminal may therefore be:

* another computer (with a full or limited range of peripherals)
* a general-purpose terminal device (e.g. a visual display unit with a keyboard)
* a special purpose terminal (e.g. cash registers, banking terminals).

As noted in Chapter 6 the terms 'intelligent terminal' and 'dumb (or unintelligent) terminal' are sometimes encountered and refer to the presence or absence of an independent processing capability at the terminal. Intelligent terminals include a microprocessor or mini-computer and can perform some processing without reference to the host processor. Clearly, all computers used as terminals fall into this category, but so do an increasing number of general and special purpose terminals.

Terminals may be able to send and receive messages to and from the host computer or only receive or send messages.

Many of the devices described in Chapter 6 may be used as terminals.

(d) Communications software

Communications software is the general term used to cover all the software used in a data communications system other than the software necessary to carry out the actual application processing on the host processor and any other processors. The main element is part of the system software on the host processor (see Chapter 7), but other elements will be found at the terminals and concentrators.

Data communications hardware and software may be combined in a wide variety of ways to support the requirements of a given application. Some of the ways in which this can be achieved will be discussed in Part V.

12 Data Management

12.1 **Data Concepts**

We have seen in Chapter 1 that data is the raw material from which information is produced and this alone gives it a major role in any organisation. Historically, data has tended to be collected, prepared and used to produce only one or at best a small range of information outputs. Thus, if the payroll department needed personnel and attendance data they arranged for it to be collected, very often in parallel with procedures for the collection of the same (or closely similar) data for the personnel and cost accounts departments. This attitude was initially perpetuated in computer data processing with each development project leading to the collection, preparation and storage of data specifically for the application. This approach is inherently wasteful. Not only are there the direct costs associated with the collection and storage of basically the same data, but there are also the indirect costs involved in reconciling information derived from different sources. Even more importantly, this approach to data management makes it difficult to extract information from the data in ways other than that envisaged when it was collected.

At first sight this may seem surprising; the data is after all in computer readable form and computers are designed to manipulate data at high speed. In practice, however, the need for extensive sorting and especially the lack of the appropriate keys to the data required means that requirements for information not foreseen when the data storage format was designed are all too often impracticable, uneconomic or just not possible quickly enough to enable them to be of use.

To realise the latent information which is contained within an organisation's data requires a change of attitude to data itself. It needs to be recognised that data has a value independent of its immediate originator, user and above all use. Data has to be regarded as a resource which should be available to anyone within the organisation who is authorised and has 'a need to know' the information contained in it. The data resource should be managed in such a way as to facilitate the realisation of that potential.

A further concept significant in data management is that within any given organisation, data will tend to be static while the processes that use that data will tend to be more dynamic. That is to say, the *entities* or things (persons, places, objects, events or concepts) about which an organisation wishes to keep data will normally change more slowly than the processes to which those entities are subjected. For example, most organisations will always keep data on employees, products, suppliers, customers, etc; the data maintained, called *attributes* (address, reference number, and so on) will, for the most part, be constant, although the actual addresses etc., i.e. the *values* or *occurrences* of that data, will change constantly. The processes, on the other hand, will typically require frequent modification as the business and its environment evolve.

Data has already been described as the raw material from which information may be produced, but in the real world it does not exist as a single amorphous mound of alphabetic, numeric and special characters which can be selected at will, but is grouped into recognisable and useful units such as words, names and numbers. Before describing how data may be managed it is important to look at the composition of these units.

The smallest unit of data with any meaning is called a 'data element'. Thus a surname, a reference number, a department name, a company name and a product code are all data elements.

Two or more data elements may be combined to form a *group*. The elements so combined are logically related but do not themselves form a complete unit of information. One example of a group might be an address combining the data elements: number, street name, town or city, county or state and post code.

Two or more data elements (which may or may not be associated into groups) which are linked to a common identifier are called a '*logical record*'. A typical example of a logical record is personnel data. A personnel data record might include: works number (a data element), name (a group with family and given names), address (a group with number, street name, town and post code), department number (data element), national insurance number (data element), tax code (data element), sex (data element), marital status (data element), and number of dependent children (data element). This logical record is represented graphically in Figure 12.1.

An organisation may have only one logical record type for personnel data, but it will have many employees and therefore many occurrences of the basic record, each containing a unique combination of values for the data elements.

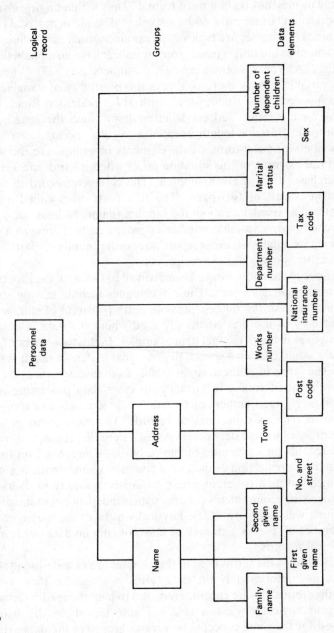

159

Fig 12.1 a typical logical record

The values associated with any given occurrence of a data element may or may not be in a fixed format. Thus within an organisation, a works number may always be a six-digit data element (fixed format), whereas addresses are typically of variable format (some houses have no number but only a name, some numbers have an alphabetic suffix, e.g. 23A, whereas others have only numbers, e.g. 127). Where there is variable format there is always the possibility of variable length (compare 1, Dee Road, Mold, with 117, Cliddesden Road, Basingstoke – the latter address is more than twice the length of the former). Variable-length records may also occur when variable numbers of fixed-format data elements or groups are included. A typical example of this situation arises where records are kept of all purchases from a given supplier. The complete record in this case might consist of two parts. The first part, often called a *header*, containing fixed data about the supplier (name, address, etc.) and the second part, a variable number of groups each relating to a specific purchase (date of order, purchase order number, part number, quantity, price, date of receipt, etc.).

Special techniques have been evolved to facilitate the processing of *variable-length records*. These techniques include leaving sufficient space to take the longest possible entry (wasteful of storage space, but easy to use and commonly used where the data is of variable length as in the personnel data example). In this case the last group of data would contain a special flag or signal to denote that it is the last.

The terms introduced so far enable us to discuss data at the record level, but of course in virtually all cases data processing is about handling large numbers of records. A large number of terms are in use to refer to collections of records. The most common of these terms are files and data bases. As used here *files* refers to a collection of records on a common theme or basis. A *data base*, on the other hand, is a collection of data on a common theme or themes which is conceived as a coherent whole to satisfy a variety of users and/or processing requirements (i.e. the data is independent of the programs which will make use of it). Physically a data base may consist of a number of 'files' which may or may not contain data associated into logical records.

Although the terms used in this chapter are in widespread use they are not unfortunately the only terms in usage for these concepts! Other terms may be encountered, and to help the reader through this terminological jungle the table in Figure 12.2 shows the main terms used for the same concepts by various groups in the data processing industry.

Terms used in this book	Terms used by Codasyl Data Base Task Group	Terms used in COBOL	Terms used by IBM in their IMS DBMS
Data element	Data item	Elementary item	Data element
Group	Data aggregate	Group item	Segment
Record	Record	Record	Record
File	File	File	——
Data base	Data base	——	Data base (data bank)

Fig 12.2 *table of terms used in data management*

When discussing data bases it becomes important to distinguish between the logical and physical structure of data. The *logical structure* of data refers to the way it appears to the user of that data (be he programmer, systems analyst or end-user), whereas *physical structure* refers to the way the data is actually stored on computer readable media (principally disks and tapes).

The trick is to make the physical structure transparent so that all users can see the data exactly as they want it oblivious of the fact that it is all obtained from a 'common pool'. Indeed the data a particular user wants may not be stored at all, but derived from other data every time he uses it (e.g. summary totals may not be stored as such, but may be calculated on request for that data).

The way in which different individuals 'look at' the same data is shown in Figure 12.3. The picture which a user has of 'his' data (i.e. the logical structure which it has rather than the values it contains) is called a data model, user view or 'sub-schema'. The picture of the complete data which is normally only available to the data administrator and systems programmer (see Chapter 13) is often called a 'schema'.

Such an approach to data management is extremely flexible in meeting the differing routine and *ad hoc* requirements of users. It reduces the unnecessary storage of 'duplicate' data and facilitates the

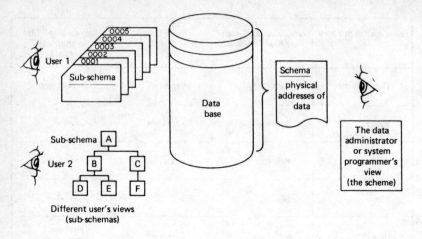

Fig 12.3   *differing views of data*

development and maintenance of programs since data storage is no longer closely linked to them as it would be if conventional file techniques were used. On the other hand, the data-base approach introduces a level of complexity to the data management process which is easily underestimated and requires significant investments in computer hardware and software and in personnel training.

The extent of a data base (i.e. the range of activities within an organisation for which it includes data) is a matter of judgement. Data-base implementations within an organisation are normally limited to specific subject areas, e.g. purchasing, production, etc., although they can and should be conceived as part of a coherent data base for the whole organisation. Subject data bases support multiple applications without becoming unmanageable or impossibly expensive and yet enable theoretical benefits to be largely achieved. For example, a Human Resources data base may support: payroll, personnel statistics, labour costing and career planning as well as *ad hoc* demands for information on a wide range of personnel and labour cost-related topics such as 'what if' questions about pay negotiations.

In this chapter two of the main elements of data management (file organisation methods and data models) will be described, and reference will be made to the fact that the latter can be implemented by means of DBMSs. The data model represents the way in which the users of the data can view or visualise it and it is, therefore, a representation of how the user wants it organised for processing purposes. The DBMS provides a link, allowing the user to access the data as represented by one of the models (hierarchical, network or relational) and in turn controlling the physical storage of the data on the storage devices in use. Physical storage utilises one or more of the file organisation methods (sequential and its derivatives, indexed sequential or random) which enable the user to carry out the fundamental processing tasks of data management which are:

* fetching a specific record from storage
* inserting a record into a logical file
* modifying a record
* reading a complete logical file
* reading the next logical record in a file
* deleting a record
* reorganising a logical file.

In practice there is another level between the file organisation method and physical data storage, sometimes called data structure (although this term is also used as a synonym for group as used in this book). This is, however, generally transparent to the analyst and will not be discussed here. For a more detailed treatment of this topic the interested reader is referred to the appropriate works listed in the Bibliography.

12.2 File Organisation Methods

The user views of sub-schemas in Figure 12.3 do not exist as a physical reality as far as data storage is concerned; they are concepts or abstractions. What does exist is a physical collection of records or files. In this section we will consider the main types of file organisation methods that are used to store data. In practice, these have to reflect the attributes and limitations of the storage device (usually tapes or disks as described in Chapter 6). The main types of file organisation method are:

* sequential (and its derivatives list and ring)
* indexed sequential
* random.

(a) Sequential, list and ring structure
If we return to our personnel data example and imagine that the details of each employee were recorded on an 8" × 5" card, each card would represent a logical record (and in this case a physical record too). The cards for a group of employees would typically be arranged

into a sequence on works number or be in alphabetical order. Sequential data structures are common in the real world and include large numbers of lists.

In the early days of data processing this sequential organisation of data was readily converted to punched card and later magnetic tape systems with the data element or group on which it was sorted becoming known as the *key*. To find any particular record the file is read until the required record is found (with direct access devices it is possible to use a technique known as a *binary search* or *binary chop* to reduce this process somewhat). To find a record on the basis of information contained in it, but not part of the key, two approaches were available. First, the entire file could be read and each record processed, those meeting the selection criteria being set to one side. Alternatively, the entire file could be sorted on the new key field and the file then processed in the usual way.

Sequential files are thus easy to use for the purpose for which they were originally intended, but cumbersome for most other purposes. *Sorting* became a major activity in most early commercial data processing installations as files were continually rearranged for different purposes.

With the advent of *direct access storage devices* (DASDs) (see Chapter 6) it became possible to divorce the physical from the logical structure of data by using *pointers* (i.e. automatically generated labels embedded in the record, which show where the next logical record is physically stored) and indexes to replace physical proximity. The way in which this is achieved is shown in Figure 12.4. This technique also makes it possible to construct multiple lists (i.e. multiple logical sequential files) using only one physical representation of the data – see Figure 12.5.

With multiple lists through the same physical data it is necessary to maintain an index of the start point for each list or *chain*. Even this can be avoided, however, by the simple expedient of causing the pointers on the last record in a list to point to the first record in that list. This 'closed list' is in fact a *ring* in which any record may be found by searching along it in either direction. Figure 12.6 shows multiple rings in an extended version of the example given in Figure 12.5.

It should not be thought that the ability to use pointers and therefore multiple list and ring structures has made sequential files obsolete. For many applications, especially those where there is naturally only one key and the volume of data is not large or it is infrequently used, or when most records in a file need to be accessed, sequential organisation continues to be widely used. It is also the only practical way of using files held on magnetic tape. A variant of the

Fig 12.4 *the list structure of data illustrated using simplified personnel records*

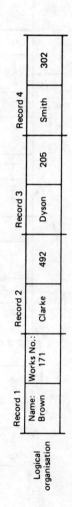

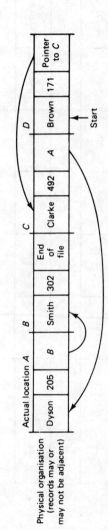

Fig 12.5 *multiple lists*

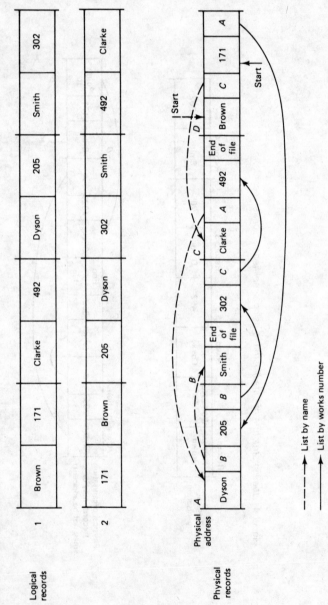

Logical records

| 1 | Brown | 171 | Clarke | 492 | Dyson | 205 | Smith | 302 |

| 2 | 171 | Brown | 205 | Dyson | 302 | Smith | 492 | Clarke |

Physical records

Physical address

| | A | B | | | B | | End of file | | C | | A | | End of file | | C | | | A |
| Dyson | 205 | Smith | | 302 | Clarke | 492 | Brown | 171 |

Start

- - - → List by name
———→ List by works number

167

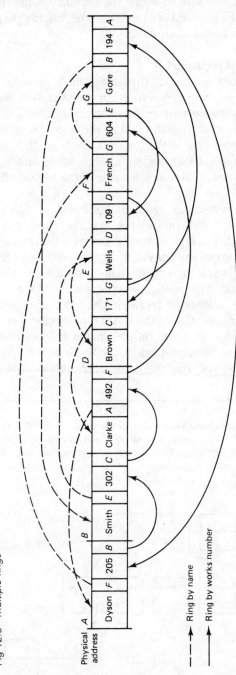

Fig 12.6 *multiple rings*

sequential structure in which the only key is the date the record is added to the file (and even this is not necessarily part of the record) is sometimes called a *serial file*.

(b) Indexed sequential

The indexed sequential structure (which must be implemented in DASDs) may be likened to a conventional dictionary. An indicator (usually a thumb tab) enables the right section of the book to be found without leafing through all the pages. A secondary index (the words in bold type at the top of the page) is then used to locate the correct page without reading all the entries under the initial letter. Finally a sequential search is made of the page until the sought word is located.

With the indexed sequential method of file organisation any number of levels of indexes may be used and a dictionary is maintained. The highest-level index gives the last key entry in each of the next lowest-level physical subdivisions of the file. At each level the index is searched sequentially until a value above the required key is found. This process is represented diagrammatically in Figure 12.7. The number of levels of the index is usually related to the physical organisation of the DASD, i.e. volume, cylinder, track, etc. (see Chapter 6). Care must be taken to ensure that the *overflow records* (i.e. insertions into the file for which space in the proper location is not available) are correctly located. Difficulties are

---

Fig 12.7   *the indexed sequential organisation structure. The search to find the record for Smith is shown by the dotted line. The physical addresses of the beginning of the track to be searched are associated with the key values*

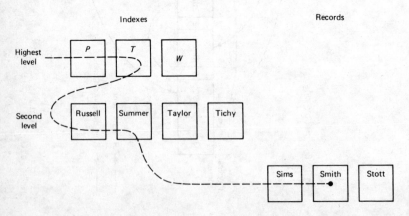

encountered when the overflow areas themselves become full and a feature of this type of organisation is the need for regular reorganisation runs if the data contained in the file is at all dynamic (this restriction is no longer true of the modern, hardware-independent versions of this organisation structure). The particular advantage of the indexed sequential organisation is that it permits both sequential and quasi random access to the data with reasonable efficiency. It is thus especially suitable for the many commercial applications which combine an element of on-line processing with a volume of batch type work (see Chapter 16). For this reason the indexed sequential organisation of its various forms has for many years been the workhorse of most data processing departments.

(c) Random
Strictly speaking, a random file organisation is not a structure at all, but it is often convenient to be able to store data in a random way so that each and every record may be independently accessed. The ability to access any record independently obviates the need to find that record by looking at the complete file as a whole. Random storage is, therefore, particularly well suited to events or processes which occur in unpredictable sequences and/or at unpredictable time intervals. Random storage is therefore commonly used in real-time systems (see Chapter 18).

Given that it is often convenient to locate data randomly over the storage space available on a DASD so that any individual record or unit may be independently accessed as readily as any other, there remain the problems of deciding where to store the data and, perhaps even more importantly, how to find it when it is needed! The two most commonly used approaches to this problem are:

* algorithmic (also called hashing)
* relative addressing.

In the algorithmic approach, an algorithm or formula is used which converts the key on which retrieval is to be made into a physical address on the DASD. When the data is stored the algorithm is used to calculate where the data is to be stored; when it is to be retrieved the same algorithm is used to find out where it has been stored and thus enables it to be retrieved. Many algorithms have been proposed and tested. Care is needed in selecting the appropriate algorithm or different key values may generate the same physical address. The most successful are the *remainder methods*. In these a prime number close to the number of buckets (addressable storage locations) needed for the volume of data anticipated is divided into the key of the record to be stored or retrieved (if the key is alphabetic it must first be converted to a numeric value). The remainder from this division is used at the relative bucket address, i.e. the record is located in the nth bucket of the area reserved for that type of data where n is the remainder. A random storage system must also be able to deal with those cases where a duplicate address will naturally arise: for example, if the key to a set of personnel data is name, how are the second and subsequent John Smiths to be dealt with? The usual approach is to introduce overflow routines which move records with keys which duplicate one already in use to another bucket and introduce a pointer into the first bucket indicating where the overflow data is located. (If the bucket size is a multiple of the record size, this is only necessary when the bucket is full, but multiple record buckets mean that the bucket has to be searched to find the specific record required.)

In the relative addressing approach, each record again has a number associated with it which gives its position relative to the beginning of the physical file, e.g. it is the xth record but in this case the programmer has the responsibility for retaining control of the relative address and, therefore, the accessibility of the data. It follows from the way that data is stored/retrieved using random storage techniques that only a single key is practical. Random storage using the algorithm approach tends to be relatively inefficient in its use of storage space as the algorithm will not spread the data uniformly over the space available. Moreover, as soon as overflow buckets are required, performance (access speed) starts to deteriorate. Programmer-controlled relative addressing imposes a significant overhead on the programming task and is only justified in special circumstances. Although random storage offers rapid access to any record, it does not permit the data to be accessed sequentially.

Since the reason for storing data is to be able to use it when required, it is important to consider the ways in which the physical file organisation may be accessed. The alternatives are sequential (in which each record is processed after its logical predecessor) or random (where each record for processing is required independently of the one before). The way in which the file organisation methods discussed above support these two access modes is shown in Figure 12.8.

12.3 **Data Models**

A data model is a representation of the data used within an organisation. As such it may be regarded as being an intermediate

Organisation	Access methods supported	
	Sequential	Random
Sequential	Yes	No
List	Yes	No
Ring	Yes (bi-directional)	No
Indexed sequential	Yes	Yes (strictly sequential in small units)

Random
  Algorithmic
 	
  Relative
	No
	Theoretically possible but impractical
		
		Yes
		
		Yes

Fig 12.8   *access methods for physical data organisations*

between the specific user views (see Section 9.9 for a description of the bubble chart technique for documenting these) and the physical organisations discussed above. Data models are concerned with the way in which data appears to be structured when viewed by the organisation. Three of the most powerful models used for this purpose are:

* hierarchical
* network
* relational.

(a) Hierarchical data models
In the real world a hierarchy (also called a 'tree') is a familiar structure. Consider, for example, the case of a car manufacturer who wants to keep track of all the parts used to manufacture a vehicle. It would, of course, be possible to make a list, but this would not reflect the fact that parts are grouped into sub-assemblies before manufacture. The natural arrangement for this type of data (commonly called a bill of materials) is a *hierarchy*. The model for a hierarchy may be represented as in Figure 12.9, which shows two notations for the logical data model (one using the same rules for relationships as in bubble charts) and a way in which this might be implemented physically on a DASD (it can be seen that the physical implementation is a list or a chain). For strict hierarchies this mode is an excellent

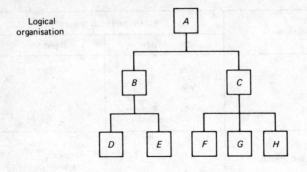

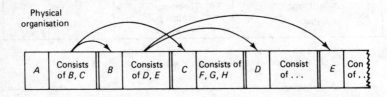

Fig 12.9   *diagram of an implementation of the hierarchical structure in a data processing environment*

---

fit and readily implemented in a data processing environment. It will be noted that one of the user views in Figure 12.3 is a hierarchy. Many hierarchies are not, however, strict in their decomposition. Returning to our bill of materials example, what happens if the same item, e.g. a bolt or other fastener, is used not only in a sub-assembly but also for joining together the final assembly? Graphically, this might be represented as in Figure 12.10, and it will readily be appreciated that such a model would lead to a very complex physical implementation. One way to overcome this problem is to limit each record or item in the hierarchy in such a way that it only has one parent. That is to say, *each record has only one one-to-one or one one-to-many relationship entering it from the next higher level in the hierarchy*, i.e. it *belongs* to only one record at the next highest level. To resolve complex real-life hierarchies such as the bill of materials in Figure 12.10 into hierarchies obeying the 'one-parent' rule is possible if redundancy is introduced (i.e. separate occurrences of the same subordinate record are introduced). When resolved in this way, Figure 12.10 becomes as shown in Figure 12.11. It will be noticed that the twelve boxes have become sixteen, i.e. four redundant records

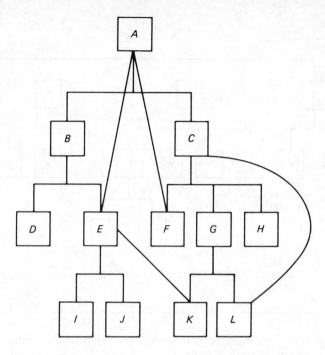

Fig 12.10   *graphical representation of a (simplified) bill of materials*

(one quarter of the new structure) are necessary in this particular case. Clearly, where the level of redundancy is high, this imposes a severe burden on physical implementation. Moreover, there are other practical problems associated with the implementation of hierarchies. First, it may be necessary to introduce dummy nodes into the hierarchy to show relationships between records at the same level; for example, if there was a relationship between H and F in Figure 12.11 as well as the relationship with L and G to C, then a dummy node linking H and F would need to be added. Such dummy nodes are, in practice, fairly frequently required. Secondly, when searching for a record, hierarchies are normally searched from the highest level (or root). Real-world queries often require searching hierarchies from both top down and bottom up. Consider again our bill of materials. While the production manager may well want to know 'What does product X consist of?', the inventory manager faced with an impending stock out of a part will want to know where it is used, i.e. he or she will want to follow the upward paths of the hierarchy from each occurrence of that part.

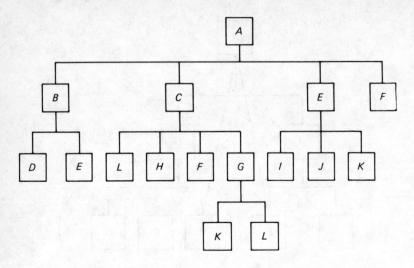

Fig 12.11   *the bill of materials example in Figure 12.10 redrawn observing the 'one-parent' rule*

For some types of organisation, the hierarchical data model represents a very good fit to reality, and some of the most popular data base management systems (DBMSs, see Chapter 7), including IBM's IMS and Intel's System 2000, are implementations of this model.

(b) Network data models
In general terms a network is another familiar structure encountered in real life. More formally we may say in data management terms that a network is similar to a hierarchy (indeed a hierarchy is actually a special case of network) in which the 'one-parent rule' is not enforced. A network data model is shown in Figure 12.12.

Most implementations of the network data model in DBMSs are in fact a sub-set of a full conceptual network. There are two main types; the limited network and the CODASYL (Conference of Data System Languages) Data Base Task Group implementations. In the limited network implementations, all record types are classified as either *master* (also called *master* or *owner*) or *secondary* (also called *transaction*, *member* or *detail*). Each secondary set may have multiple masters and each master may have multiple secondary sets associated with it.

To model many types of data in a limited network of this type, it is necessary to introduce intersection records which provide the

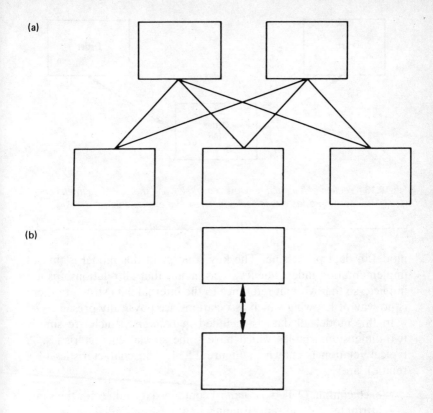

Fig 12.12   *two representations of a complex network*

relationships between master sets. An example of a limited network model using intersection records in secondary sets is shown in Figure 12.13.

Cincom's TOTAL and Hewlett Packard's IMAGE are two of the widely used DBMSs which incorporate a limited network model.

Numerically, most DBMS implementations of the network data model use a simplified version of the conceptual model which was proposed as a standard by CODASYL. This model does not support direct many-to-many relationships which are instead resolved with intersection records. Implementations of the CODASYL standard include Cullinet's IDMS, ICL's IDMS, Honeywell's IDS II and Unisys' DMS 1100.

(c) Relational models
In recent years much emphasis has been placed on the relational

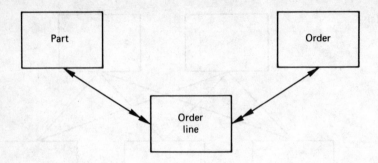

Fig 12.13   *section of a limited network model showing the use of an intersection set to provide a relationship betwen two master sets*

model in data processing. The key concept in this model is that of implementation independence. This means that all relationships are implicit, so that without reference to the internal data structure there is no way of knowing which associations are physically present.

In this model all data is included in *relations* which are simply two-dimensional tables which have some special characteristics. A typical relation is shown in Figure 12.14. The characteristics of a relation are:

* each column (called a *domain*) contains data values for the same attribute, e.g. all the surnames in a personnel relation.
* there is no significance in the order of the rows or colums
* each row (called a *tuple*) is unique (there are no duplicates in selected key attribute columns)
* there is only a single value associated with each cell (intersection of row and column): put another way this means that each row is in first normal form (see Chapter 9).

Tuples are, therefore, records in first normal form (1NF). It follows that the column (or more than one column) headings which identify the key attributes which are not duplicated are the primary key for that relation. Thus, in Figure 12.14, supplier number and part number form the primary key, since neither supplier number nor part number alone uniquely identify price and description, i.e. there is a many-to-many relationship between supplier number and part number. A relational data base consists of multiple relations which may be visualised as a stack of cards or spreadsheets (Figure 12.15), each of which contains a different relation. In essence these relations represent basic building blocks of data which may be merged, analysed and cross-referenced to produce 'views' or arrangements of

Supplier relation

	Supplier number	Part number	Unit price	Description
A tuple	1234	A12654	£15	Steel widget
	1356	A27984	£10.50	Aluminium widget
	1356	B18964	£8	Brass gland
	1459	A12654	£14.50	Steel widget

a domain

Fig 12.14   *a relation*

Fig 12.15   *a representation of a relational data base*

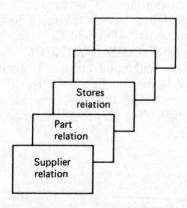

data to satisfy a wide variety of information needs by the use of a limited, rigorous and easy-to-use set of processing commands. The two main sets of processing commands for this purpose are *relational algebra* and *relational calculus*.

Relational algebra uses three basic commands; SELECT, JOIN and PROJECT to manipulate relations. The SELECT command retrieves all tuples from a relation that meet specified criteria, e.g. a particular key value or with a particular field (cell) value above or below a specified limit, and constructs a new relation with the retrieved tuple(s). The Boolean algebra AND, NOT and OR statements can be used to link the criteria used with a SELECT command. The JOIN command creates a new relation from two or more relations by combining them on the basis of common values in a domain, i.e. it merges two relations. The PROJECT command extracts specific domains from all tuples to form a new relation.

Relational calculus achieves functionally similar results to relational algebra using powerful commands which may involve attributes from different relations.

Although the relational model and, therefore, relational data bases have been readily accepted as powerful tools for the processing of data to answer *ad hoc* or irregular demands for information, there has been considerable debate about the suitability of relational DBMSs for routine high-volume data processing applications such as payroll, accounting and inventory control systems. Some authorities have maintained that production data processing is better supported by hierarchical or network data bases from which a relational data base is extracted at intevals to enable *ad hoc* enquiries to be satisfied; others maintain that careful physical implementation of a relational data base makes it as effective as any other for routine data processing 'production'. At the time of writing, IBM market their relational DBMS DB2 in parallel with their hierarchical DBMS IMS, with the former supporting both decision support and operational systems while the latter is oriented more towards high volume production requirements. ADR and Cullinet, on the other hand, market their relational DBMSs (DATACOM and IDMS/R respectively) for both *ad hoc* and production use. In addition to the DBMSs already mentioned as implementations of the relational model, there are many others which claim to be full or partial implementations of the relational model. One of the latter group is Software AG's ADABAS DBMS.

12.4 **Data Dictionaries**

One of the essential tools of modern data processing is a data dictionary. Simply put, a data dictionary is a data base of data about data, and the term *metadata* is sometimes used to describe its contents. Four distinct types of use may be identified for a data dictionary:

* for change control
* for documentation support
* as a design aid
* for data management.

The systems analyst will be a major user of the data dictionary in the first three of these usages.

(a) For change control

Part of the contents of a comprehensive data dictionary will be up-to-date formats and descriptions of the data elements used within the data processing systems of the organisation, together with a cross-reference to their storage and the programs in which they are used and processed. When any change is proposed to the format, capture or definition of a data element, the impact of that proposal on other systems can readily be assessed.

At another level the data dictionary can also be used to identify and record current versions of programs and all changes that are made to them (including by whom, on whose authority, a record of the tests conducted, the nature of the change, and the date on which the change became effective). Records of this nature not only reduce the risk of deliberate fraud but also greatly improve the operational efficiency of a data processing department.

(b) For documentation support

As the data processing department's data base, the data dictionary will contain much of the documentation generated by systems analysts (indeed it is increasingly the basic tool they use for creating much of their documentation using the so-called 'analysts' work-benches' and computer-based systems development aids now available). For documentation support of systems analysis a good data dictionary will include the process, data flow, external entity and data store descriptions generated when using data flow diagrams (see Chapter 9) as well as data element descriptions, user views, etc. In this role the data dictionary is a prime communication medium for all those concerned with systems development and maintenance.

(c) As a design aid

The data dictionary is, as implied above, a major design aid to the analyst in enhancing productivity in its documentation support role, but it also aids the design process in other ways. For example, as it is the repository of information about all applications, it provides the basis for analysing interfaces between computer systems and the source of data element definitions.

(d) For data management

As described in Chapter 13, data management as a function is a prime responsibility of one or more senior members of the data processing department who plan, develop and implement an organisation's approach to data. The data dictionary is for such staff a prime working tool and also their major 'product'.

Part IV

Making Data Processing Work

13 The Data Processing Department

It is one of the paradoxes of automation that it is a labour-intensive activity. That is to say the basic process of identifying, designing and creating automated systems requires considerable effort by people with many different skills. Commercial data processing is no exception to this general statement and in fact adds another dimension to it inasmuch as the operation of a commercial data processing centre also requires a considerable range of skills.

In this chapter four separate though interrelated subjects will be discussed. First, the skills necessary to provide a comprehensive data processing service will be identified. Second, ways in which staff may be organised will be considered. Third, approaches to monitoring and controlling the work of the data processing department will be discussed; and, fourth, the role of standards and documentation in the total management process will be reviewed.

13.1 The Skills Required

The majority of data processing departments have two distinct responsibilities:

* the design, development and commissioning of new data processing systems
* the routine operation of data processing systems.

To reflect these responsibilities it is convenient to consider the skills required under two broad headings. The groupings of development skills and operations skills will be used for this purpose, although it should be recognised that in some cases there is an overlap between them. There is also a third responsibility: that of overall data processing management which encompasses both the responsibilities and which will therefore be discussed first.

(a) Data processing management

The only skill that embraces both development and operations in most data processing departments is that of data processing management. The emphasis in this role should be on the general management skills rather than data processing techniques although a good level of understanding of the technical aspects of the work is obviously a prerequisite.

Among the particular tasks performed by data processing management are:

* overall monitoring and control of data processing development and operations

* personnel management of departmental staff including:
  — recruitment
  — training (both technical and general)
  — career planning

* resource management, including:
  — allocation of resources between development and routine operations
  — allocation of resources between the various departments in the organisation as a whole
  — use of hardware
  — use of human resources

* planning, including:
  — applications development planning (in consultation with senior management and user departments)
  — hardware requirements planning
  — personnel requirements planning (qualitative as well as quantitative)
  — financial planning including departmental budgets
  — facilities requirements planning (e.g. need for extended premises, installation of additional telephone lines, etc.)
  — long-range planning on the role and development of data processing within the organisation
  — organisation planning for the data processing department

* liaison with user departments, senior management, other companies, industry sources, etc., on all facets of data processing activities (current, planned and possible).

Data processing management is then a wide-ranging function with long-term and short-term planning and staff management responsibilities, as well as the more obvious technical aspects. Recruiting a suitable person to fill this demanding position often presents difficulties, not least because the position requires qualities which are not always required in the immediately subordinate positions where the balance between technical and purely management aspects are usually tilted firmly in favour of the former. There is thus no single obvious source of future Data Processing Managers, who may be drawn from the ranks of systems development and routine operations as well as from other management science disciplines, managers of small data processing departments (inside or outside the organisation) and even from outside data processing. The emphasis should always be on the personal characteristics and general management capabilities rather than on specific technical experience.

(b) Development skills

Even within the specific area of development work there is a wide range of skills required and in addition many of these are necessary at a variety of levels.

The main skills required are:

* development management
* analysis and design
* programming
* data administration
* quality assurance and standards.

(i) Development management. In the smaller data processing . installations the direct management of the development function will often be the responsibility of the Data Processing Manager. In medium-sized or larger installations, however, the management and co-ordination of development work will invariably require the appointment of a full-time manager. In addition to understanding the specifically developmental work described under the functions of the Data Processing Manager, the manager of the development function (often called Systems Manager) will be particularly concerned with systems development planning, project monitoring and control, staff training and development and the formulation of standards.

(ii) Analysis and design. This activity requires a spectrum of skills ranging from a high-level business-oriented view of systems ideas and opportunities through conventional organisation-and-methods work to the technical design of computer systems. Depending on the size and organisation of the department these functions may be the responsibility of separate individuals or groups or may be combined. The business analyst skill, for example, is often, *de facto*, provided by a combination of development group and user department management activity though this cannot be considered a fully satisfactory solution for any but the smallest organisations.

In Figure 13.1 outline job descriptions together with a summary of personal qualities required are given for Business Analysts, Organisation and Methods Practitioners and Technical Analysts.

(iii) Programming. As we have seen in Chapter 10, programming is more than the translation of specifications into computer code and embraces a wide range of tasks. Inevitably these tasks overlap with those of the Technical Computer Systems Designer and indeed many organisations split the tasks identified under that description between the Computer Systems Analyst and Programmer. Still other organisations allocate the technical design functions to senior programming saff, using such titles as Senior, Chief and Design Programmer. Perhaps more than any other skill within data processing, programming includes a vertical range of expertise between trainees or junior coders to highly experienced professional staff. An outline job description and summary of personal qualifications required for programming are given in Figure 13.2.

(iv) Data Administration. In Chapter 12 the importance of data management has been stressed and the recognition of the importance of this work has been matched by the rise of a sub-discipline of data administration within data processing. In fact a number of roles may be distinguished in this field, ranging from that of Data Strategist (responsible for the long-range planning of data administration) through Data Administrator, to Data Base Administrator or Data Base Designer. These roles may all be performed by one person or performed by fewer individuals than the number of distinct roles would suggest. Figure 13.3 outlines the job descriptions and personal qualities required for these roles.

(v) Quality assurance and standards. The fifth area of skills required in systems development is quality assurance and standards. It is also the most neglected area. Yet to ignore this function is tantamount to running a production line without inspectors, or an accountancy department without auditing. There are two aspects to this function: first, establishing recommended codes of practice (standards) and, second, that the work produced both adheres to those standards and reaches acceptable quality levels (quality assurance). As with other skill groupings in data pro-

Fig 13.1 *analysis and design skills*

Job description	Personal qualifications

Business Analyst

Identifies the business functions which may be and/or need to be supported by improved systems (both manual and automated). Establishes economic feasibility of such systems development. Reviews existing systems. Reviews new innovations with a view to establishing their applicability within the organisation. Liaises with user management on all facets of systems work. Responsible for collection of data about systems requirements, its analysis and the logical design of systems. Participates especially in the feasibility study, detailed analysis and design phases of the systems development methodology. May lead project teams.

Degree, professional qualification, HND, HNC, or equivalent together with extensive practical experience within the organisation and/or the business area(s) in which he is operating. Wide knowledge of systems approaches and modern systems techniques. Good analytical and communication skills

Organisation and Methods Practitioner

Specialises in the human, workflow and non-computer aspects of systems, including; the design of the man-machine interfaces (terminal procedures, input and output forms design, data collection), user manual preparation, documentation and archival systems, etc. Applies modern technological but non-computer solutions to administrative and other problems especially in the fields of office systems (word processing, microfilm, printing and reproduction, 'office of the future concepts', personal computing, etc.).
    Participates mainly in the feasibility, detailed analysis, design and implementation phases of systems development.

Degree, professional qualification, HND, HNC or equivalent together with extensive experience of business procedures. Wide knowledge of office equipment. Good communications skills including ability to write unambiguous instructions. Ability to evaluate alternative solutions to problems. Ability to collect and analyse data.

Technical Designer (the term Systems Analyst is often used to cover the role of Technical Designer and parts of the work of the Business Analyst).
    Participates in the analysis, design and building of systems. Analysis data obtained and specifies interfaces between proposed and existing systems. Prepares detailed specifications for programming. Work may include: design of data storage, subdivision of system into computer runs and programs, identifying work to be programmed and that which can be achieved by use of existing modules. Liaises closely with programming staff. Senior technical Designers may be in charge of small teams and involved in the training of junior staff. Works especially in the detailed analysis, design and systems-building phases of the systems-development methodology.

Degree, HND, HNC or equivalent. Extensive knowledge of computer technology including computer processing opportunities, available software packages and programming. Detailed knowledge of data-base theory and practice and data communications capabilities as they pertain to the organisation. Task requires methodical work and great attention to detail. Must be able to document work accurately.

Job description	Personal qualifications

Programmer

Job description	Personal qualifications
Responsible for program design, coding and testing. Works on the maintenance of operational systems. Senior program-mers may be in charge of teams of pro-gramming staff and involved in the training of junior staff. Participates mainly in the systems building and implementation phases of systems development.	Degree in computer science, mathematics or science-based discipline, HND or HNC in similar disciplines or equivalent qualifications (trainees may be recruited at 'A' level standard). Extensive experience in programming, technical design and program testing. Ability to use and to evaluate use of programming languages and software aids in use within the organisation. Must be able to document his/her work effectively.

Fig 13.2   *programming skills*

cessing, these functions may be combined in many operations. Figure 13.4 outlines the job descriptions and personal qualifications required for these roles.

Fig 13.3   *data administration skills*

Job description	Personal qualifications

Data Strategist

Job description	Personal qualifications
Plans the long-term evolution of data management within the organi-sation. Liaises with Business Analysts and users on fugure data requirements. Analyses requirements for DBMS and impact on data processing plans.	Degree, professional qualification, HND, HNC or equivalent qualification. Wide knowledge of data analysis techniques and DBMS capabilities. Good communications skills.

Data Administrator

Job description	Personal qualifications
Defines and models data, using data analysis techniques. Prepares logical data-base designs. Liaises with users in the resolution of conflict over data definitions. Responsible for maintaining the data dictionary.	As above. Requires detailed know-ledge of data dictionary capabilities

Data Base Administrator (also called Data Base Designer)

Job description	Personal qualifications
Builds physical data bases, using the facilities of available DBMSs. Concerned with performance and fine tuning of data-base organisation and software.	Degree in computer science, mathematics or science-based discipline, HND or HNC in similar disciplines or equivalent qualifications. Detailed knowledge of DBMS and related software. Able to assess interactions between hardware and software in achieving acceptable performance.

Job description	Personal qualifications
Quality Assurance Officer	
Reviews work performed by development staff to ensure that it meets published standards and conforms to best industry practices.	Extensive knowledge of all aspects of data processing. Tactful manner. Must be capable of explaining why changes should be made. Attention to detail.
Standards Officer	
Reviews available standards and arranges additions, deletions and amendments to them as necessary. Ensures that standards are properly promulgated and the reasons behind them adequately understood.	Extensive knowledge of international, national, industry, trade and in-house standards. Must be able to write clear, concise and unambiguous instructions.

Fig 13.4   *quality assurance and standards skills*

(c) Routine operations

As with development work the routine operations of data processing require a wide variety of skills. Routine data processing operations may be likened to a production function (in contrast to the 'design function' of development work). The skills required therefore, have a strong practical and management aspect and in general are concerned with shorter time horizons than those involved in systems development work.

The main skills required are:

* operations management
* computer operations
* scheduling and control
* data preparation
* technical operations support
* ancillary operations.

(i) Operations management. As with development management, direct management of the operations function will normally be the responsibility of the data processing manager in the smaller data processing installations. In medium-sized or larger installations, however, it will be found necessary to appoint a person whose sole task is the management and co-ordination of routine operations. In addition to carrying out those of the general departmental management functions which specifically relate to operations, the Operations Manager should liaise with user departments on the scheduling and performance of systems in use. It is also important that the Operations Manager becomes involved in the development of new applications at an early stage to ensure that they are both operationally viable (i.e. can be operated efficiently on a routine basis) and fit into the longer-term schedule of computer usage. The Operations Manager controls and integrates the work schedules of the individual sections of the operations departments to ensure that as a whole they meet quality and timing requirements of the users and senior management.

The quality of the operational system is the standard by which the data processing department is most often judged. Development skills are, for most of the time, transparent to the users. It is therefore essential that the management of this function has the organisational skills to provide and maintain a high level of operational performance.

(ii) Computer operations. As the name implies, this family of skills is concerned with the physical operation of the computer or computers and the peripheral equipment attached to it. As computers have become more powerful the role of the Operator(s) has become steadily more crucial. Even with machines having highly sophisticated operating systems, operators can have a significant impact on throughput and efficiency. In all but the smallest installations there will be a hierarchy of Operators starting with Junior or Trainee Operators and rising to Senior Operators and Shift Team Leaders.

(iii) Scheduling and control. Organising the workload of a computer centre on a day-by-day basis is important if maximum throughput is to be obtained. Even where the basic workload is unchanged inasmuch as the same applications are in use, variations or delays in input, the need for monthly or other cycle end-processing, problems and errors necessitating the re-running of applications will require dynamic scheduling.

The sheer volume of data being processed by a computer also makes data control a vital function. Control has two aspects: keeping track of all batches of work as they pass through the data processing centre and providing control totals for each batch so that individual transactions do not get lost during processing.

Even in installations where there is a preponderance of on-line or real-time applications there will be considerable volumes of data processing by batch methods and it is in this area that data control plays the most significant role. Data is tracked from the moment it is received in the data processing centre to ensure that it progresses through data preparation or any other preliminary stages to reach the computer on schedule. Similarly output is tracked until it leaves the data processing centre or is handed over to the user.

Data control also plays an important role in integrating program testing, systems testing and other *ad hoc* or irregular demands for computer time into the schedule without detriment to routine applications.

It will be clear from the foregoing that this function plays a significant part in maintaining harmonious relations between the users and the data processing centre. This factor should be reflected in the choice of staff, who in addition to having the necessary skills should have an appropriate personality.

(iv) Data preparation. *Data preparation* is the task of translating documents from a human to a machine readable form suitable for input to the computer. The increasing tendency is for *data capture* to be a by-product of another activity or for it to be integrated into a work process or for human readable documents to be machine translated into computer readable (see Chapters 6 and 16). Most data processing installations nevertheless still have a significant element of work that needs to be 'translated'. This process usually involves a specialised keying function requiring a high degree of manual dexterity. The machines most commonly used for this purpose are described in Chapter 6.

(v) Technical operations support. Operations support covers a range of activities which have in common the fact that they are a necessary adjunct to computer operations. The main skills involved are:

* systems programming
* data communications expertise
* network control
* data librarianship.

Systems programming is the skill associated with the operational use within a data processing centre of the operating system and other system software (see Chapter 7). The implementation, maintenance, 'fine tuning' and utilisation of this software is a significant factor in establishing the efficiency of a computer and generally increases with the capacity and complexity of the computer.

As systems programming is to systems software so is data communications expertise to the hardware and software specific to data communications. As has been pointed out in Chapter 11 this is a specialised field within data processing requiring a high level of specific technical skills.

Closely related to data communications expertise is network control which refers to the day-to-day operational management of a network.

Data librarianship is, as its name implies, the custodial responsibility for data. In any data processing centre there are large quantities of data to be stored in both computer and human readable forms. The care of data in transportable computer readable form, e.g. demountable disk packs, reels of magnetic tape and hard copy documentation, e.g. operating manuals, is usually the responsibility of a specialist data librarian function.

Job descriptions and a summary of the main personal qualifications for the various roles in the operations field are shown in Figure 13.5.

(vi) Ancillary operations. In addition to the functions discussed above, nearly every data processing installation requires a number of ancillary operators. These personnel will be responsible for such tasks as: bursting, decollating and guillotining computer printouts (i.e. separating them into separate sheets, separating multiple copies and cutting the margins), delivery of computer output to users, the collection of computer input and the operation of any non-computing machinery in use, e.g. developers used for computer output on microfilm.

(d) Career development

One persistent myth within data processing is that there is a natural progression from operations to programming to analysis work. An examination of the personal qualifications required in each field shows, however, that they are markedly different and although individuals may progress from one function to another this should not be considered the normal career progression. Typically this approach results all too often in the 'promotion' of excellent and experienced operators and programmers to become mediocre programmers and analysts. It has, moreover, served to depress the relative status of both operations and programming *vis-à-vis* analysis work.

Career development in data processing should, therefore, be seen as having three separate paths rather than being a single one covering the areas of analysis, programming and operations. The need for separate career paths is becoming steadily more evident with the increase of technical specialisation in each field. It follows that the most senior positions in each field should provide a level of status and financial reward to satisfy the reasonable career expectations of the

Fig 13.5 *operations skills*

Job description	Personal qualifications

Computer Operator

Operates computer and peripheral equipment. Works from schedule of jobs prepared by schedulers.

ONC or GCE 'A' level standard (preferably with bias toward mathematical or scientific subjects) or equivalent qualifications. Ability to master detail quickly and to make decisions. Junior positions often require considerable dexterity. May be required to work shifts.

Schedulers and Controllers

Prepare detailed schedule of work to be performed on a computer and control work being processed through a data processing centre.

Educational level as above. Ability to master detailed information and make logical assessments. Ability to work accurately and methodically with limited direct supervision. May be required to work shifts.

Data Preparation Staff

Operate data preparation equipment.

CSE or equivalent. Operation of data preparation equipment requires ability to work quickly and methodically and possession of above-average dexterity.

Systems Programming

Responsible for the generation, maintenance and 'fine tuning' of systems software. Advises development staff of impact of systems software on applications. Usually involved in computer capacity planning.

Degree in computer science, mathematics or science-based discipline, HND or HNC in similar disciplines or equivalent qualifications. Extensive knowledge of systems software (both installed and available). Detailed knowledge of specialised programming techniques.

Data Communications Specialist

Responsible for planning, evaluating, installing, commissioning, maintaining and operating data communications hardware and software to form a data communications facility. Advises development staff of capabilities and limitations of installed and planned facilities. Works closely with telecommunications engineers from common carrier systems programmer and computer hardware engineers.

Degree in computer science, electronics, mathematics or science-based subject, HND or HNC in similar disciplines or equivalent qualifications. Detailed knowledge of data communications, facilities (hardware, software and links) and the interfaces between them.

Network Controller

Operates a data communications network. Liaises with schedulers and operators on detailed performance of workload.

GCE 'A' level, ONC or equivalent qualifications. Practical knowledge of the operation of data communications hardware, links and software. Ability to master detailed information quickly and make logical deductions.

Fig 13.5 *cont.*

Job description	Personal qualification
Data Librarian	
Maintains records of use and availability of demountable computer storage media. Controls physical movement of such media between computer room and safe storage location. Monitors preparation and storage of security copies of data media.	GCE 'A' and 'O' levels or equivalent. Methodical worker capable of maintaining detailed records accurately.

people recruited to junior or trainee positions in that field. Not every recruit will achieve a management position, but senior analysts, programming and operating staff should all enjoy rewards commensurate with a high level of technical skill and/or responsibility.

13.2 Organising the Data Processing Department

In this section the internal organisation of a data processing department will be discussed. The following section will consider the way in which the department fits into the complete organisation. As has been noted above, there are two readily discernible functions in most data processing departments, and this is almost invariably reflected in the organisation structure.

(a) Routine operations
Within the routine operations side of data processing the organisation usually consists of one or more computer operating teams, together with a number of support groups. Where the computer centre operates on a single-shift basis only one computer operations team will be needed, but where extra shifts and/or weekend working is the rule, additional teams will be required. The support groups reflect the skills needed and usually consist of a data preparation group, a scheduling and data control group and a systems programming team. The data librarian function should report to the scheduling control group. The scheduling and data control group may or may not work shifts on the same pattern as the operating team, depending on the nature of the work being processed. Scheduling and data control may also be separate functions. A typical organisation structure for an operations department is shown in Figure 13.6.

(b) Systems development
There is probably more diversity in the organisation of systems development than there is of routine operations reflecting, at least in

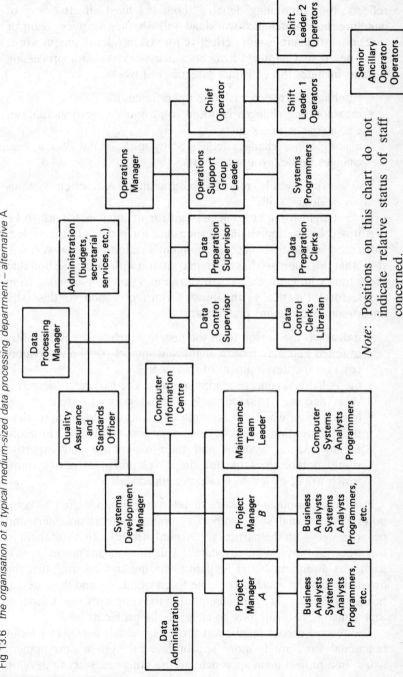

Fig 13.6 the organisation of a typical medium-sized data processing department – alternative A

Note: Positions on this chart do not indicate relative status of staff concerned.

part, the less-structured nature of the work itself. This diversity reflects, too, continuing debates about the most effective way of handling the maintenance workload and whether a project team or functional structure is more effective for systems development work.

As noted in Chapter 10 maintenance work on data processing systems includes three distinct categories of work:

* eliminating errors revealed in operational use
* incorporating changes imposed from outside the organisation, e.g. a change in tax rules
* making minor changes requested by users of the system, e.g. changes in the layout of reports.

This work typically requires programming and often systems analysis or design skills.

At first sight it might seem prudent for maintenance work to be performed by the individuals responsible for producing the system concerned in the first place. A moment's reflection, however, will show that this approach has much in common with the suggestion that every time your car breaks down you should summon someone from the factory! Practically, the most serious objection to this (still unfortunately common) practice are:

* it distracts the person from the task to which he/she is currently assigned and may have a significant impact (time and possibly cost) on the development of that task
* the individual concerned may not have the particular 'detective skills' necessary to trace faults in an operational system
* in time those who have done most systems development work in the organisation would become very heavily involved in maintaining existing systems and their experience and expertise would not be available for the development of new systems which would be left to less-experienced staff!

For these reasons a specialist maintenance group staffed by computer systems analysts, technical computer systems designers and programmers with the particular personal attributes that suit them to this work is always to be advocated. This does mean, however, that particular attention should be paid to testing and ensuring that the original programs reach acceptable levels of quality and documentation since there is always the temptation to skimp work if it is thought that someone else will have to clear up the problems.

The second debate mentioned above is whether a *project team* or functional structure is more appropriate for system development work. In a project team approach, all the skills necessary to develop the system are brought together under a single manager (who may be from either data processing or the user department principally concerned). This project team has a single responsibility and, it is argued, is much more committed to the project than is possible with any other organisation. The *functional approach*, on the other other hand, separates the development staff into sections or departments according to the disciplines of the individuals. Thus there is a programming section, a systems analysis section, etc. In this organisation structure work is passed from section to section and allocated to individuals in accordance with section workloads. Advocates of this approach maintain that it provides higher standards of professionalism (a programmer is always judged on his programming performance and not on other duties he performs as a team member) and in the more efficient use of skilled resources (there is no temptation to switch analysts on to programming work because that phase of the work is running late) and that it is easier to plan careers for the staff concerned.

Figures 13.6 and 13.7 show two typical data processing department organisation structures, the former with the systems development activity organised in project teams whereas in the latter the systems development activity is organised functionally. Figure 13.8 summarises the major points for and against each approach.

It will be noted in the two alternative organisations shown there are common elements. In both cases the Quality Assurance and Standards Officer is shown as occupying a staff position showing not only the need for this function in both cases, but also the desirability of separating it from the normal line management structure. This ensures that any problems in this area are brought to the attention of the Data Processing Manager. It will also be noted that there is a need for a separate data administration group in both organisations although in the project team approach this may be reduced to data strategy only with data modelling, etc., being performed within the project group. The third element the two organisations have in common is a computer information centre. This group assists end users in making use of computers. Depending on the environment, this may include assisting people to use and develop applications on personal computers, teaching users fourth generation languages and helping them use high-level languages for information retrieval and *ad hoc* reporting. Such requirements do not require the full rigours of the system development methodology and provided that careful control is maintained to prevent abuse such a group can have a very beneficial impact on the image of the data processing department.

In theory a project team is a transient structure that is dismantled

Fig 13.7 the organisation of a typical medium-sized data processing department – alternative B

Project team approach	Functional approach
* All team members 'goal-oriented'.	* Highest standards of technical competence because people work in peer groups and not mixed-discipline teams.
* Project lead times and costs may be shortened because of high level of motivation, simplified decision making and flexibility in use of resources.	* Easier to train new staff.
	* Easier to enforce standards.
* Facilitates liaison with users.	May lead to excessive interdepartmental bureaucracy.
* May lead to erosion of standards and documentation to get work done to a time limit.	* May cause problems if each department liaises separately with end-users.
* May cause problems in career planning because staff allocated work in accordance with project needs and moreover they may, over a period of time, report to many different managers, none of whom has any control over career development.	

Fig 13.8   *the project team and functional approaches to systems development*

when the project is completed. In practice there is a tendency in data processing to have 'permanent project teams' in which a 'project team' is assembled to support a functional area of the complete organisation on a continuing basis. Thus, for example, a financial applications or production applications group may be established. These groups, which are almost invariably staffed solely by data processing personnel, may also include the maintenance function as well as new systems development. Whilst overcoming some of the objections raised to pure project teams, such organisations re-introduce much of the rigidity that is inherent in the functional approach.

13.3 Monitoring the Work of the Data Processing Department

In most organisations today the data processing department accounts for a significant part of the total budget and payroll. It is clear that this expenditure and use of resources should be carefully monitored, the more so since data processing in most cases is providing a service to other departments within the same organisation.

There are two aspects to monitoring the work of the data processing department. The first of these may be called 'external control' and is concerned with seeing that the right things are being done (is data processing effective?). The second aspect may be called 'internal control' and is concerned with seeing things are done correctly (is data processing efficient?).

(a) External control

External control starts with the structure of the organisation and in particular the Manager to whom the Data Processing Manager reports. Typically this will be a Senior Manager or Director responsible for a range of service functions and having a title such as Management Services Manager, Administration and Services Director or the like. Whatever external control is exercised over data processing it is important that the function serves the organisation as a whole and it should not, therefore, report to a manager having specific departmental responsibilities, e.g. the Chief Accountant or Engineering Manager. Such an arrangement almost always leads to allegations that data processing is serving that department alone.

This reporting structure is not, however, the only means of external control on the data processing function. Many organisations have a *Computer Steering Committee* charged with the high-level identification of areas in which computer technology may be applied and the allocation of systems development resources between such areas. Such a committee is typically composed of senior managers from the most important computer-using departments (actual and potential) within the organisation. Terms of reference for a computer steering committee are shown in Figure 13.9.

(b) Internal control

As with most other aspects of data processing there is a dichotomy between the control of development work and routine operations.

The most important aspects in controlling systems development work are project progress control (time and budget) and quality assurance. The quality assurance function has already been discussed above, and project progress control will be considered in Chapter 14.

Within routine operations, control takes the form of measuring the performance of certain key indicators and examining trends over time. Thus, for example, the availability of an on-line system may be targeted for 35 hours per week and performance will be measured against that target. Where possible these measurements should also be compared against absolute standards. 'Absolute standards' in this context may refer to industry averages, the achievement of other users of the same equipment or manufacturer's specifications. Some of the key performance indicators that may be monitored are listed in

1. The function of the committee is to determine information systems development plans

2. To monitor progress against previously established plans

3. To assess priorities for systems development

4. To allocate priorities to systems development

5. To allocate resources to the systems development process

6. To establish time scales, scope, budget and terms of reference for feasibility studies

7. To resolve policy disputes relating to systems development planning

8. To ensure that short-term developments are compatible with long-range corporate plans

9. To ensure an appropriate infrastructure for data processing development exists within the organisation

Fig 13.9   *typical terms of reference for a computer steering committee*

Figure 13.10. It will be noted that these are oriented towards the end-user and thus emphasise the services orientation of most data processing departments.

13.4 **Standards and Documentation**

A major role in the internal operation of a data processing department is played by the twin topics of standards and documentation.

Standards are the systems and procedures applied to the work of data processing staff. The case for standards has been argued many

---

Fig 13.10   *some key performance indicators for data processing operations*

* Average response time for on-line systems

* Percentage of planned time for which on-line systems are available

* Percentage of output reports delivered more than (say) four hours after scheduled time

* Volume of transactions processed for each on-line system

* Percentage of batch jobs rerun (by cause) (causes include: user data error, data preparation error, data control error, operator error, data librarian error, application software fault, system software fault, hardware fault, etc.)

times and it is probably only in the younger disciplines like data processing that the debate continues. The case for standards is the case for professionalism and it is particularly valid in a discipline which, like data processing, draws its practitioners from a wide variety of backgrounds rather than having a universal training programme.

Not every department has to start from scratch and create its own standards. In fact, if a professional approach is to evolve with data processing, then it is important that they do not! Proven standards are available from many sources and each organisation should be able to select from the wide range available, tailoring or adapting them to the specific needs of the organisation where necessary.

Among the sources of standards and examples of the standards which may be obtained from them are:

* national and international standards groups which may provide standards for data communications codes and flowcharting symbols
* user groups which may provide programming standards for specific languages
* published material which may provide data analysis techniques
* consultants who may provide formalised systems development methodologies.

This brief list illustrates, *inter alia*, the wide scope of standards which should cover the full spectrum of work in a data processing department including all aspects of systems development and operations.

There is a risk that because data processing is a (relatively) young profession and since its standards, like its personnel, are drawn from a wide range of sources, the result will be a miscellany of unconnected parts. It is one of the roles of the Standards Officer within a data processing department to ensure that this does not happen and that the individual standards are part of a coherent whole. In this task the adoption of a methodology for systems development such as that outlined in Chapter 8 is of major importance.

14 Implementing Systems

14.1 **The Implementation Phase**

No matter how good the design work and programming that has been carried out, or how good a functional fit a purchased package may be, no system makes any contribution towards the effectiveness of an organisation until it has been brought into use. This process is a difficult one since systems are rarely installed in 'green field sites' and careful transition from an existing system or set of procedures to the new system has to be achieved.

Making a system work has many facets. The obvious one is sorting out the technical problems associated with the computer part of the system, but this is only a fraction of the total workload. Other major activities of the implementation phase include:

* the thorough testing of the system
* training user staff
* training computer operations staff
* acquiring the necessary supplies to make the system work (e.g. special stationery)
* converting data files and historical records to the format required by the new system
* recoding information to suit the new system
* installing new equipment needed to support the new system (e.g. installing terminals in work stations)
* reorganising user work routines and organisation.

Not all these activities will occur in every system implementation, nor will they all necessarily be the responsibility of the data processing staff. However, unless someone makes sure that all the required tasks are performed, the system may well fail or fail to realise the economic or other benefits envisaged. It is therefore incumbent upon the data processing staff to ensure that the work is carried out and, if necessary, draw the attention of management to the outstanding items.

The implementation phase, therefore, places heavy demands on the non-technical skills of data processing staff.

14.2 **Planning for Implementation**

A sound plan is a prerequisite for successful systems implementation and itself depends on two factors. The first factor is the accurate identification of the tasks to be carried out, and the second is the realistic estimation of the resources (both manpower and other) needed to perform them.

Many techniques are used for planning purposes, including the familiar bar charts and critical-path-analysis charts, but it cannot be stressed enough that no planning technique can make up for inadequacies of the data contained in it. Thus, if the basic tasks are not identified correctly or the estimates of the resources required to perform them are inaccurate, the plan cannot possibly be expected to be realistic. This is not to say that any plan can be expected to be 100 per cent accurate – rather it is an assessment of what may be expected to happen and should be sufficiently accurate to enable management to allocate resources.

Estimating the work content of tasks to be performed is a particularly difficult task. Although many formulae have been developed for this purpose the only universally reliable method is to break the task down into sufficiently small units to enable a realistic assessment to be made of their work content by comparison to similar, well-established activities.

Planning, of course, is not necessary only during the implementation phase of systems development; it is needed for all phases of the methodology described in Chapters 8 and 10. The need for planning, however, becomes particularly acute during the implementation phase. It is for this reason that planning is discussed in this chapter, but the reader is reminded of the fact that it is not solely applicable to this phase of systems development. This is because the number of tasks and organisational units involved in the implementation phase usually increases and the interrelationship between tasks tends to become more critical. For example, installing a new terminal may require: building work (say, installing a new conduit), electrical installation (providing a new power source), telephone installation (providing communication links), purchasing terminal equipment/ new forms, user staff training (in terminal operation), computer staff training (in network control) before it can be considered to be operational. Some of these tasks can be performed in parallel (like staff training and building work) while others require one or more to be completed before another can begin (for example, redecoration of offices must follow the building work). Planning tasks in the most efficient way can not only make the whole process more likely to occur on schedule, but will also reduce the elapsed time necessary.

14.3 **Project Management and Control**

As with planning, which in fact as we shall see is an integral part of the complete project management and control process, this topic is not limited to the implementation phase of systems development. Discussion of the topic has been delayed until this stage because it is desirable to have a good appreciation of what has to be done before consideration is given to the control process.

It is implicit in the systems development methodology described in this book, and indeed in the nature of most systems development work, that the tasks to be performed naturally lead to an identifiable target or conclusion; for example, implementing a new computer-based system, rather than representing a continuous activity. In this way systems development may be likened to civil engineering, with its emphasis on the construction of discrete items (buildings, bridges, etc.). In the case of systems development the realisation of its objectives is achieved by bringing together people with a variety of skills (systems analysis, programming, user management, etc.).

This approach to work imposes rather different requirements on management than conventional continuous operations. The particular requirements of management in a project environment may be identified as:

* identification of targets
* progress monitoring and reporting
* team selection
* quality control.

(a) **Identification of targets**
A plan by itself is only of limited use: one further step is necessary to turn it into a useful part of the project management process. This additional step is the identification of intermediate targets against which progress may be monitored. These targets must be frequent enough to be useful for monitoring purposes and be events that can clearly be described as completed or not completed so there is no ambiguity about whether they have been achieved. Thus 'submit report for approval' would be a good target while 'complete investigation' would be a poor choice since it is more difficult to ascertain whether it has actually been achieved. The term 'deliverables' is increasingly being used to describe the outputs to be produced on or by a target date.

(b) **Progress monitoring and reporting**
Closely related to plans and targets are the mechanics for monitoring

and reporting progress. The purpose is not only to check what has been done, but, more importantly, the plan is on schedule. Identifying what remains to be done to achieve a target is necessary to provide early warning to management that the target may not be met (or will be met ahead of schedule). This enables plans for subsequent stages to be revised and/or the resources allocated to the task leading up to the target to be reviewed for either quantity or quality.

It is a common phenomenon in systems development work that the stage of 90 per cent completion is soon reached, but the remaining 10 per cent of the work takes rather longer! It is only by measuring what remains to be done that this consequence of over-optimism can be avoided. One reason for failing to meet targets is that the specification of the system has been revised during its development. Although it is clearly necessary to allow changes to be made whenever possible (especially where these reflect the changing environment rather than merely changes of opinion) there are times when changes cannot be entertained without modification to project cost budgets and/or deadlines. Such 'frozen' periods should be clearly identified (program coding and systems testing are two obvious examples) and communicated to user management and any changes during these periods avoided. Amendments requested during the 'frozen' period should be documented and implemented as soon after the system goes 'live' as is practical. It is also important that all amendments are evaluated in the same way as the original systems proposal to avoid the possibility that the scope of the system is not inadvertently extended beyond economic limits.

(c) Team selection
An important part of the project management task is selecting the appropriate human resources to meet the project objectives. In addition to ensuring that the necessary skills are available in the right quantities, this also means that the staff concerned should be capable of working together to achieve the project goals.

(d) Quality control
Quality control is an essential element of good project management and has to be introduced through the use of sound development approaches and effective monitoring. The development approaches to be followed (methodologies and techniques to be used and documentation to be produced) should be subject to clear standards or codes of practice which must be communicated to all staff concerned in advance of the commencement of work on the project. Effective monitoring entails the use of both normal supervision

methods and also the use of such techniques as '*walkthroughs*'. Walkthroughs are a formalised approach to peer group evaluation in which staff of a similar status in the organisation critically evaluate each other's work in a structured way. The key points to remember when using walkthroughs are:

* the size of the group should be large enough to permit all involved to participate, but small enough that it does not become a formal presentation. In practice 6 to 8 persons is usually most effective
* all attenders must be sufficiently involved in the detailed work being discussed to enable them to make a meaningful contribution
* the discussion should be based on a chart or other document which must have been circulated to all attenders sufficiently in advance to enable them to familiarise themselves with it
* the time available should be limited to prevent open-ended discussion. About 2 to $2\frac{1}{2}$ hours is normally sufficient
* the person or group whose work is being 'walked through' should be given the opportunity to describe *why* they have done things in a particular way as well as *how* they have represented them on the chart in question
* walkthroughs should be held after the individual or group has had a chance to formulate (and document) ideas, but before being totally committed to the particular solution presented
* walkthroughs are only practical if the same individuals take turns at being 'presenters' and 'audience'
* all the 'audience' should participate. 'Observers' are not to be encouraged
* the walkthrough should have a chairman who should seek to ensure that all points raised are relevant and satisfactorily resolved. The chairman should also control the length of discussion on each topic to ensure that the complete subject of the walkthrough is considered and should identify what action is to be taken on all the points raised
* a secretary should be appointed to record the points raised and their resolution
* no personal comments are allowed
* at the end of the walkthrough the possible outcomes are: acceptance of the chart without modification, acceptance of the chart or document subject to modifications agreed at the meeting or rejection of the chart, which is then subject to rework or additional investigation. In this latter case a date should be established for a further walkthrough on the same subject.

In addition to their role in promoting quality control, walkthroughs are extremely valuable as a communication tool and way of ensuring liaison between people working on different but related parts of a project.

14.4 Systems Testing

Before any new system is introduced it must be subjected to thorough testing. It has already been noted in Chapter 10 that programs are subjected to tests to ensure that they perform their functions satisfactorily, but this is only part of the testing necessary before a new system is implemented.

Thorough systems testing includes four separate stages:

Stage 1 The system is tested using 'clean' data to allow accurate comparison between known input and expected output.

Stage 2 The system is tested using the same data as in the previous stage with the addition of known error data to test the error routines and reporting to verify that corruption of good data does not occur.

Stage 3 The system is tested using greater than operational volumes to ensure that it is capable of handling such volumes without operational problems, e.g. excessive file sizes or run times

Stage 4 The special month or other period end-routines are tested.

Ideally the test data should be prepared and the system test carried out by user and normal computer operations staff rather than by the staff who designed and built it.

After the test has been completed the results obtained should be carefully verified before the system is passed for operation.

After systems testing is complete the test data and verified results should be retained. In this way information is available to prove the accuracy for audit or other purposes. New test data does not have to be re-created after each modification to the system and moreover a proven set of results is available for comparison with the results produced during such tests.

In many organisations systems tests are used for three purposes (and may require three separate tests). These purposes are:

* for the development team to satisfy itself that the system is complete and ready for operation
* for acceptance by the user organisation to establish that the system meets user requirements

* for acceptance by the computer operations and/or programming maintenance sections to show that the system is capable of being operated on a routine basis. This check will involve detailed examination of the system documentation to establish that it is satisfactory for the resolution of normal operating problems.

14.5 Introducing the New System

There are three basic ways in which a new system may be introduced into an organisation. These are:

* direct implementation
* phased implementation
* parallel running.

(a) Direct implementation

The most obvious approach, that of introducing the new system in its entirety on a given date to replace the existing system, is, in practice, usually only adopted for small systems. The reason is that the early days of operation of a new system normally reveal many practical and/or technical problems. The systems staff are limited in number and are only able to attend to a few of these problems and assist a limited number of the users of the system at any time. Moreover, direct implementation removes the 'safety net' provided by the existing system which can no longer be used even if the problems associated with the new system prove significant. Direct implementation can therefore be a dangerous practice and should only be used after careful consideration of all the circumstances.

(b) Phased implementation

As an alternative to direct implementation a phased approach may be used. In this case the new system replaces the existing system in a series of steps or phases. The steps may be functional (e.g. initially introducing only the receiving part of a warehouse system, then, after that has been established, introducing the new issuing procedures) or concern a part of the total extent of the system (e.g. all the transactions for a given branch of a company or all transactions relating to a small part of the total range of products). Phased implementation significantly eases the problem of training staff and facilitates the solving of operational problems before they become too serious. On the other hand, it does serve to extend the implementation period (and thus delay obtaining full benefits).

(c) Parallel running

The third possible way of implementing a new system is to operate in parallel to the system it is to replace. This approach means that the existing system may be used in the event that problems are experienced in its replacement and moreover provides a ready source of comparison to validate the results obtained using the new system. Despite these apparent advantages, parallel running is not the answer to all implementation problems. By definition it requires double work and, moreover, depending on how much change the new system introduces to working methods, may be impractical or may overload the resources (human and/or machine) available. Parallel running tends to be used for accounting applications in order to ensure the accuracy of the new system before it is accepted as part of the organisation's financial control.

The choice of approach (or combination of the two latter approaches) will depend on the particular circumstances encountered in any given case. Systems personnel should never forget that they are agents of change and care in introducing that change is an essential part of ensuring the success of their work.

14.6 The Conversion Process

No word is calculated to strike more terror into an experienced data processing professional than 'conversion'. Conversion has many connotations including the notorious and unproductive process of changing from one type of computer to another. In the context of system implementation the usual manifestation is that of 'converting' data from one form to another. This may mean collecting data currently in hard copy form and transferring it to a computer readable medium; changing from one computer medium to another and reorganising existing files or data bases to meet the requirements of the new system.

None of these activities is simple and most are underestimated. Not only does plenty of time have to be allowed to plan and carry out the conversion, but great care must be taken to ensure that it is carried out accurately.

Concurrently with conversion the opportunity should be taken to 'clean' the data – especially when inaccurate data is known to be one of the problems of the existing system. This activity is not only time-consuming, but requires experienced and committed staff.

14.7 **Training**

Training in the implementation phase means the training of two groups of staff: the users and the computer staff responsible for routine operation. Within each of these groups there will be specific requirements. For example, the training needs of a clerk who will use a terminal to enter transaction data into a system are quite different from those of the manager who will be using reports generated by the system. Training therefore requires careful preparation, considering the specific needs of the trainee.

There is a tendency for this activity to be given insufficient attention, being rushed and/or conducted 'on the job' without proper documentation or any teaching aids such as sample forms, special terminal dialogues, etc. Such an attitude on the part of the systems development staff is indefensible and leads almost inevitably to additional difficulties in the early days of the operational use of the system.

14.8 **The Sixth Decision Point**

At the end of the implementation phase there is a sixth decision point at which the system is reviewed. It is admittedly rare though not completely unknown for a system to be cancelled at this stage, but nevertheless the review should be carried out to ascertain that the system is properly operational and that the anticipated benefits will be realised.

A further important part of the review stage is that it enables a comparison to be made between the estimates made at stages throughout the project and the actual performance. Almost invariably systems development will be found to have taken longer and cost more than estimated. This information is itself valuable and should be furnished in a clear and simple manner to the estimators to help improve the accuracy of future estimtes.

14.9 **Post-Implementation Follow-up**

After implementation every project should be reviewed periodically (say every two or three years) to ensure that it is still meeting its objective and performing both efficiently and effectively.

This review should establish, *inter alia*, whether the benefits still outweigh the running costs of the system or whether it has reached a point where it has become uneconomic. This situation may arise because benefits are no longer being realised (for example, reports are being produced, but no longer used) or because the costs of keeping the system running are too high. This in turn may be due to the need to retain otherwise unneeded equipment or the high cost of maintaining an old and much modified system.

As has been remarked above, a system is like a capital asset and as such needs this type of review to ascertain that it is still 'paying its way' and has not outlived its economic working life.

15 Taking Care of Data

15.1 **The Different Aspects of Care**

Having gone to considerable trouble and no little expense to provide a means of processing data it is obviously incumbent upon the data processing department to exercise great care whilst the data concerned is in its stewardship. In this chapter the principles of security will be outlined, the ways in which a data processing centre is organised to protect data is discussed and finally the specific ways of protecting data will be examined. First, however, it is necessary to consider what is meant by 'taking care of data'.

Data may, in fact, be exposed to a number of separate risks and although the measures adopted to protect against them may be the same, it is important that they are distinguished from each other:

* accidental loss
* accidental damage or corruption
* theft
* deliberate damage or corruption
* unauthorised disclosure.

Although it is the spectacular events of fraud, theft, natural disaster or deliberate sabotage that attract the most publicity, it is probably true to say that the biggest risk faced by most data processing centres is human error leading to accidental loss, damage or corruption of data. Considerable attention has also been paid in the press to the topic of *privacy*. The perhaps understandable fear that large data bases and powerful computers can at least theoretically combine data provided by the individual to different organisations has led to demands for legislation to prevent unauthorised disclosure. To this demand has been added such refinements as the right of the individual to inspect the data held and/or the appointment of a 'data inspectorate' coupled with the registration or licensing of specific types of data bases (notably those containing data on individuals). Many countries, including the UK (where the Data Protection Act was passed in 1984 and came into full effect in 1986) have such legislation.

15.2 **Principles of Data Security**

There are a number of principles of data security which might almost be considered axioms. The most important of these are:

* * security should be provided throughout the data cycle
* * the security measures should not cost more than the value of the data being protected
* * the security measures adopted should be appropriate to the risks faced
* * there is no such thing as absolute security
* * security measures must include recovery procedures.

(a) Security should be provided throughout the data cycle
If data is worth protecting at all it is worth protecting throughout its life-cycle. Despite the obvious nature of this statement it is amazing how often examples may be found of it being ignored. Data which is kept under lock and key in rooms with special access procedures when it is in computer readable form is all too often left lying around on office desks when in human readable form as a computer printout. It is as if a householder bars the upstairs windows to his home but leaves the front door open!

(b) The security measures should not cost more than the value of the data being protected
The problem with this axiom is assessing the value of data. For most commercial data this is simply the cost of recovering it, but in some cases the value is a great deal more. In the case of national security or commercial confidentiality where there is a risk that someone would want to steal the data because it is 'secret' the value usually approximates to the costs that the other party would incur by finding out the same data by legitimate means (doing his own research).

(c) The security measures adopted should be appropriate to the risks faced
Another obvious point, but again one that is often neglected. If your computer centre is near a river and on the ground floor, guard against floods – a precaution not likely to be necessary on the tenth floor! Yet examples abound of expensive precautions being taken against risks with a very low probability while much larger risks are not protected against. Thus many data processing installations have elaborate access control systems, but only basic levels of fire protection or environment control.

(d) There is no such thing as absolute security
The point here is that no matter what security measures are taken, protection is not absolute. The approach must be to ensure that deliberate intrusion is too expensive (in time as well as money) to be worthwhile and to reduce risks of accidental loss, damage or corruption to acceptable levels.

(e) Security measures must include recovery procedures
Closely following from the preceding point is the principle that since all risks remain (even though at diminished levels) no matter what security precautions are taken, any comprehensive security plan must include *recovery procedures* to ensure continuity of processing in the event of a security incident.

15.3 General Data Processing Security Measures

General data processing security measures are those that are applied as part of the regular operations of a data processing department. As such they do not have to be specified for each new application developed, but will be automatically applied. They fall into two broad categories: physical measures which are either present or absent and which cannot be selectively applied to individual applications, and procedural controls which although theoretically capable of selective application are by management decision universally applied within an organisation.

The main controls included in the category of general data processing controls are:

* access control
* environmental control
* hardware back up
* data management procedures
* data control procedures
* program maintenance procedures
* disaster recovery procedures.

(a) Access control
Most commercial data processing installations impose limitations on the number of individuals who may freely enter the computer room and other sensitive areas such as the tape library. The main purpose is security, although there may also be productivity reasons by limiting the distractions suffered by operators. Access control may be enforced by supervision or by the installation of special door locks and

limiting the issue of 'keys' (often in the form of plastic cards) to those needing to enter the computer room.

It is important to remember, however, that computers may be accessed by terminals. Where terminals are installed it makes relatively little sense in terms of data security to control carefully access to the computer centre but allow free access to the terminals attached to it. Consequently, terminals are often lockable using conventional keys and, more commonly still, access to programs and/or data from a terminal is protected by the use of passwords.

Passwords are effectively software 'keys'. They consist of a short combination of alphabetic and/or numeric characters which the terminal user must enter into the computer and have verified by it (against a central file of valid passwords) before he or she is permitted access to specific data or programs. Password protection may be very extensive, limiting access to specific data within a data base and distinguishing, for example, between those who can update and those who can only read data. The disadvantage of passwords is that to be effective they need to be changed regularly and that people tend to write them down to eliminate the risk of forgetting them.

Although access control is important its effectiveness tends to be overestimated and it must be supplemented by other measures.

(b) Environmental control
Mainframe computers in general require a specific environment in which to operate and as a result are usually housed in a specially prepared facility incorporating not only air-conditioning, but also 'filtered' electrical current, smoke detection and fire extinguishers. All these features help reduce risks from certain types of threats.

For smaller installations and where the equipment installed does not require such a carefully controlled environment, provision of appropriate substitute measures should be arranged. Such measures should include, for example, regular checking by watchmen or security personnel outside normal working hours and the provision of manual fire extinguishers.

(c) Hardware backup
Another way in which the continuity of processing can be assured is by having extra hardware for back-up purposes. In extreme cases this will entail the provision of duplicate computers (possibly even housed in separate buildings and staffed by separate personnel). Such extreme measures are, however, only justified where the system concerned is absolutely central to the organisation's operations and where no *down time* due to hardware failure can be tolerated.

Examples of this type of system include airline reservations systems, the control of space flights and on-line banking systems.

For other applications some limited form of hardware back-up may also be justified. Many computer installations have their own electrical generation systems to ensure that they can continue processing even if the main power supply fails. Computer dependency on power refers not only to its availability, but also to its quality. Minute fluctuations in power supplies, unnoticeable for normal electrical equipment, may cause loss or corruption of data. To alleviate this problem many data processing installations use alternators or buffer supplies through a bank of batteries to ensure a constant power supply. The number of disk drives and other peripheral equipment installed (especially those with electro-mechanical elements) may also be in excess of those theoretically required in order to provide some 'safety margin' against failure. A number of organisations also choose to install two medium-sized computers rather than a single large machine so that even if one breaks down essential processing can continue (albeit on a reduced scale).

Many organisations negotiate mutual back-up arrangements with other nearby data processing installations equipped with similar computers. The basis of these arrangements is that in case of need due to prolonged inability to process, the organisation can 'borrow' computer facilities to run at least its essential applications. To be worth while such arrangements need to be regularly tested and should be subject to annual ratification and detailed procedures. Although such arrangements sound practical and economic in theory, in practice they are often of little value. Small differences in the alignment of tape and especially disk drives and in the operating system may make the running of applications difficult or even impossible. Moreover, when urgently required it may be found that the other computer centre is already fully loaded and little if any capacity is available for back-up purposes.

(d) Data management procedures

One form of data management security procedure has already been discussed in the form of password control over access to data. A second form is the control over the issue and use of the data media (magnetic tapes, demountable disks, etc.) exercised by the data librarian function and discussed in Chapter 13. Among the other data management procedures having an impact on security are:

* the periodic dumping of data
* the keeping of hash or control totals

* the provision of log records, and
* the keeping of 'generations' of data.

(i) Periodic dumping of data. It is standard practice in most data processing installations to 'dump' data held on-line to tapes at regular intervals. Where the activity on the data dumped is high (i.e. there are many updates) the frequency of *dumping* should also be high (daily or even more frequently). Where activity is low, dumps may only need to be taken weekly or even monthly. The purpose of the dump is to have a basis from which to begin restoration work on the event of failure or loss. It is therefore vital to record exactly when the dump was taken and the information retained must include all the files and data required to restore the situation to the point *immediately prior* to the failure. Dumping data should not be carried out indiscriminately, but should follow specific procedures and guidelines as should the recovery procedures; these forming part of the operations standards discussed in Chapter 13.

(ii) Keeping hash or control totals. Totals are normally kept of all records in a file and of a specific field within every record on that file. Where this latter total is meaningful, e.g. the sum of all the money values in a stock file, it is a control total, but where it is meaningless, e.g. the sum of the part numbers in a stock file, it is called a *hash total*. Both control and hash totals may be used before and after any processing to check whether data has been corrupted or lost.

(iii) The provision of log records. For all except simple sequential files the process of updating a file or data base means that the file or data base itself is changed. It is therefore standard practice to keep a record (the *log file*) of all transactions processed against the main file or data base. Such a log file may be used in conjunction with the dumped version of the file or data base to recover if data is lost or corrupted. The log file is also an important part of the *audit trail*, which enables auditors to trace the processing of individual transactions through the system.

(iv) The keeping of 'generations' of data. It is standard practice to keep at least three *generations* of a file or data base, the third (and any subsequent generations maintained) providing a further level of security in the event that restoration is not achieved using the first back-up copy. The principle can perhaps be most readily illustrated by considering a sequential file held on magnetic tape. When an *updating run* occurs a new tape is written, combining the previous *master tape* and any updates and leaving the previous master tape unchanged. Both the previous master (now the 'father' tape) and the new master (now the 'son' tape) are retained, together with the actual transactions processed. In the next updating run the 'son' tape is used as the master and a new (blank or scratch) tape is used to become the new master. At the completion of the second run the *'father'* becomes the *'grandfather'*, the *'son'* becomes the 'father' and the scratch tape becomes the 'son'. If only three generations are to be maintained the 'grandfather' can become the *scratch tape* for the next updating run. At any time it is possible to re-create the 'younger' version by using the next older generation plus the appropriate transaction log.

(e) Data control procedures
In Chapter 13 the role of data control was introduced and it will be readily appreciated that it has an important part to play in data security as well as its basic work-control and progress-monitoring functions. Although in some degree the process may be automated the bases of data control are good manual procedures coupled with accurate clerical work that progress batch work on a step-by-step basis through the data processing department.

(f) Program maintenance procedures
One of the risks faced by a data processing installation is that of fraud perpetrated by someone who can manipulate a computer system. No one is better placed to carry out fraud than an inadequately supervised programmer who can theoretically make fraudulent changes to a program (for example, automatically paying extra amounts to his or her bank account in a payroll application) and just as easily reversing the changes just before the annual check by the organisation's auditors. The checks against this type of activity are, however, simple:

* quality assurance checks on all code written
* no amendments to operational programs without specific authority
* no permanent allocation of programmers to specific programs
* program amendment runs logged and controlled by data control
* random spot checks by auditors.

(g) Disaster recovery procedures
The near universal applicability of Murphy's Law means that no security program is complete without *disaster recovery procedures*.

These procedures should be written, cover as many eventualities as can be reasonably foreseen and must be periodically tested. The procedures should include the criteria by which work should be identified for processing (given inadequate facilities for processing both, which takes precedence, payroll or invoicing?), emergency procedures, persons to be notified, etc. This latter point is especially important. As each successive level of back-up or recovery is activated a higher level of management should be involved in authorising the move. Thus while a Shift Leader may authorise the use of a 'father' file the Chief Operator's permission should be necessary to release the next level of back-up and so on.

The disasters considered will depend on circumstances, but fire, prolonged machine failure and prolonged absence of certain key individuals (e.g. the one trained Librarian or Network Controller) are obvious contenders. Tests should be carried out unannounced so that a realistic exercise can be performed using available staff and unforeseen problems rectified before the procedures are used in earnest.

15.4 System Specific Security Measures

The security measures considered in the preceding section were general in that they applied to all applications in operation in a given data processing installation. Some applications have, however, specific requirements which go beyond the general measures provided. Such specific requirements should be identified during the feasibility study stage of the systems development methodology and taken into account when assessing the economics of the system.

Many system specific requirements can be met by relatively simple measures such as the provision of extensive data validation routines and the use of check digited numbers for such data as customer reference number, account number, part number, etc. (Check digits are calculated by a mathematical formula and added to the original number. By recalculating and comparing results whenever the number is used, the accuracy of the data entry, transcription or other process can be checked.)

Specific security requirements may be mandatory in that they are included in legislation (e.g. privacy laws in many countries) or imposed by an external body (e.g. the organisation's auditors). Alternatively, they may be requirements that are introduced by an organisation's general or departmental management to guard against a perceived threat relevant to that application (e.g. industrial espionage in conjunction with computer-aided design work).

Occasionally such specific security requirements will entail the installation of additional physical security measures, e.g. the installation of an electrical generator when the first real-time application is introduced and such measures then apply to all existing applications and consequently upgrade the overall security of the installation. More typically, however, the measures are confined to tightening data management and data control procedures. It is essential that these requirements are met if the users are to accept the system for regular operational use.

Part V

The Applications of Data Processing

16 Applications Requirements

Within the field of data processing there is a wide diversity of applications and an almost equally wide range of environments in which they operate. Given that data processing extends into almost every facet of commercial and industrial life it might seem difficult, if not impossible, to identify any general requirements for applications. Experience shows, however, that a number of features are common to the majority of successful applications. It is therefore important that these features receive special attention during the systems development process.

Success can be measured in a number of ways. All too often the only one considered is the technical efficiency of an application – the amount of computer resources it uses, the speed of execution of the constituent programs, etc. While not unimportant, such factors are of much less importance than the *effectiveness* of the system – is it performing a useful function for the organisation as a whole? What is really needed, of course, is a balance between these two factors – an effective system which is also efficient.

In the following section some of the key characteristics of successful applications will be identified and discussed. In the final section of this chapter the various types of application in use will be introduced.

16.1 Characteristics of Successful Applications

As noted above, it is possible to identify a number of characteristics shared by successful applications. Among the most important are that the application:

* helps meet the organisation's objectives
* has a realistic scope
* has a sound economic base
* has a long life-expectancy
* makes use of sound management techniques
* is easy to use
* is designed with full user co-operation.

(a) Helps meet the organisation's objectives

It is implicit in the concept of effectiveness outlined above that no application can be considered successful unless it is performing a useful function. Yet all too often the objectives of a system are considered on a narrow and/or short-term basis. What is needed is a systems development programme which is related to long-term organisational objectives rather than short-term departmental goals. This is not a plea for grandiose or all-encompassing information systems, but rather a statement that the most successful systems can be seen to form part of the 'big picture' of the organisation's operational requirements. The role of the computer steering committee identified in Chapter 13 can be valuable in ensuring that this criterion is met and it should be part of the feasibility study described in Chapter 8 to identify how, if at all, the specific application relates to the organisation's information systems development plan.

(b) Has a realistic scope

Closely related to the previous point is the question of the scope of a system. This has two aspects, which may be termed the 'breadth' and the 'depth' of the system.

(i) Breadth of system. The breadth of a system refers to its extent or the number of business functions included within it. Thus a human resources system which includes personnel statistics, labour costing, career planning and payroll processing is broader in scope than a system which provides only payroll and labour costing. Similarly, a materials management system which embraces purchasing and expediting, inventory control, warehouse management and distribution functions is broader in scope than one which provides only storehouse control and registration of receipts and issues of material.

Up to a certain point increases in scope are advantageous inasmuch as they reduce interfaces between separate systems. Beyond that point, however, any benefits gained are more than outweighed by the problems encountered. Difficulties are invariably experienced with overly broad systems during the development cycle for two main reasons. First, widely defined systems inevitably increase the number of the organisation's line managers and other staff who have to be consulted and whose agreement needs to be obtained. Almost inevitably this leads to a long and reiterative cycle of reports, meetings, subcommittees and memoranda in an effort to resolve contentious points. Consequently systems development can easily become stalled.

Second, the realisation of large-scale systems within a reasonable time frame requires (assuming constant levels of productivity) a larger systems development team and consequently an increased percentage of the total effort must be devoted to team briefings, administration, control and management. This in turn means a yet larger team and yet more internal briefings, administration, control and management!

Having identified the dangers of systems that are too broad it remains to consider what is an appropriate scope for a system. The answer will depend partly on the nature of the system. The simpler or more routine the business functions covered by the application, the broader the scope it will generally be possible to handle without difficulty. Similarly, if high productivity and/or extended deadlines make it possible to handle the development with a small or medium-size team, then again the breadth of the system may be extended without difficulty. The point at which the size of the development team becomes too large is again a matter of judgement and will depend in part on the organisation structure, the experience of the staff concerned, the cohesion (or otherwise) of the team and the development methodology in use. As a rule of thumb any system which requires a team of more than six or seven people for a period of eighteen months or longer (i.e. approximately ten man-years' effort) should be considered for possible subdivision into sub-projects. Each sub-project must have identifiable objectives, targets and its own allocation of resources. Where a total project is divided into sub-projects it is not always practical or necessary to start work on all the sub-projects simultaneously. The priority attached to each should be assessed and those with the highest priority tackled first, subsequent sub-projects being progressively included until the total project is complete. In this case, the priorities should reflect the operational viability of the sub-projects as well as their value to the user.

(ii) Depth of system. The depth of a system refers to the degree to which the business function is automated. It is a commonly experienced phenomenon that the major effort in a project is expended to provide solutions for a small percentage of the total activity. Sometimes referred to as the '80/20 rule' (i.e. 80 per cent of the systems development effort relates to 20 per cent of the occurrences) this phenomenon has an important impact on systems development effort (and hence systems economics).

It will often be found worth while to restrict the depth of a system so that the less-frequently encountered or more complex exceptions are not handled automatically, but are set aside for manual processing. Clearly care needs to be taken that summary records and audit trails are correctly preserved in such cases but these are usually more readily catered for than trying to automate the full exception processing. In addition to simplifying the work required in developing the system such an approach may have a secondary benefit in providing job satisfaction to the user staff concerned with the operation of the system since they are required to deal with the more complex or exceptional transactions. As a guideline any exception that is forecast to occur once in every two hundred transactions or less should be considered for processing manually or in a partly automated manner.

Systems specified with both realistic breadth and depth are more likely to prove successful than those that are too grandiose in scope.

(c) Has a sound economic base

To be successful an application should not only be effective but be economically viable. That is to say that the amortised development costs and the running costs together should be less than the value of the output produced. Output in this context may include direct savings, e.g. in manpower, or indirect savings achieved through the provision of improved information. We have already discussed in Chapter 8 the need to consider the economic viability of a proposed system, here it may be observed that unless a sound economic base is realised the application cannot be considered fully successful.

(d) Has a long life-expectancy

Systems development is a labour-intensive and, therefore, expensive activity. Moreover, it is often a protracted exercise and makes use of resources (both human and financial) which might be used for other purposes. It is therefore invariably more rewarding to deploy these resources on applications which are likely to be of benefit to the organisation over a considerable period of time. Two advantages may be realised: first, benefits will be maximised and, second, the cost of development can be amortised over a longer period, thereby effectively reducing the cost of outputs, be they measured by transaction or by report. From time to time exceptions to this general statement may be found. Some applications may be expected to have only a limited life, but are, nevertheless, so beneficial that their development costs are justified. It should be stressed, however, that such applications are exceptions.

(e) Makes use of sound management techniques

Successful applications are not only effective and efficient ones, but also make use of sound management techniques. A number of these may be cited by way of example:

* information is provided to the person or persons accountable for the process or procedure concerned
* data is captured as close as possible to the point of origin to minimise the cost, delay and possibility of error introduced in transcription and similar intermediate processes
* there is a division of responsibilities in all financial and financially related applications to obviate the possibility of fraud
* there is an effective audit trail in all commercial applications
* reports are provided on an exception basis to highlight the need for action or attention
* proven formulae are used in all calculations, e.g. as in the calculation of economic order quantities in a purchasing system.

(f) Is easy to use

A number of features make a system easy to use (both from a users' and from a computer operations viewpoint) and help to contribute to its success. Many of these points have already been discussed, but all are listed here for completeness. The main features which make a system easy to use are:

* it is user friendly
* it is reliable
* it fails safe
* it interfaces well with other systems
* it is operationally viable.

(i) It is user friendly (see Chapter 10). In particular this means that the man–machine interface is carefully designed so no difficulty is experienced in generating input to the system or interpreting output received from it. Well-structured user manuals and training programs are also important in securing user friendliness.

(ii) It is reliable. Reliability is a prized feature in any application. Apart from the avoidance of difficulties it engenders a feeling of confidence in users, which greatly increases the credibility of the system and indeed the data processing department as a whole.

(iii) It fails safe. In the event of hardware or software errors the application fails in such a way that restoration is not difficult. This will mean that good logging procedures, checkpoint and restart facilities are included in the system and that all key fields in the transaction data are validated prior to the processing to prevent corruption of the master records.

(iv) It interfaces well to other systems. Many difficulties will be experienced with applications that do not interface well with other systems. From an operational point of view this will often mean problems with data sets; for the users it may mean problems with reconciliation of results, transcription of input formats, use of differing codes for different systems or, for data communications systems, awkward terminal procedures when the interface between communications and applications software is negotiated. Needless to say successful applications are those with well-designed and simple interfaces to other systems!

(v) It is operationally viable. Operational viability in this context relates to the ease with which the computer operations department can operate the system on a routine basis. Here again good documentation (including instructions) is important, but to this must be added, *inter alia*:

* good output stationery design (to facilitate accurate printing and subsequent decollating, guillotining, etc.)
* good input forms design and accurate form completion (to facilitate accurate data capture)
* intelligent use of checkpoint and restart facilities
* sensible division into separate jobs (to obviate unnecessary operator intervention or time-consuming set-up)
* clear diagnostic or error messages
* maintainability in the event of failure.

(g) Is designed with full user co-operation

In the last resort data processing is almost always a service function and the applications developed are and will remain the user's systems. Full confidence on the part of the users that the system will indeed meet their requirements is, to say the least, unlikely unless they (or members of the same user organisation) have been actively involved during its specification. There is also a psychological point in that most people tend to be nervous about using new tools especially if these tools (as is often the case with computer systems) are of a type basically unfamiliar to the user. Such nervousness or fear can be most readily dispelled by the familiarity that comes from close and continuing involvement in the development phases.

Active involvement in systems development should therefore be sought from all levels of user staff: from user management to demonstrate their commitment to the system (and therefore implicitly to the changes it will necessarily introduce) and from other grades to reduce or eliminate the fear of change as well as to ensure the design of a system which truly meets user needs.

16.2 Types of Application

Applications of data processing may be classified in many ways, but three of the most useful are:

* system purpose
* processing mode
* processing location.

(a) System purpose

Applications systems can usually be categorised as being either routine operational systems or information systems. Routine operational systems are those from which the output directly satisfies an identifiable business function such as the printing of invoices, the preparation of payslips, acceptance of orders, etc. Information systems, on the other hand, produce information which is subsequently used to administer, manage, control or decide upon some facet of the business activities of the organisation. Examples include sales and personnel statistics systems. In many cases systems will include elements of both categories, but one will usually be found to be more important than the other.

The significance of the distinction lies in the way in which the data is regarded. For routine operational systems accuracy and economy are usually of paramount importance, but in many instances information systems may be more valuable if they sacrifice some level of accuracy for timeliness. This is because information of this type tends to lose value the longer it is delayed. To borrow a concept from nuclear physics, the 'half life' (i.e. the time which it takes to decay to half its original value) is short. Where it is difficult or impossible (or just too expensive) to collect all the original data in a short time frame there may be a trade-off between the delay incurred by demanding higher levels of accuracy and the value of the information produced. For example, sales statistics in the food-processing industry assume particular importance during special sales campaigns (e.g. television advertising, point-of-sale displays and/or special offers). Early information can help decision-making on production and distribution questions. It may therefore be worthwhile to produce statistics for either a limited region or ignoring some of the slower-to-

Fig 16.1 principal modes of data processing

Mode	Sub-modes	Major characteristics	Typical use
Batch		Periodic processing of grouped or batched input	Financial systems, payroll
	Remote batch	As above, with input generated, batched, controlled, entered and output remotely from the computer on which processing is performed	As above – especially where the organisation concerned has a central head office or administration centre and remote operational units, e.g. factories
	Off-line data transmission	As above, with the remote equipment off-line from the host computer	
On-line		Operation or equipment directly linked to a computer system which immediately accepts any stimulus from that operation or equipment	Data collection, order entry, etc., with subsequent processing on a periodic basis
	Interactive systems	Operator and computer respond to stimuli from each other so that process is completed in a series of small steps	Problem-solving applications, complex calculations, inquiry systems using data banks maintained as a commercial or public service
	Time-sharing	As above with multiple individual users	
Real-time		An on-line system with immediate processing and/or control as a result of the data input	
	Human intervention systems	As above, with a human being included in the complete processing loop, e.g. a clerk, using a terminal as an intergral part of the work performed	Airline and other reservation systems
	Process control	As above, without human intervention in the processing loop	Industrial process control, e.g. water treatment, monitoring and control, chemical plant control, etc.

arrive data (e.g. sales returns from remote districts) rather than wait for 100 per cent accuracy. The balance between accuracy and timeliness is one that can only be decided by the user management concerned, but in these circumstances it should be among the alternatives offered by the data processing department.

(b) Processing mode

To meet the diversity of applications requirements that exist a variety of data processing methods or modes have been developed. Three principal modes may be distinguished:

* batch
* on-line
* real time.

The major characteristics of these modes and their principal subdivisions are shown in Figure 16.1 and will be discussed in detail in Chapters 17 and 18.

(c) Processing location

Applications may also be categorised by the location at which they are processed. The two main classifications in this category are centralised and distributed. Centralised processing referrs to applications for which all the data is channelled to a specific computer or location for processing. *Distributed processing* refers to the situation where different elements of the same application are carried out on different computers usually, though not always, with selected or summarised data being forwarded to another computer (which may or may not be one involved in the initial processing) for further computation. The specific characteristics of distributed systems will be discussed in Chapter 19.

17 Batch-Processing Systems

The initial applications of computers to commercial data processing were all of a batch nature and although the other processing modes have gained in importance much of the routine work in most installations is still performed in this way. Nor can this be considered as merely a legacy from a less-sophisticated age of data processing since for some types of application batch processing is the natural and most effective approach.

What are the characteristics of the batch-processing mode? Batch processing means that individual transactions are grouped or batched and processed together periodically. The frequency at which the batches of transactions are processed will depend on a number of factors including the nature of the application, the volume of transactions and the loading of other work being performed on the computer. Daily, weekly, four-weekly, calendar month, quarterly and annual intervals are all common.

A further characteristic of batch processing is that each transaction in turn is subjected to a series of processing steps and the processing of that transaction is completed (or at least reaches a definable intermediate stage) before work starts on the next transaction. There is thus a repetitive sequence in which processing takes place.

17.1 The Advantages and Disadvantages of Batch Processing

A number of distinct advantages and disadvantages flow from the very nature of batch processing and it is important to understand these if the best use is to be made of this processing mode. The main factors concerned are:

* the division of work into runs
* the timing of processing runs
* recovery techniques
* economics.

(a) The division of work into runs

The essentially sequential nature of batch processing readily permits the total processing requirement to be divided into separate segments or computer runs (indeed the capacity of early computers and the data storage and media available usually necessitated this). In some ways this is a disadvantage in that it breaks the flow of operations and requires more activity by the computer operators, but from other viewpoints it is a positive advantage. Thus it is possible, for example, to separate all data validation and editing into a separate computer run. This routine can then be performed using all the transaction data: the 'clean' data (i.e. that which passes all the checks) can be set aside (usually on a tape or disk file) for future processing. Any transactions which produced error conditions can then be vetted and amended as necessary and subjected to a further validation run. This process can be repeated until all the transaction data is 'clean' and then, and only then, is the main processing carried out.

The division of computer processing into discrete runs also makes the reconciliation of data produced from different sources somewhat easier. Because processing only occurs at discrete intervals it is possible to pinpoint the status of a record (for example, a customer account) more easily than if it is constantly subject to change as in the other processing modes.

(b) The timing of processing runs

The division of the processing work into separate runs and the fact that these only take place at defined intervals introduces a number of other points beyond those already considered. The first of these concerns the frequency of the runs themselves. In some cases this is almost self-evident. For example, where staff are paid weekly, a weekly interval for payroll processing is natural. On the other hand, for transactions which occur more or less continuously, periodic processing introduces a delay between the origin of the data and the availability of the information derived from it. In general the longer this delay the less valuable the information becomes. Stock records produced monthly, for example, are soon too inaccurate to be of use if stock movements occur on a daily basis. Conversely, there are operational inefficiencies if batch runs are scheduled too frequently, computer set-up, data control and scheduling overheads being incurred. Striking the correct balance between these two conflicting factors is not easy and requires careful thought during the systems development process.

A second point associated with the periodic nature of batch-processing runs is that there is tendency for the computer workload to peak at intervals. Most weekly reports run from Monday to Friday and are therefore processed on the computer on the Monday or Tuesday of the following week. Similarly, most monthly reports run from the first to the last day of the calendar month and are processed on the computer during the first week of the following month. Imagine the first week of a new month when the computer centre has to process both month-end and weekly reports; the situation becomes even worse at quarterly or year-end periods! Installed computer capacity and staffing levels often respond to these pressures, but it should be noted that in many cases there is little or no need for all applications having the same cycle (weekly, monthly, etc.) to be processed at the same time. Thus it may be possible for statistical reports on salesmen's performance, for example, to be prepared on a monthly cycle say from the 15th of the month to the 14th of the month. Indeed there may even be an advantage in this case because bonuses could then be paid at the month end, i.e. two weeks after the end of the sales performance cycle rather than the more common four weeks! Although a little planning and imagination can do much to alleviate this problem (performing validation runs throughout a period as data accumulates is another worth-while move) it is likely to remain the case that the bulk of batch processing will tend to peak at intervals. The need to reconcile many types of records, and the fact that all accounting or financial management systems are likely to be given equal priority, are prime reasons for this situation.

(c) Recovery techniques
The very nature of batch processing tends to simplify the provision of recovery procedures. It is always possible to restart the process if, for any reason (e.g. hardware or software failure), it is unsuccessful, by going back and repeating the whole process. This requires, of course, that the original data and security copies of the files used have been retained as discussed in Chapter 15. This is invariably simpler than keeping track of a moving target, as is necessary in the other processing modes. Where a batch-processing run is known to take a long time it is common practice to establish *checkpoints* at intervals. Such a practice entails dumping security copies of the files in use, together with any necessary control totals or *restart* data, at the defined checkpoints. In the event of a failure it will not be necessary to restart the run from the beginning, but merely from the last checkpoint. This technique can be valuable, but should be thoroughly documented to ensure that the computer operators know exactly what is required when performing the dumping or restart operations.

(d) Economics
The inherent simplicity of batch-processing systems especially in regard to recovery procedures and testing means that, in general, they are quicker and therefore cheaper to develop than systems using the other processing modes.

17.2 Applications of Batch Processing

From the foregoing it will be appreciated that there are particular types of systems to which the batch-processing approach is most suited. In general these are systems which have a natural cycle, e.g. weekly payroll, or those which produce results which are only meaningful if accumulated and/or compared with other similar periods such as many statistical and trend analysis systems. Thus to tell a sales manager that 100 cases of product X have been sold in the past hour may not be very meaningful but to say 500 cases have been sold during the week and this compares with a weekly average of 400 cases and the figure of 350 cases in the same week last year may be very significant.

Most *transaction-oriented* systems incorporate a significant batch-reporting element. Thus in an on-line inventory control application, daily, weekly or other reports summarising stock movements are produced in batch mode.

It follows therefore, that batch processing tends to be most widely used in accounting and reporting types of application. Among the applications frequently processed in this manner are:

* payroll
* salaries
* sales statistics and analysis
* personnel statistics
* production recording
* bought ledger
* sales ledger
* customer accounts and invoicing
* invoice payment
* maintenance and other scheduling applications
* performance reporting
* bonus calculation.

In Figure 17.1 a simplified systems flowchart indicating the main features of a generalised sales statistics system is shown. It will be noticed that this flowchart illustrates the principle of having separate data validation runs before clean data is submitted for processing.

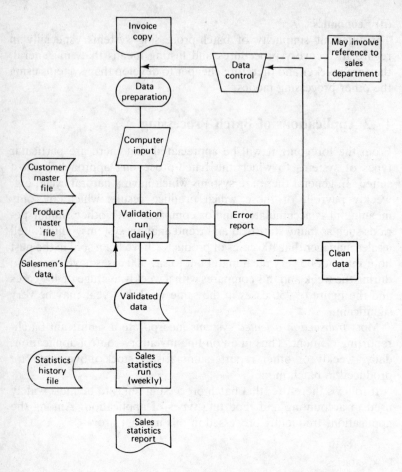

Fig 17.1   *a system flowchart for a typical batch processing sales statistics application (simplified)*

18 On-Line and Real Time Systems

18.1 **The Concepts of On-Line and Real Time**

Much confusion exists between the terms 'on-line' and 'real time', which are often used indiscriminately. The two concepts, are, however, quite distinct and though a system may be on-line it need not be real time. Conversely, a real-time system must, of necessity, be on-line so the term sometimes seen, 'on-line real time' (OLRT), is in fact tautological.

On-line may be defined as the direct linking of an operation or equipment to a computer system so that any stimulus provided by that operation or equipment is immediately *accepted* by the computer system ('acceptance' in this context may also include certain types of rejection where, for example, the computer system is overloaded).

Real time, by contrast, is the mode of processing where the stimulus provided by the external operation or equipment is immediately accepted *and processed* by the computer system.

Thus the key distinction between the two modes is the immediacy of processing of the input data by the computer. Moreover, in real-time systems the results of the computer processing are often, though not invariably, fed back to the source equipment or other output device to produce an action at that point.

It is sometimes difficult to determine in practice whether a commercial data processing system is actually operating in real time. Input messages may be queued awaiting processing if the computer system is already busy. It therefore becomes difficult to judge if the system is always real time or merely sometimes real time. There is thus a case for describing all such commercial data processing systems as on-line and reserving the term 'real time' for industrial process control and similar systems where processing (often used using a dedicated computer or a *high-priority interrupt*) is immediate. In practice, however, both terms are in such widespread use that there is little likelihood that the terms will always be correctly distinguished. The term *transaction processing* is also used to distinguish on-line and real time processing from batch processing.

18.2 **On-Line and Real Time Applications**

There is a wide and increasing range of both on-line and real time applications and in this section it is only possible to outline some of those that might be encountered.

(a) Interactive systems

An increasing amount of computer processing today is being performed in an *interactive* or *conversational* manner. In this approach a person seated at a VDU or other terminal device is provided with the full power of a computer. After the initial formalities of signing or *logging on* to the terminal and specifying which of the available options available on that computer he wishes to use, the individual is 'prompted' by the computer 'asking' for a response to a particular question. After the response is provided the computer will 'ask' for another response (perhaps more data or the specification of a parameter or the choice between specified options). The 'conversation' thus proceeds by a series of steps to the goal. The success of this approach is clearly dependent on the skill of the designer in providing a logical series of steps which is neither too stilted nor too rushed for the users concerned. The series of steps or choices is generally referred to as a '*menu*' and forms the basis of the operator/computer dialogue. Systems of this nature have been implemented on all types of computer from micros to the largest mainframes and cover a wide variety of uses. Among the uses are:

* statistical calculations
* stress and other engineering calcualtions
* discounted cash-flow analysis
* program writing
* inquiry response systems.

(b) On-line order entry with batch updating

One of the simpler applications of the on-line mode of processing is that of order entry with batch updating. In this application the objective is to provide quick acknowledgement to the customer that the order is being processed and that the goods will be dispatched as ordered. Variants of this approach are in use by a wide variety of companies in the food and distributive trades.

A typical implementation of this approach would involve the customer or perhaps the salesman when at the customer's premises ringing the company concerned. The phone call would be routed to a sales clerk with a VDU on his or her desk. The customer would provide certain basic data (customer identity code, etc.) which the sales clerk would key into the terminal. The computer would check that the identity code was valid and display the name and address of the customer on the VDU so that the sales clerk could positively confirm this data. After identity has been established, the customer reads out his order, item by item, specifying product number and quantity required. As each item is keyed in, the computer checks if stock is available and either acknowledges the order or displays a list of alternatives so the clerk can advise the customer along the lines: 'The medium-size package of Brand X is out of stock but we do have the small and large sizes.' The customer can then decide whether or not to choose one of the alternatives before proceeding to the next item on his order. The computer may also display details of any special offers or discounts currently being offered which the sales clerk can relate to the customer in an effort to increase the size of the order. When the order is complete the computer will calculate its value and check whether this and any outstanding balance on the customer's account exceed the approved credit limit. The sales clerk will then acknowledge the order and ring off.

The order which has been entered on-line will then be held on a computer file until later (probably immediately after office hours) when the actual processing takes place. This will include: printing instructions to the warehouse to pick the items ordered, printing dispatch documents and invoices and updating the customer account, the sales ledger, stock account and sales statistic files.

Note that, as outlined above, the on-line part of the system was only reading data and the actual updating of the files took place later. This approach avoids much of the complexity incurred (particularly in ensuring recoverability) when files are updated on-line.

It may be argued that by avoiding on-line updating much of the benefit of the system is lost. In the example given, what happens, for instance, if sales of the small-size pack of Brand X mean that it too is sold out by midday? This sort of problem can, however, be circumvented without going all the way to on-line updating of the master stock record. One approach is to produce a copy of the master stock record which is updated on-line and read to ascertain the availability of stock. Then when the end-of-day processing takes place to use the master stock record, and either reconcile that to the working copy or else create a new working copy for the following day. A second approach is merely to keep a running record of what has been sold during the day by item and each time an item is ordered to compute whether the balance of the overnight stock less orders so far today is sufficient to meet the current customer's demand.

Developments of this approach include the elimination of the sales clerk and the customer communicating directly with a 'talking computer'.

(c) On-line systems with on-line updating

Sometimes the data in the master files is so volatile that the approaches outlined above are not suitable and it is necessary that they are updated on-line. At this point there is a quantum jump in application complexity since it is not only essential to keep track of which transactions have been processed, but also what stage they have reached in processing. This is necessary since software or hardware failure may occur during the processing of any transaction.

Special care also needs to be taken where there are multiple users (e.g. several clerks using terminals) to prevent two or more updates occurring simultaneously – a situation which could lead to most inaccurate results. This potential danger may be guarded against by '*locking*' parts of the data to prevent others using them at the same time. Even here care must be taken to avoid a situation where all users are waiting for one another to finish with some 'locked' data – the consequence of this so-called '*deadly embrace*' being that no one can continue processing!

Where truly critical it may also be necessary to provide instantaneous change-over from one computer to another as, for example, when a hardware fault occurs. This requires not only duplicated hardware, but also software and data and complex switching equipment and programs to transfer processing to the standby computer.

Techniques to overcome all these problems exist and are in regular use. The point is that anything which creates complexity will significantly increase the development and operating costs of the system and should not, therefore, be incurred unless absolutely necessary.

(d) Data logging

One of the simplest types of on-line system is a data-logging application. In these applications one or more recording devices are on-line to a computer which either '*polls*' them regularly to check and record their status, e.g. checking temperatures at intervals or alternatively recording data when it is supplied by the recording device. Many of the recording devices used in this type of application are of an analog rather than a digital nature; the systems problems are often those of interfacing the hardware rather than those more commonly encountered in commercial data processing.

(e) Process control systems

The true real time systems are those that react immediately to a stimulus provided by an operation or piece of equipment linked to the computer. A major category of real time systems is that of process control. These applications carry the concept of real time one step further in that they react to the stimulus in such a way that a physical action is taken automatically and immediately.

For such systems the typical input/process/output sequence of data processing becomes: measure/process/react.

Some examples will provide an indication of the systems in use.

In many kinds of industrial process heating is a crucial factor. Not only is the heat attained during the process critical, but the duration for which it is applied and the evenness with which it is applied are also vital. These parameters are important in such diverse processes as industrial baking, steel furnaces, glass furnaces and brick kilns. These factors can not only determine the point for completion of the process, but also the quality of the product and the economics of its production (excess energy inputs increase costs but may not affect either quantity or quality of the product. Moreover, extra time spent on production means less product in any given period.)

For processes of this nature the development of process control systems which monitor temperatures at different parts of the oven, furnace or kiln and control the heating of it and determine the optimum time for terminating the process are a major contribution to efficiency.

Here again the major problems are likely to be encountered in interfacing the monitoring equipment to the computer (which is often dedicated to that process) and especially in determining the parameters governing the production of the optimum product mix.

Another application of process control is the monitoring of industrial effluent. Many of these applications started as relatively simple data logging systems monitoring the levels of various chemicals in effluent and have since been upgraded to control the release of the effluent so that specified levels of the chemicals are not exceeded. As well as controlling the release of effluent some systems also control the flow of water or other fluid to dilute its concentration. Process control applications can also be found in chemical plants, controlling conveyors and warehouses in manufacturing plants, in aircraft and increasingly in houses and cars providing such specialised services as environmental control (air-conditioning, exhaust pollution control) and energy-saving (optimising fuel flow). Few, if any, of these are data processing applications in the normal, commercial meaning of the term, but they do represent an important and increasing part of the total field of computing.

A final category of system which should be mentioned at this point is numerical control of machine tools. This application which was among the earliest developments of industrial computing provides as output from highly specialised computer programs, instructions which enable a machine tool to carry out a complex sequence of operations. Again, such applications are outside the realm of conventional data processing, but in some organisations impinge on the work of the data processing department.

18.3 The Advantages and Disadvantages of On-Line and Real Time Systems

The above examples should have served to highlight the most important characteristics of on-line and real time systems and therefore draw attention to their major advantages and disadvantages.

The overwhelming advantage is that of timeliness. Both the on-line and real time approaches harness the power of computing to problem-solution when it is needed – a feature that batch processing can only provide for some categories of application. Taken together, the on-line and real time modes of processing offer a range of approaches which can be tailored to suit a wide variety of situations.

The major disadvantage is that of complexity and hence cost. Although with modern equipment (which may in any case be set up especially for this type of work) the simpler forms of on-line system may be little if any dearer than the equivalent batch application, this is not true for the more sophisticated approaches. It is thus more than ever important that the systematic evaluation of the alternatives available and their economics, described in Chapter 8, are followed.

19 Distributed Systems

19.1 **Distributed Processing**

In the preceding chapter we mentioned in passing that many real-time systems, especially those of a process control nature, operated on dedicated computers. Part of the data produced in such dedicated systems may, however, be important input to one or more conventional data processing systems. Such a situation leads naturally to demands to link the dedicated system to the main data processing computer, perhaps initially by means of off-line data communications, but before long by means of on-line or even real time communication.

At the same time the increasing use of remote terminals connected to a central computer will often result in a situation where large volumes of data are transmitted to the central location and large volumes of information need to be returned from it. Much of the information is typically only of use at the terminal location. There is thus pressure to relieve any overloading of the communications link of the central computer by performing, at the remote location, such part of the processing as is of local interest only.

Both the situations outlined above (and which may be experienced at the same time within an organisation) tend to lead to the development of a network of computers, terminals and communications links in which the transmission and processing of data is optimised to meet the needs of individual locations. A distributed system is then an approach to data processing in which processing and data storage tend to be located at or near the points where the data occurs or the information is used, but with communications links to allow access to and from other processing facilities and data storage as required. Depending on the applications requirements of the organisations the resulting distributed system may be:

* hierarchical
* star type

(i) Hierarchical distributed systems. Hierarchical distributed systems are the more frequently encountered and a typical example is outlined in Figure 19.1. This shows the type of distributed system that might be used by a manufacturing concern with a head office and three separate factories. Component parts are produced in factories A and B and assembled in factory C.

The head office mainframe computer is used to establish a production schedule, use the sales forecasts produced and then process the schedule against the bill of materials (listing the quantity and type of each sub-component required) and the company's stock record, to order the materials to be delivered to the separate factories at the correct time. The central computer also communicates that part of the production schedule and details of the goods on order to the appropriate factory computer (which may be another mainframe, a maxi or large minicomputer). The factory computers monitor the receipt of material and also the production achieved at that factory. Summary or exception data (i.e. variations from the plan) are provided by the factory computer to the head office computer and are used as input to the next iteration of the production schedule.

Using this approach the organisation concerned can provide computing support at a local level and yet retain control of production. Any spare capacity on the factory computers may be utilised on applications of purely local interest, e.g. scheduling the machine shop within factory A, or for processing applications which although common are sufficiently different to prevent centralised processing. An example of this type might be payroll if the employees at head office are salaried while those at factory A are on piece rates, those at factory B on an individual bonus system and those at factory C are paid according to a group bonus system. Alternatively, where all input is generated locally and most if not all the output is required locally, but the application is common to all locations, then a common system may be developed and implemented separately at each location. A system of this type, operating in the environment described above, might be employee time recording or warehouse control.

Hierarchies may have more than two levels. In the example above, each of the factory computers might in turn have subordinate mini- or microcomputers to perform specific aspects of the work delegated to the factory computer. Thus a mini computer to control an automatic warehouse might be attached to the computer at factory A. Similarly, the head office computer might in its turn be connected to a group headquarters computer to which it periodically reports production and sales data.

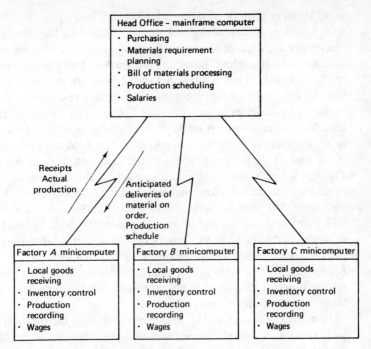

Factories *A* and *B* produce components, for example engines and bodies respectively, which are assembled at factory *C* (in this example into cars).

Fig 19.1   *a typical hierarchical distributed processing system in a manufacturing environment (simplified overview)*

(ii) Star-type distributed systems. Star-type distributed systems arise when there is no constant hierarchical dependency betwen the applications run at one location and another, as in the example just considered. Thus they arise when any work not performed at its own geographical location or system is just as likely to access another computer or the data held on it as that computer is itself likely to access the first one. The purest form of star-distributed system is shown in Figure 19.2.

As remarked above, such systems are less commonly encountered than hierarchical distributed systems, but they do exist both in pure and modified forms.

One example might be where each computer is located at a university or research establishment. The majority of processing will be performed locally so that most routine computation work will be performed on the computer geographically closest to the user. However, to avoid duplicating special data by storing it at each location it may be agreed to hold such data for different disciplines at different locations. Students, research workers and staff for each discipline, however, are spread at all the locations in the network. Thus a student located near computer *A* may want to access data held on computer *D* while a research worker located physically near to computer *C* may need to add to the data held on computer *B* while another research worker located near computer *D* might want to correlate data held on computers *A*, *C* and *D*. If all computers are interconnected as shown in Figure 19.2 then each individual can access the data he or she requires by means of a terminal attached to the 'local' computer. Not only data can be accessed in this way. Special programs which are only run on one of the computers (perhaps because it is larger or faster than the others or has a particular software package or compiler which the others lack) can also be accessed. Moreover, at least in theory, if one computer is overloaded while one or more of the others is underutilised, work can be diverted from one computer to another.

In many of these cases the source of the data or the location at which work is actually processed may be transparent to the actual user. That is to say the individual user may not know where his data comes from or where his work is processed.

Fig 19.2   *a simple star-distributed system*

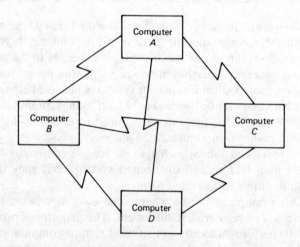

19.2 **Designing distributed systems**

The impression may have been gained so far that distributed systems are not designed, but like Topsy they 'just growed'. No doubt some do evolve in this way, but if they do the achievement of a system which was both functional in meeting the users' requirements and did so economically would be a matter of pure luck.

To be both effective and efficient distributed systems require very careful design. This is not easy, especially since the development of the technology may be altering the economics of the system very rapidly.

In addition to all other problems and considerations that need to be taken into account as for any other system, distributed systems also require detailed considerations of:

* control software
* network design
* standardisation
* application software
* data storage.

(a) Control software
It will be readily appreciated that data cannot go from place to place within a network without some form of control. With the first type of distributed system considered this is not much of a problem since the rigid hierarchy and the *de facto* 'master' status of the head office computer naturally leads to a solution in which that computer controls the movement of data within the hierarchy. In more complex networks, however, it is not so easy. One solution is to designate one computer as the 'master' for this purpose, but this of course tends to undermine the reliability and security inherent in the structure since in the event of failure by that computer the entire network collapses. The solution to that particular problem is usually to duplicate the essential elements of the control software and to maintain them on several computers in the network activating them in a predetermined manner in the event of failure.

An alternative approach which may be adopted if the volume of traffic between computers is low is to have a series of 'bilateral agreements' whereby traffic between any two computers is regulated by them without recourse to a 'master'. This approach, however, requires that each computer maintains an up-to-date record of the availability of data and facilities elsewhere and is not a practical approach in many situations.

(b) Network design

Network design is a delicate and changing balance between communications, hardware and software costs bounded by the parameters of application requirements and technical feasibility. The trick is to create a framework in which individual components can be changed without disturbing the entire structure should this become necessary for applications or economic reasons. Thus, for example, it should be possible to upgrade the data storage associated with one computer in the network without causing difficulties elsewhere. Similarly, the relative processing capabilities of the various computers should be changeable without difficulty.

The details of network design are beyond the scope of the present work, and the reader who needs further information on this topic is referred to the Bibliography. The type of network that may be developed to support a variety of applications in a distributed processing environment is shown in Figure 19.3.

(c) Standardisation

In practice the solution of many of the problems outlined in the preceding paragraph is achieved by standardisation. In a distributed system standardisation is required at many levels, including:

* line protocols
* hardware interfaces
* software access control methods
* recovery procedures
* inquiry languges
* file access methods
* data coding systems.

Standardisation may, to some extent, limit the choice of equipment considered for inclusion in a distributed system. For example, a minicomputer purchased from company *X* may not use the same *line protocols* (data transfer standards) as a mainframe computer supplied by company *Y* (or even for that matter supplied by company *X*). Although ways round such apparent incompatibilities can usually be found, the cost and technical difficulty (i.e. the allocation of resources that could be used for other purposes) will only rarely make such moves advisable.

(d) Application software

Since the concept of distributed processing is to put computer power where it is needed, it follows that the applications designed to work in such an environment should more than ever reflect the needs of the

Fig 19.3 a network developed to support a variety of data processing applications

- Remote mainframe
- 200 bps — Multiple data collection devices
- 4800 bps (leased line) — Minicomputer
- 40 Kbps (leased line)
- 4800 bps (leased line) — Minicomputer — 200 bps — Multiple data collection devices
- Mainframe computer (with back-up)
- 9600 bps (leased line)
- 4800 bps (leased line) — Minicomputer — 2400 bps — Multiple inquiry, response and file updating terminals
- Concentrator
- 4800 bps (leased line) — Minicomputer — 2400 bps — Multiple inquiry, response and file updating terminals
- 4800 bps (leased line) — Minicomputer — 2400 bps — Multiple inquiry, response and file updating terminals
- 600 bps (dial up) — Time-sharing terminal
- 600 bps (dial up) — Time-sharing terminal
- 600 bps (dial up) — Time-sharing terminal
- 600 bps (dial up) — Time-sharing terminal
- 600 bps (dial up) — Time-sharing terminal

end-user. This outcome, however, may run contrary to any desire the organisation as a whole has to uniformity or standardisation of approach and can certainly lead to 'reinventing the wheel' many times. There is thus a requirement in most distributed processing environments for some uniformity or common approach to systems development. This may take the form of centralised development being imposed on the individual locations, co-operative development between locations or the adoption by other locations of an application already developed elsewhere. In turn this may also lead to requirements to standardise equipment.

In our manufacturing company there was no requirement for the computers installed at the three factories to be the same – still less identical. If, however, applications are developed to run at each factory, e.g. time recording, then it is pointless to have to recode the same programs merely because another type of computer is in use. Thus there will be applications pressures (as well as commercial and staffing pressures) towards the adoption of common equipment.

(e) Data storage

Throughout this book the advantages of modern approaches to data management have been highlighted and it might be thought that many of these could be sacrificed if a distributed system is implemented and data is returned as far as possible to the location at which it is most frequently used. This fear is not, however, substantiated: modern data management approaches and distributed systems are compatible. What is required is a two-level approach to the problem. First, an overall organisation view is required and it should be part of the function of the data strategist (see Chatper 13) to determine what data is required to be stored at which location. Security and operational requirements (access time or cost of transfer) may dictate that some data is held in more than once place but the essential point is that data is still managed as a resource. Second, at each individual location the physical storage of data (the concern of the data-base designer) should reflect the applications requirements and be subject to the disciplines discussed in Chapter 12.

19.3 The Advantages and Disadvantages of Distributed Systems

In the preceding sections the characteristics of distributed systems have been discussed and illustrated by means of some examples. In this section the principal advantages and disadvantages of the approaches will be reviewed. The main points are:

* user convenience
* flexibility
* complexity
* staffing
* economics
* organisation impact.

(a) User convenience

In the last resort the purpose of a distributed system is to improve the data processing service to its users. If this is achieved in the broad sense then the system is basically a success. The ability to place computing power where it is required must therefore be judged an advantage. It should be noted, however, that if the same results from the user's viewpoint can be achieved by using a terminal to a remote computer, then the decision whether to adopt a centralised computer with terminals or a proper distributed system is essentially transparent. The choice should be based on economic or reliability grounds rather than user convenience.

(b) Flexibility

As we have seen a feature of a well-designed distributed processing network is its ability to respond readily to changing applications requirements. Combinations of processing capabilities and data are placed at the user's disposition in a flexible manner which may be used as requirements dictate.

(c) Complexity

It has already been commented that designing networks is not an easy task. Moreover, the discussions on control software and standardisation should have indicated that distributed processing can introduce a level of complexity into data processing that had not previously been reached. The compensating advantage is that in many cases distribution may be introduced incrementally with the installation of intelligent terminals being succeeded by microcomputers and communications links being upgraded or changed as required (although such items often have a long lead time between order and installation).

(d) Staffing

Distributed systems require some form of distributed staffing. At the operational level each computer obviously requires its own operating staff, but problems may arise in terms of development staff. If all development staff are centralised urgent maintenance can become a problem and one of the user's benefits of control over his (computing) destiny is to a considerable extent eroded. Conversely, if all development staff are decentralised problems will be encountered in establishing and maintaining standards and in data management. At first sight the idea of a central cadre of staff to deal with such matters as data management, standards (see Chapter 13 for a description of these tasks) and common application development with small decentralised teams to deal with purely local applications and essential maintenance might appear to offer the solution, but this too presents problems. With such an arrangement it is all too easy to create first- and second-class analysts and programmers, differing not so much in ability or objective worth to the organisation, but in terms of breadth of training, status, grading, opportunities for promotion and other personnel distinctions.

There is no ideal solution to this problem, but a centralised team with a few decentralised members, coupled with careful training, job rotation, career development and planning can provide a satisfactory compromise between the pressure for full centralisation and total decentralisation.

(e) Economics

It was long thought that economics of scale applied to computers. Indeed *Grosch's Law* (so named after Dr Herbert Grosch, who first enunciated it) stated that computing power increased fourfold when hardware cost doubled. Such a 'law' would seem to offer overwhelming support for centralisation of all possible data processing on to the smallest number of mainframes. Yet distributed processing effectively seeks to reverse this situation and distribute computing power to locations as near as possible to the end-user. The answer to this conundrum lies in the fact that Grosch's Law does not take into account the costs of moving data to a centralised processor or in transporting the information to the place where it is required. Moreover, since it was formulated the improvements in the price/performance ratio of medium-size and small computers have, if anything, been even more impressive than those of large-scale computers. At the same time as large-scale computers have become even larger, increasing requirements of the operating systems and the specialist staff necessary to support them have altered the economic comparison *vis-à-vis* the smallest computers where much if not all of the necessary support can be provided by less-specialised staff – perhaps even the user himself! At the same time because of their development history micro- and minicomputers rarely require specialised environments in which to work.

All these factors adjust if not refute the basic conclusion from Grosch's Law that as much work as possible should be centralised.

What needs to be carefully evaluated before implementing a distributed system is the total cost of hardware, software, communications links and support staff for each of the alternatives considered. There is a tendency for the support costs to be underestimated and it is particularly important that these are realistically estimated.

(f) Organisation impact

One often unforeseen result of the introduction of a distributed processing system is a shift in the power balance within the organisation. 'Knowledge itself is power' is Bacon's well-known phrase; the distribution of knowledge means a distributed system may therefore move power away from the centre of the organisation to middle or local management. To this extent distributed systems can modify the impact of data processing on the organisation discussed in Chapter 3.

The considerations of the balance of organisational power should be outside the purely objective considerations of data processing. All too often they impinge on the way in which technical decisions are resolved, and the data processing practitioner is advised to be aware of these considerations.

Bibliography

This bibliography is divided into six parts. The first five parts correspond to the five parts of the book and list material which complements the treatment of the specific topics covered. Part VI of the bibliography lists glossaries and dictionaries of data processing terms.

Part I   An introduction to data processing

Boehm, B., *Software Engineering Economics* (Englewood Cliffs, NJ, Prentice-Hall, 1981).

Buchanan, D. A., Boddy, D., *et al.*, *Organisations in the Computer Age* (London, Gower, 1983).

O'Leary, T. J. and Williams, B. K., *Computers and Information Processing* (Menlo Park, Ca., Benjamin Cummings, 1985).

Strassman, P., *Information Payoff* (London, Gower, 1985).

Part II   The tools of data processing

Aitkin, J. K., *Computer Science*, 2nd edn (Plymouth, Macdonald & Evans, 1980).

Lee, G., *From Hardware to Software – an Introduction to Computers* (London, Macmillan, 1982).

Morris Mano, M., *Computer Systems Architecture*, 2nd edn (Englewood Cliffs, NJ, Prentice-Hall, 1982).

Petersson, J. L. and Silberschatz, A., *Operating Systems Concepts*, 2nd edn (Reading, Mass., Addison-Wesley, 1985).

Wright, G. G. L., *Mastering Computers* (London, Macmillan, 1982).

Part III   Development systems

Boar, B. H., *Application Prototyping* (New York, Wiley, 1984).

Deen, S. M., *Principles and Practice of Data Base Systems* (London, Macmillan, 1985).

Galitz, W., *Handbook of Screen Format Design* (Amsterdam, North-Holland, 1985).

Gane, C. and Sarson, T., *Structured Systems Analysis: Tools and Techniques* (Englewood Cliffs, NJ, Prentice-Hall, 1979).

Gosling, P. E., *Mastering Computer Programming*, 2nd edn (London, Macmillan, 1985).

Keller, R., *The Practice of Structured Analysis* (New York, Yourdon, 1984).

Martin, J., *Computer Networks and Distributed Processing* (Englewood Cliffs, NJ, Prentice-Hall, 1981).

Martin, J., *Strategic Data Planning Methodologies* (Englewood Cliffs, NJ, Prentice-Hall, 1982).

Martin, J. and McClure, C., *Diagramming Techniques for Analysts and Programmers* (Englewood Cliffs, NJ, Prentice-Hall, 1985).

Martin, J. and McClure, C., *Structured Techniques for Computing* (Englewood Cliffs, NJ, Prentice-Hall, 1985).

McFadden, F. R. and Hoffer, J. A., *Data Base Management* (Menlo Park, Ca., Benjamin Cummings, 1985).

Page-Jones, M., *The Practical Guide to Structured Systems Design* (New York, Yourdon, 1980).

Sherman, K., *Data Communications – A User's Guide* (Reston, Va., Reston, 1981).

Stallings, W., *Data and Computer Communications* (London, Collier Macmillan, 1985).

Yourdon, E. and Constantine, L. L., *Structured Design*, 2nd edn (New York, Yourdon, 1978).

Part IV   Making data processing work

Brill, A. E., *Building Controls into Structured Systems* (New York, Yourdon, 1983).

Brooks, F. P. Jr, *The Mythical Man Month* (Reading, Mass., Addison-Wesley, 1975).

DeMarco, T., *Controlling Software Projects* (New York, Yourdon, 1983).

Donaldson, H., *Successful Management of Computer Projects* (London, Associated Business Press, 1978).

Graef, M. and Greiller, R., *Organisation and Management of a Computer Centre* (London, Collier Macmillan, 1985).

Lane, V. P., *Security of Computer-based Information Systems* (London, Macmillan, 1984).

Myers, G. J., *The Art of Software Testing* (New York, Wiley Interscience, 1979).

Roeske, E. G., *The Data Factory* (New York, Yourdon, 1983).

Yourdon, E. *Managing the Systems Life Cycle* (New York, Yourdon, 1983).

Part V   The applications of data processing

Anderson, R. G., *Case Studies in Systems Design* (Plymouth, Macdonald & Evans, 1980).

Gessner, R. A. (ed. Cerra, F.) *Manufacturing Information Systems* (New York, Wiley, 1984).

Goldstein, L. J., *Computers and their Applications* (Englewood Cliffs, NJ, Prentice-Hall, 1986).

Hirschheim, R. A., *Office Automation* (Reading, Mass., Addison-Wesley, 1985).

Kroeber, D. W. and Watson, H. J., *Computer Based Information Systems* (London, Collier Macmillan, 1986).

Martin, J., *Design and Strategy for Distributed Data Processing* (Englewood Cliffs, NJ, Prentice-Hall, 1981).

Wilson, P., *Designing Systems for People* (Manchester, NCC, 1980).

Part VI   Glossaries and dictionaries

Chandor, A., with Graham, J. and Williamson, R., *The Penguin Dictionary of Computers*, 3rd edn (Harmondsworth, Penguin Books, 1985).

Longley, D. and Shain, M., *Dictionary of Information Technology*, 2nd edn (London, Macmillan, 1985).

Rosenberg, J. M., *Dictionary of Computers, Data Processing and Telecommunications* (New York, Wiley, 1984).

Glossary

access time. The time between the issuing of an instruction to move data and the moment that data has arrived in its new location. Used for both backing and mainstorage. Access time is measured in milliseconds, microseconds, nanoseconds or picoseconds as appropriate.

acoustic coupler. A device attached to a terminal which accepts the handset of a standard telephone and enables a free-standing device to be used in conjunction with a telephone as a computer terminal.

ALU see ARITHMETIC LOGIC UNIT

analog digital converter. A device that converts analog (i.e. continuously variable) signals into discrete or digital signals for use in a data processing computer.

application package. A generalised software package (or series of programs) produced to meet the needs of a variety of data processing users. Thus a commercial organisation may produce a system for calculating pay in the belief that this is a requirement of many companies and offer it as an applications package which the users can run on their own computers.

arithmetic logic unit (ALU). That part of a central processor which performs the arithmetic and logic functions.

assembler. A computer program which converts a program written in an assembly or low-level language into machine code that the computer can understand. Conversion is mainly on a one-for-one basis, i.e. each statement in the program is converted into a machine instruction.

audit trail. The path or series of procedures and records by which any single transaction can be traced through a computer system. Audit trails are of particular importance in financial systems.

backing store. Any storage device added to a computer beyond the immediately usable main storage. Backing store includes peripheral devices as well as additional memory banks added to the central processor.

bar code. Codes consisting of light and dark marks which may be optically read.

baud.   Measure of speed at which data may be transmitted over a communications link. In most cases the baud rating is the same as the BITS PER SECOND (bps) rating.

binary.   The system of arithmetic using only the digits 0 and 1. Used extensively on computers because the digits may be represented by the electrical states ON and OFF.

bits.   The term BITS is often used as a contraction of BINARY DIGITS.

bits per second (bps).   Measure of speed at which data may be transmitted over a communications link.

Boolean algebra.   System of logic developed by George Boole in which an algebraic notation is used to express logical relationships. Boole expressed these relationships in such a way that results can be expressed in a simple YES or NO manner. Widely used in computers for the same reason as binary arithmetic.

buffering.   The technique whereby data or information is stored for a short time before being released for the next process. May be used, for example, on a terminal to enable error correction to take place before data is input into a computer or to enable a comunication link to be utilised efficiently.

bus.   A path by which communication is achieved between a central processor and other devices.

byte.   A group of BITS (usually 8) taken together and treated as a unit in a computer.

Central Processor Unit (CPU).   That part of a computer configuration which controls the operation of the entire system and executes the instructions contained in the programme. The CPU includes a CONTROL UNIT, ARITHMETIC LOGIC UNIT and MAIN MEMORY.

channel
  1. a longitudinal subdivision of a magnetic tape used to record bits of data at a density depending on the device in use.
  2. A path along which data is moved between a central processor and peripherals.
  3. A communications link (either radio or line) allowing one way communication.

checkpoint/restart.   A point in a program at which the status of all files, working stores, etc., is recorded. In the event of subsequent failure of either hardware or software it is not necessary to go back to the start of the run of that program, but merely to the CHECKPOINT and to RESTART from that point.

COM   see COMPUTER OUTPUT ON MICROFILM

compiler. A program which translates a high level language into machine code.

computer output on microfilm (COM). The process of producing computer output on microfilm or microfiche. The peripheral equipment used in this process may be on-line or (more usually) off-line.

concentrator. A communications device that allows data transmitted over a number of lower-speed links to be combined and immediately retransmitted over a single higher-speed link. As a programmable device the concentrator is more flexible in use than the MULTIPLEXER, which performs a similar function.

configuration. The term used to denote the combination of hardware devices used to make a computer system.

control unit
1. That part of the CPU that accesses instructions, interprets them and initiates action.
2. A device that controls data flow between a peripheral and a CPU. May be mounted between the peripheral and the channel or physically attached to a peripheral or housed in the central processor.

conversational computing. A method of computer operation in which the user, operating a terminal, engages in a dialogue with a computer. Each input made by the user produces a response from the computer. Also known as INTERACTIVE COMPUTING.

CPU see CENTRAL PROCESSOR UNIT

cursor. Indicator appearing on a VDU showing where the next data entry is to be made.

cylinder. A set of corresponding TRACKS on different surfaces of a DISK PACK.

DASD see DIRECT ACCESS STORAGE DEVICE

data analysis. A collection of techniques including data modelling and normalisation which assist in converting a collection of data elements into a data-base structure.

data base. A collection of data on a common theme or themes and which is conceived as a coherent whole to satisfy a variety of users and/or processing requirements.

data-base management system (DBMS). A software package to implement a data base.

data dictionary. A means of recording and tracking the usage of data. Usually used to describe a software package used in a data processing environment and used in conjunction with a DBMS, a data dictionary may also be maintained manually.

data element.   The smallest unit of data with any meaning.

data model.   A representation of the data used within an organisation. See also SUB-SCHEMA and USER VIEW.

DBMS   see DATA BASE MANAGEMENT SYSTEM

deadly embrace.   A condition which arises when two or more
programs using a computer at the same time are all suspended
waiting for the same data which has been locked by one of them.

debugging.   The process of removing errors from a program.

digital analog converter.   A device that converts digital (i.e. discrete)
signals into continuous or analog signals. Used to enable digital
computers to control analog devices.

direct access storage devices (DASDs).   Any type of backing store in
which any unit of storage may be addressed directly. Usually used
to refer to magnetic disks, drums and similar devices.

disk drive.   A PERIPHERAL. device in which the medium used is
a magnetic disk which may be either fixed or demountable.

disk pack.   The demountable element of a non-fixed-disk drive.
Includes the recording surfaces and usually the spindle on which
they are mounted. Some types of disk pack (WINCHESTER
DISKS) include the read/write heads. The disk pack may be in the
form of a cartridge.

diskette.   A small ($5\frac{1}{4}''$ and $3\frac{1}{2}''$ are typical sizes) magnetic disk used
for data storage and/or transfer. Diskettes are a form of removable
BACKING STORE and may be either semi-flexible or rigid.

distributed processing.   An approach to data processing in which
processing and data storage tend to be located at or near the points
where the data occurs or the information is used, but with
communications links to allow access to and from other processing
facilities and data storage as required.

downtime.   The period during which a computer is inoperable due to
mechanical or other failure. The term UPTIME is sometimes used
to refer to the period the computer is available. Either term may
refer to the computer configuration or a single unit of it.

drum.   Also called MAGNETIC DRUM. A type of BACKING
STORE PERIPHERAL device in which data are recorded on the
magnetised surface of a drum which is rotated at high speed.

field   see GROUP

file.   A collection of RECORDS on a common theme or basis.

firmware.   An element of HARDWARE included in a computer
which performs a function traditionally performed by SOFT-
WARE.

floppy disk.   A magnetic disk made of semi flexible material. Floppy disks may be handled and transported with less difficulty than conventional disks.

flowchart. A diagram which shows the sequence or flow of events. Usually drawn using a standard set of symbols and obeying some widely accepted conventions (e.g. flow is from top to bottom, left to right, unless otherwise stated).

front-end processor. A computer dedicated to communications functions which act as an interface between a HOST PROCESSOR and the network. It is normally situated close to the HOST PROCESSOR and carries out such functions as line control, message queuing, etc.

grandfather, father, son. A way of cycling tapes in a data processing centre to provide security in the event of hardware or software failure. The master tape in one processing run becomes the back-up tape in the next run (FATHER) and second reserve (GRANDFATHER) in the subsequent run. Only when a new SON has been created successfully is the GRANDFATHER tape released for re-use.

group. A combination of two or more DATA ELEMENTS which are logically related but do not constitute a record. An address consisting of street, town and county is an example of a GROUP. Also called a FIELD.

hard copy. Printed output from a computer.

hardware. All the physical elements of a computer configuration. Includes the central processor, backing store, peripherals, cables, supports, etc.

header
1. A record at the beginning of a file which identifies the data on it, its generation, retention period, control totals, etc.
2. The first part of a record containing fixed data which is followed by a number of groups containing specific data.

high-level language. A programming language in which each statement in the SOURCE CODE is equivalent to many statements in MACHINE LANGUAGE. Examples include: ALGOL, BASIC, COBOL, FORTRAN and PL/1.

highway. Synonym for BUS or TRUNK. See also CHANNEL and MULTIPLEXER.

host processor. The main computer in a network. In some types of networks, several computers may act as host processors. A host processor performs the applications workload of the network and may be assisted in the communications role by a FRONT-END PROCESSOR.

instruction set.   The list of operations that a computer can perform.

interactive   see CONVERSATIONAL COMPUTING

inter-block gap.   A space left on a magnetic file between records or blocks of data to allow the tape drive to accelerate/decelerate (also called INTER-RECORD GAP).

interpreter.   A program (which may also be firmware) which interprets a program written in a high level language into machine code at execution time.

inter-record gap   see INTER-BLOCK GAP

interrupt.   A signal (e.g. from terminal or other peripheral) which tells the control unit that control should temporarily pass from the current program to another. The interrupt enables the discontinued program to be resumed as soon as the interrupt has been dealt with.

I/O.   Short for *I*NPUT/*O*UTPUT

JCL   see JOB CONTROL LANGUAGE

job control language (JCL).   A special programming language to enable the operators of a computer to communicate with the OPERATING SYSTEM about resource allocation, priorities, etc.

K.   Short for KILO (one thousand). In data processing used as a prefix, especially for measures of main or backing storage capacity. Because of the addressing system of computer memory 1 K of main storage equals 1024 bytes or words.

key.   That GROUP or FIELD of a RECORD which is used to provide access to the entire record.

kiloHertz (kHz).   Hertz (Hz) is the international standard measurement of frequency of a communications link, expressed in cycles per second. 1 kiloHertz is one thousand cycles per second.

LAN   see *Local Area Network*

leased line.   A communications link which is provided by the telecommunications authority for the exclusive use of a particular customer.

light pen
  1. A hand-held optical scanner for reading bar and similar codes (also called WAND).
  2. A hand-held optical device which can be used in conjunction with a VDU to select or modify data presented on the screen.

line printer.   A computer peripheral that prints one line of output at a time.

Local Area Network (LAN).   Generic term for a variety of hardwired techniques for linking computing devices and PERIPHERALS within a limited geographical area (normally a few hundred metres).

log file. A file which records all transactions in a system to provide both recovery back-up and history records. Also called LOG TAPE since such files are frequently made on tape.

logging on–off. Logging on is the sequence of operations which a user must go through at a terminal before he can make use of the programs or data he requires. Usually this will entail identification of both the user and the system. Logging off is the reverse operation conducted at the end of a terminal session.

low-level language. A programming language in which each statement in the SOURCE CODE is equal to one or at most a few statements in MACHINE LANGUAGE. See also ASSEMBLER.

machine language. The internal code of a computer. Binary patterns may be used to represent the INSTRUCTION SET of the computer and thus it is possible (but not easy) to program in machine language.

magnetic ink character recognition (MICR). A technique for reading characters printed with a special magnetisable ink in a special fount. Widely used on cheques as a means of improving data capture.

mainframe. Data processing computers built to (relatively) conventional architecture. Used to distinguish this class of machines from minicomputers and microcomputers.

main storage. That part of the total storage of a computer from which instructions are executed.

mark reading. A technique for reading marks made on computer input documents. Both optical and electrical (mark sensing) techniques may be used.

media. The material on which data is input to, stored on or output from a computer. Thus magnetic tape, punched cards, floppy disks and magnetic disks are all media.

megabyte. A million bytes.

memory. Synonymous with MAIN STORAGE. Sometimes used loosely to include BACKING STORE as well.

menu. A list of alternatives or choices presented to a user at a terminal from which a selection can be made by use of keyed input, light pen or other means.

metadata. Term sometimes used for information about information – see also DATA DICTIONARY.

methodology. The process and procedures used in carrying out systems development or other activities. A methodology will usually involve the application of a number of techniques.

MICR see MAGNETIC INK CHARACTER RECOGNITION

microcomputer. A fully functional computing device containing all the elements of a computer which is built around a MICRO-PROCESSOR.

microprocessor.   A LSI (Large-Scale Integration) circuit design that provides on one or more chips, similar functions to those contained in the central processing unit of a computer.

microsecond.   One millionth of a second.

millisecond.   One thousandth of a second.

minicomputer.   A class of computer derived from the miniaturised computing devices developed for industrial applications. Mini-computers do not require the specialised environments (air-conditioning, etc.) associated with MAINFRAMES and offer a wider range of computing capabilities and peripheral options than MICROCOMPUTERS.

modem (*Mo*dulator *Dem*odulator).   A device providing an interface between a digital device (terminal, concentrator or computer) and an analog communications link. Modulation is the process of loading the digital signal on to the analog carrier wave and demodulation is the process of stripping the signal from the carrier.

mouse.   A roller device for inputting data on a VDU. As the mouse (which is connected to the VDU) is moved across a surface (usually the desk adjacent to the VDU) it causes the CURSOR to move on the screen. A button (or buttons) on the mouse enables an action to be entered when the cursor is in the correct position (e.g. to select an option from a MENU).

multiplexer

1. A communications device that allows data transmitted over a number of lower-speed lines to be combined and immediately retransmitted over a single higher-speed link. Although per-forming essentially the same function as a CONCENTRATOR, the multiplexer is inherently less flexible.
2. A type of CHANNEL used to connect a central processor and peripherals which uses multiplexing (i.e. interleaving of data from different sources) principles.

multiprocessing.   A configuration in which two or more separately usable MAINFRAMES access common MAIN STORAGE.

multiprogramming.   The technique whereby two or more programs are processed by a computer in an interleaved manner so that it appears to the user that they are running concurrently. Multi-programming enables the resources of the computer to be used more effectively as processing for another program can be conti-nued while a program is waiting for a relatively slow operation (e.g. reading of input) to be completed.

nanosecond.   One thousand millionth of a second.

NCR paper   see NO-CARBON-REQUIRED PAPER

no-carbon-required paper.   Paper which is chemically impregnated so that impact on the top sheet produces an image on the second and subsequent sheets without the use of interleaved carbon paper.

number cruncher.   Loose term used to refer to any very large MAINFRAME super-computer especially if optimised for computation as opposed to data processing.

object program.   A program in MACHINE LANGUAGE achieved by processing the SOURCE PROGRAM with a COMPILER or ASSEMBLER.

OCR   see OPTICAL CHARACTER RECOGNITION

off-line.   Equipment, operations or procedures not operating under direct computer control.

OLRT   see ON-LINE REAL TIME

on-line.   Equipment, operations or procedures directly connected to a computer.

on-line real time (OLRT).   A mode of data processing whereby the input data arising from an external event or process is immediately accepted and processed. OLRT is a tautology in that real-time operations are necessarily on-line.

operating system.   The program(s) that manage the use of the computer's resources. Functions performed include: supervision of CPU operations, control of input and output transfers and, where appropriate, multiprogramming and virtual storage operations and control.

optical character recognition (OCR).   The technique whereby stylised characters printed using special founts may be read by optical means as a way of capturing data for use in a computer system.

overflow.   Data which cannot be accommodated in the physical location on a DASD to which it would normally be assigned is called 'overflow data' or 'overflow records' and the routines to locate such data in specially reserved overflow areas are called 'overflow routines'.

package.   Generic term for an application program or suite of programs marketed for use by multiple organisations.

page printer.   A printing peripheral or stand-alone system which produces one page of printed output at a time.

passwords.   A combination of alphabetic and/or numeric characters used as a 'key' to enable a user (usually via a terminal) to have access to computer held data or programs. Passwords act as the equivalent to the key to a conventional lock.

PC   see PERSONAL COMPUTER

peripherals.   Collective term for input and output devices connected to a computer together with those types of BACKING STORE which are connected to but not fully integrated into the CPU.

personal computer (PC).   A MICROCOMPUTER normally used in a stand-alone manner or linked to similar devices via a LAN to provide an individual with computing power to assist in one or more aspects of his/her work.

picosecond.   One million millionth of a second.

plug-to-plug compatible.   Hardware which can be substituted for that installed by the original supplier simply by unplugging the original and plugging in the replacement. In its strictest interpretation no further changes to hardware, software or procedures are necessary to make use of the newly installed equipment.

pointers.   Indicators added to records stored on DASDs to enable the logical structure of a FILE to be preserved irrespective of the physical location of the data. Pointers give the address of the next logical item of data in the file. Multiple pointers enable multiple logical files to be constructed using only one physical occurrence of the data.

point-of-sale terminals (POS).   Terminals used at the check out or sales point of a retail store or similar operation. In addition to providing locally required functions, e.g. cash total, such terminals capture data (either on- or off-line) for computer use.

polling.   The technique whereby a computer or other control unit 'asks' terminals if they have data to transmit. Polling may take place on a strict rotation basis, i.e. terminal *A* is polled then terminal *B*; on a clock basis, e.g. every 5 seconds, or or some other basis reflecting the relative usage of each terminal.

POS   see POINT-OF-SALE TERMINAL

printout.   HARDCOPY computer output produced on a printer. Usually reserved for fairly substantial reports produced on line or page printers rather than brief or single-page reports printed on character printers.

program.   The set of instructions used to communicate the orders of a human being to a computer. Programs are written in a *programming language* and the person who writes them (especially if he or she does so on a regular or full-time basis) is called a 'programmer'.

protocols.   A set of standards defining the procedures and format for data to be transmitted via communications links.

public switched network.   Publicly available dial-up telephone services provided by telecommunications authorities. May also be used as communications links for data.

read/write heads. That part of a PERIPHERAL which reads data from or writes data on to the media in use.

real time. A mode of data processing whereby the input data arising from an external event or process is immediately accepted and processed.

record. Two or more data elements (which may or may not be associated into groups) which are linked to a common identifier. The identifier is usually one or more of the data elements.

rotational delay. The average time necessary for the correct sector of a disk or drum track to arrive at the read/write head prior to the transfer of data.

schema. The complete picture (including the physical storage) of data stored in a data base.

scratch tape. A magnetic tape which is available to record any data as required. Distinguished from a tape which holds data subject to retention (either permanently or for a specified time).

sector. A subdivision of a track on a magnetic disk or drum.

seek time. The average time for the physical movement of the read/write heads of a magnetic disk to position them at the appropriate cylinder for the transfer of data.

software. Collective term for the instructions fed into a computer to make it work. Includes COMPILERS, OPERATING SYSTEMS, SYSTEM SOFTWARE and APPLICATION SOFTWARE.

source code. The instructions written by a programmer in a programming language before they are translated into OBJECT CODE or MACHINE LANGUAGE using an ASSEMBLER, COMPILER or INTERPRETER.

standards. The systems and procedures applied to the work of data processing staff. Standards cover the use of METHODOLOGIES and techniques as well as specific technical subjects such as interfaces and PROTOCOLS.

structured program. A PROGRAM constructed in accordance with the principles of modularity and in which each module consists of one or more of the basic logical constructions.

sub-schema. A user's view of data contained in a DATA BASE. This is a logical view of a portion of the data which may or may not be the same as the way in which the data is physically stored.

syntax. The 'grammatical rules' relating to the use of a programming language.

system. A term widely used in data processing with a series of imprecise meanings:

1. A computer configuration, e.g. the *system* is down; that is, the

computer has developed a fault.

2. An application, e.g. a payroll *system*.
3. An abbreviation of operating *system* as in *systems* generation, i.e. the installing of an operating system on a computer configuration.

system software.   A portmanteau term used to mean all programs used within a computer installation which are not applications programs (i.e. those that produce directly useful output for the user of the computer). Compilers and analogous programs may or may not be included in the term.

tape deck (also called TAPE DRIVE and TAPE TRANSPORT). A PERIPHERAL device in which the storage medium used is magnetic tape.

terminal

1. Any device which is used for computer data input and/or output via communications links.
2. An interactive peripheral.
3. A peripheral forming part of an interactive work station.

third normal form (TNF).   The third and usually final stage in the quasi-mathematical transformation process of normalisation which is used to combine groups of data in a stable way prior to the development of a data-base structure.

time-sharing.   A mode of data processing in which two or more computer users may simultaneously make use of the resources of a computer via communications links. The resources of the computer are allocated in brief intervals to each user.

touch screen.   A VDU in which the display screen is surrounded by a series of photo-electric cells. When a finger or pointer touches the screen, it intercepts the beams from the cells which enables the computer to record the intercepts. This can be used to record an action, e.g. select an item from a MENU.

track

1. Synonym for CHANNEL when this term is used in conjunction with magnetic tape.
2. The path on a magnetic disk or drum on which data is stored.

trailer.   A record at the end of a file which contains control totals and may also mark the end of that file.

transfer rate.   The rate (usually expressed in characters per second) at which data may be transferred between the main memory of a computer and a peripheral device. Transfer time is the time taken to effect the transfer of a given amount of data.

trunk.   Synonym for BUS or HIGHWAY. See also CHANNEL and MULTIPLEXER.

turnaround document.   A document produced by a computer which, after some intermediate action, is subsequently used for computer input purposes. Such documents may be in the form of punched cards which are also printed with human readable characters or forms printed (in whole or part) in OCR founts. Such documents are often used as part of an invoice and subsequently as a remittance advice accompanying the payment.

turnkey.   A project or system, usually involving both hardware and software, which is completed by a software house or other con-tractor and then turned over in a completed state to the customer.

user view.   A graphical representation of the way in which data appears to be logically related for one or more users of that data. See also SUB-SCHEMA.

utility programs.   Generalised programs which manipulate data independently of the content of specific files. Used for such frequently required operations as sorting and dumping data. Utility programs obviate the need to write separate programs each time these standard functions are used. Utility programs are usually considered to be part of SYSTEM SOFTWARE. Also called UTILITY ROUTINES.

VAN   see VALUE ADDED NETWORK

Value Added Network (VAN).   A subscriber service making use of computer and communications technology to provide an informa-tion dissemination (and/or capture) service to remote users.

VDU   see VISUAL DISPLAY UNIT

virtual storage.   A technique, implemented via an OPERATING SYSTEM, which enables users of computers to make use of much larger areas of MAINSTORAGE than is physically available. Data is *paged* and *rolled* between MAIN STORAGE and BACKING STORE as required. Also called VIRTUAL MEMORY.

visual display unit (VDU).   A TERMINAL and/or PERIPHERAL that consists of a cathode ray tube (CRT) to show or display data and usually some form of input device to enable data to be entered (most commonly a keyboard or light pen). Many VDUs incor-porate a certain amount of *intelligence* (processing power) and may be used off-line as well as on-line. Also called CRTs.

walkthroughs (also spelt WALKTHRUS).   A formalised peer group evaluation of work.

WAN   see WIDE AREA NETWORK

wand   see LIGHT PEN

Wide Area Network (WAN).   Generic name sometimes given to data communications system or network linking geographically remote computing devices and/or TERMINALS. Many use hardwired, satellite or radio links and may be dedicated or use public facilities.

Winchester disks.   A type of magnetic disk device in which the DISK PACK and READ/WRITE HEADS are sealed in a demountable or exchangeable unit.

word. A group of characters treated as an entity within some computers.

Index

Also available in the Macmillan Professional Masters series

JOHN ALDER
Constitutional and Administrative Law is a clear and readable account of the basic principles of UK constitutional law. It will be an invaluable introduction to the subject for first-year law-degree students and a self-contained text for 'A'-level and Part One professional examinations, as well as for the interested general reader.

MARISE CREMONA
Criminal Law provides a short but thorough overview of the fundamentals of English criminal law as required for degree courses and professional examinations. It will also prove invaluable reading for magistrates, police officers, social workers and others who need an introduction to the key features of this subject.

E. C. EYRE
Office Administration is suitable for all syllabuses in office administration and relevant parts of business administration and management courses. It is an invaluable text for students studying for the examinations of the Institute of Administrative Management, the Institute of Chartered Secretaries and Administrators, the Society of Company and Commercial Accountants, BTEC and NEBBS.

KATE GREEN
Land Law provides a clear and straightforward introduction to basic English land-law rules. It will be an invaluable text for first-year undergraduates and those studying for professional examinations in both law and other subjects where an understanding of land law is essential.

ROGER HUSSEY
Cost and Management Accounting is a clear explanatory text covering the principles and techniques of the subject. It will prove invaluable for students in further and higher education, particularly those studying on accounting foundation, 'A'-level and BTEC courses. It will also suit practising managers who wish to improve their existing skills.

ROGER OLDCORN
Management is a clear, accessible text which will appeal as a self-contained text to students on BTEC, SCOTVEC, Diploma in Management Studies and Institute of Personnel Management courses and as introductory reading for higher-level courses. It will also prove invaluable reading for practising or aspiring managers.

KATE WILLIAMS
Study Skills offers students practical, step-by-step suggestions and strategies to use in their studies, whether these are academic, professional or vocational in nature.

All these books are available at your local bookshop or, in case of difficulty, from John Darvill, Globe Education, Houndmills, Basingstoke, Hampshire RG21 2XS (Tel: 0256 29242).